Chinese Rules and Procedures for Addressing Mass Actions

Cong-rui Qiao

Chinese Rules and Procedures for Addressing Mass Actions

A Juridification Account

Springer

Cong-rui Qiao
Law4Sustainability
Amsterdam, The Netherlands

ISBN 978-3-031-62200-7 ISBN 978-3-031-62201-4 (eBook)
https://doi.org/10.1007/978-3-031-62201-4

This Springer imprint is published by the registered company Springer Nature Switzerland AG
The registered company address is: Gewerbestrasse 11, 6330 Cham, Switzerland

To my dearest family Liu Cuiying (刘翠英), Qiao Congxiao (乔聪晓) and Qiao Shuqing (乔树清)

Foreword

Time and again the question what makes the Chinese system of governance tick has proved to be very challenging. The mission conducted in 1793 by George Macartney, Britain's first ambassador to China, failed, because due to a lack of knowledge he misjudged the Qing court and the Qianlong Emperor. By contrast, the Dutch mission undertaken in 1795 turned out to be a success, because the delegation members had deep knowledge of Asia and were intent on understanding China on its own terms.[1] This book written by Qiao Cong-rui, a Chinese scholar who has built an academic career in The Netherlands, is part of the Sino-Dutch understanding which started with the meeting of minds in 1795. Her profound knowledge of the Chinese governance system and her ability to vernacularize it by showing its logic to an international audience are the strong pillars of the book.

Cong-rui rightly makes the point that in order to properly understand government–citizen relations in China, one should rely on China's indigenous traditions rather than Western concepts, such as constitutionalism. Thus, the Western liberal model is based on the assumption that the government cannot be trusted and that it needs to be constrained through checks and balances and separation of powers. In China, on the other hand, the assumption is that, in order to discharge its Mandate from Heaven, the government will act in a benign way. Therefore, rather than reining it in, as is the case in liberal constitutionalism, the government should be given the room to do good for its people. To ensure benign government, the ruler should not be corrected, but be stimulated to engage in self-cultivation and moral self-improvement.

As Cong-rui also demonstrates, despite these different approaches to governance, since 'Reform and Opening-up' China has adopted many transplants from the West, such as fair trial guarantees, which enrich and strengthen its legal system. It would, therefore, be wrong to construe Western and Chinese concepts as being binary

[1] As engagingly described by Tonio Andrade, *The Last Embassy, The Dutch Mission of 1795 and the Forgotten History of Western Encounters with China*, Princeton, 2021.

opposites. On the contrary, China and the West have constantly been exchanging ideas and theories on governance. Thus, during Enlightenment European philosophers drew much inspiration from Chinese thought. They rejected Christianity's negative view on mankind associated with the fall of man. To prevent people from straying from the right path, Christianity relied on a repressive system based on guilt and sin to secure obedience. Therefore, the Confucian idea of human goodness, which presented such a stark contrast to the negativity of Christian doctrine, was appealing to them. The Chinese example showed that religion is not a prerequisite for having a sound ethical system. As a result, the concept of humaneness or *ren* became part of the Enlightenment discussions. There are even indications that it has found expression in the 'fraternity' component of France's tripartite national motto, next to liberty and equality.

Cong-rui succeeds in effectively explaining to her international readership how Chinese authorities deal with mass actions. As a detached academic, she neither condemns nor condones the practices she describes. Nor are the readers supposed to accept them uncritically. However, through her analysis she does open a new path towards understanding what is really happening in this regard in China. That demonstrations are being held in socialist China, which is being led by the Communist Party, may seem paradoxical to some, but it is a fact of social life.

Cong-rui does her readers a huge favour by providing them with the tools to properly understand the way mass actions unfold in China. In so doing, she provides an in-depth and fine-tuned analysis of government–citizens relations. She presents a clear and compelling account of the facts, distinguishing them from seemingly paradoxical myths. This is achieved through a rigorous research design and the use of compelling narrative techniques. Therefore, the book deserves a very wide audience.

Utrecht University, Utrecht, The Netherlands
17 March 2024

Tom Zwart

Acknowledgements

This book presents the findings of a ten-year study on the relationships and interactions between the Chinese government and citizens, with a focus on the evolution of government accountability law in modern and contemporary times. The contents of this book were originally developed during my doctoral and post-doctoral research and subsequently revised during my teaching at universities in the Netherlands, Belgium and China. At the start of my writing, I aimed to contribute to the research field by proposing conceptual and analytical approaches to the juridification of Chinese measures for addressing citizen complaints about government decisions. However, my ambition has shifted towards engaging a broader readership, including not only accountability or Chinese law researchers, but also a diverse array of students, policy advisors and other curious members of the public who wish to understand the features of government–citizen relations and interactions in China, the role of law in these interactions, and the institutional and social changes that shape them.

Those even with the faintest acquaintance with my personality will understand the depth of my indebtedness to, among the many who are the sunshine to which I am a seed during my academic growth, my dear colleague and inspiring mentor Professor Tom Zwart. Starting a career in a foreign environment can be challenging for anyone. It is crucial to receive recognition of one's talents and potential early on and continued support thereafter to sustain professional confidence and competence. There were no instances where I left a meeting with Tom feeling discouraged or demotivated. I greatly appreciate the trust and support of colleagues like Tom, as they enabled me to further my research and teaching on Chinese governance and legal issues with a critical view of Euro-centric notions and to develop some generalisable theories on the development of State governance and law across cultures.

It is often claimed, and I find it true from personal experiences, that following the conventional path is easier than pursuing an innovative one. In 2019, the European Union designated China as a systemic rival, leading to growing concern in European academia about China's undue influence. In this context, my work is a demanding undertaking. I would like to express my gratitude for the timely advice and unwavering help provided by my colleagues at the Free University of Amsterdam

(VU), specifically Wim Janse, Sandra Hasanefendic and Eva Meijerink. Wim provided opportunities for me to improve my academic and team management skills, while Sandra assisted me in establishing the new Asian Law Series course in 2020. In 2021–2022, Tom and I co-designed the cross-university course 'Law, Governance and Human Rights in China', which Eva helped to attract students from diverse disciplines.

I would like to express my gratitude to Carry Knoops, Geert-Jan Knoops, Stefanie Lemke, Nicole Zwart, Mimi Zou and Marijk van der Wende for their attentiveness to my career development and their generosity in supporting it. Special thanks go to Paul van den Hoven, Chang Jian, Shi Anbin, Kees van den Bos, Leo Lentz, Georg Frerks, Julie Fraser, Stacey Links and Jing Chao for their insightful comments on the foundations of this book. I am grateful to my wonderful friends in the Netherlands who have provided me with unwavering patience and trust, enabling me to sustain my wild curiosity about a multitude of subjects and refine my "unworldly" application of critical thinking in my professional and personal lives. In this regard, I am particularly indebted to Neander, Tianshu, Gaoge, Huwan, Yu, Xuelai, Kexin, Yan and Zippo.

It cannot be overstated that the institutional support of my former employers, Utrecht University and VU, was crucial to my academic growth. Their friendly staff and cross-disciplinary, cross-national collaboration resources were essential to my development through research and teaching fellowships in mainland China, Hong Kong, South Korea, the Philippines, Germany, Sweden, France and Belgium. I would also like to thank my postgraduate and undergraduate students at VU, the University of Amsterdam and the University of Antwerp for their critical remarks during each lecture. I am thankful to my editor, Laura Hofmann from Springer, for her kind assistance during the peer review, revision and publication processes.

Time and space compel me to stop here. I am deeply grateful to many more people who have left their footprints in my cherished memories. In the future, déjà vu will remind me that I once saw in you the true beauty of academic work, and the meaningful contribution of individuals to their community and society.

Written in Amsterdam, this 8th day of March 2024.

Qiao Cong-rui

Contents

Chapter 1
Introduction: Contexts, Concepts and Analytical Points

1.1 De-puzzling Government-Citizen Interactions in China

Over the last thirty years, China has emerged as a significant global economic and political force, attracting considerable attention to its governance model and the role of law within it.[1] The prevailing view is that the Chinese State governance system, centralised under the political leadership of the Communist Party of China (hereafter referred to as the "CPC"),[2] has facilitated remarkable economic growth and stability, at the perceived cost of stifling dissenting opinions and curtailing citizen rights. With China's expanding economic and geopolitical influence, there is growing curiosity, both domestically and internationally, about the sustainability of the Chinese governance model and its ability to incorporate government accountability rules in its governance practices.

The Chinese governance model has been perceived as non-rule-based, but in recent years, there has been a noticeable shift. Various areas of law are now playing an increasingly important role in holding the Chinese government accountable to its citizens, with the implementation of the administrative procedural law and the engagement of external opinions throughout the government's decision-making

[1] This book focuses on Mainland China, where the State governance system has been significantly impacted by the CPC-endorsed acceptance of government accountability rules, affecting the interactions between citizens and governing authorities. The book does not cover Hong Kong, Macau, or Taiwan, as their governance systems differ from that of Mainland China.

[2] Founded on 1 October 1949, the Chinese Socialist State, under the leadership of the CPC, currently consists of six powers: the National People's Congress exercises legislative power, the State Council is the highest administrative organ, the Central Military Commission commands the armed forces, the National Supervisory Commission serves as the highest supervisory organ that oversees the work of local supervisory commissions, the Supreme People's Court is the highest judicial organ that supervises the delivery of justice by local courts, and the Supreme People's Procuratorate is the highest procuratorial organ that directs the work of local procuratorates. In: Articles 1, 57, 58, 85, 93, 125, 132 and 137, in the 1982 Constitution of the People's Republic of China amended in 2018.

C.-r. Qiao, *Chinese Rules and Procedures for Addressing Mass Actions*,
https://doi.org/10.1007/978-3-031-62201-4_1

process more systematically and consistently.[3] This seemingly paradoxical coexistence of China's political singularity and its acceptance of government accountability law has puzzled many observers. In this context, this book serves as a gateway for international readers to understand the legislative, institutional and social developments that underlie China's approaches to addressing citizen complaints from the 1970s to the present. The book focuses on the responses of Chinese legislative, administrative, and judicial authorities to mass actions, which are defined as collective citizen complaints aimed at redressing shared grievances for which the Chinese government is allegedly responsible.

To date, the research literature on China's measures for dealing with mass actions has relied heavily on notions and assumptions drawn from European governance traditions and reflecting European governance values.[4] Unfortunately, there has been little effort to incorporate China's indigenous governance traditions and historical developments into the explanation of the current rules and practices for managing citizen disagreements and discontent. Assessing Chinese governance measures on the basis of Occidental concepts and theories assumes that China's governance development will or should emulate the examples set in the Occident. While not without a theoretical or empirical basis, this perspective is divorced from reality.

An immediate problem with the above-mentioned assumption is that it does not adequately take into account the enduring impact of indigenous Chinese traditions of State governance and government accountability on contemporary interactions between Chinese citizens and governing authorities. As elaborated in Chap. 2, the influential Chinese governance doctrine is rooted in the formally and socially ingrained norm of reciprocity. Here, the governing power is expected to demonstrate governance competence to promote the well-being of the governed. In return, the governed are not inclined to question or resist the decisions of a competent government. The norm of reciprocity continues to shape how Chinese citizens interact with their governing powers and how Chinese authorities address citizens' grievances today.

Surveys conducted by both Chinese and non-Chinese researchers consistently show that Chinese citizens express high levels of satisfaction with the CPC-led government given its commendable governance competencies. For example, a survey conducted between December 2014 and June 2016 found that an overwhelming seventy-eight per cent of Chinese respondents preferred the current government to other alternatives, and largely appreciated China's impressive progress made in various economic and social areas.[5] In stark contrast, public appreciation for governments in the European Union (hereafter referred to as the "EU"), used here as a

---

[3] Ma and Wang (2018), pp. 220–222.

[4] This book uses the term 'Occident' to refer to States and regions, such as Western Europe, where liberal governance cultures have developed that value the protection of individual liberties and legal constraints on public powers. The foundational assumption tied to this concept is that governments are inherently prone to encroaching on the liberties and well-being of individuals.

[5] The latest data of the longitudinal surveys on public opinion on political values and governance in Asia, conducted by The Asian Barometer (ABS), are not open-access. The survey results on the

comparative reference, was much lower, with only thirty-one per cent of European respondents expressing their appreciation for governments in 2016.[6]

Moreover, the assumption that one set of rules in China dominates government-citizen interactions overlooks their nuances. Over the past four decades, China has systematically shifted from a revolutionary and lawless governance system towards a rational and rule-based one. During this period, some aspects of Chinese governance practices appear to be moving closer to a rule-based model, while others are still lagging. Neglecting the transitional nature of Chinese State governance leads to overly optimistic or pessimistic views. Notably, in 2006, EU policymakers once believed that China's economic marketisation would lead to a general shift towards a liberalised governance framework,[7] and this expectation was ultimately met with confusion and disappointment. In recent years, the EU has repositioned itself to regard China as a systemic rival[8] and has been vigilant against Chinese threats to its core liberal values.[9]

Indeed, the Chinese State governance system differs from that of many Occidental States, particularly in its political form. Unlike the latter, China's leading political party, the CPC, cannot be replaced by other political parties in the country. Furthermore, the CPC retains central control over China's legislative, administrative and judicial powers. Some argue that the development of rule-based governance in China is hindered by this feature and that China's announced transition to a rule-based model is more formal than substantive.[10] However, it remains unclear whether the concepts and assumptions underlying these beliefs are valid. What is missing from the existing discourse is a nuanced account of the relationship between the political form of State governance and the development of law in it. Specifically, there is a gap in understanding the implementation of government accountability law under singular political leadership and its institutional arrangements for addressing citizen complaints.

From a conceptual standpoint, it is crucial to clarify whether the absence of legal primacy in State governance is synonymous with the absence of rule-based governance and whether the State's political system unilaterally dictates the functioning of State governance powers. At the analytical level, there is a need to broaden the scope of research data and perspectives to comprehensively capture the multifaceted

---

confidence and trust in their government by Chinese respondents in 2016 are quoted from the working paper by Weatherall and Huang (2017).

[6]Standard Eurobarometer 86 (2016) Public Opinion in the European Union (in the "Trust in Political Institutions").

[7]The European Commission (2006) EU-China Relations: Commission Sets Out Its Strategy.

[8]The European Commission (2019) Joint Communication to the European Parliament, the European Council and the Council: EU-China – A Strategic Outlook".

[9]The European Parliament (2021) The European Parliament Resolution on A New EU-China Strategy (2021/2037(INI)): A New EU-China Strategy.

[10]The notion that the political structure of the Chinese State fundamentally hinders the development of the rule of law is a conclusion shared by many scholars. For instance, Zhang (2017), pp. 394–396.

dynamics of Chinese governance rules and practices. These are developing based on diverse governance norms and institutional arrangements, which overlap and sometimes conflict with each other. Unless the oversimplified assumptions and conclusions are corrected, government-citizen interactions in China and their domestic and global implications will remain shrouded in mystery.

The rule-based transition of Chinese State governance is reflected in a variety of areas, each with varying degrees of success. Similar to the differing histories of the development of legal primacy in the Occident,[11] the Chinese governance transition is influenced by multiple notions and values. In China, both the statist and liberal approaches to law are influential. The statist approach treats law as a tool to facilitate State governance, while the liberal approach prioritises the protection of individual rights and the regulation of governing powers. Notably, China's economic laws are widely acknowledged to have played a key role in facilitating the country's successful transition from a centrally planned economy to a market-oriented one, and in consolidating its position as one of the world's fastest-growing economies.[12]

Less widely recognised is that, beyond the economic sphere, non-economic aspects of Chinese State governance are also developing in a rule-based direction. Despite its unified political leadership, China's legal system has performed remarkably well within the bloc of middle-income countries, particularly in terms of the quality and effectiveness of China's legal institutions.[13] Millions of complainants actively seek legal remedies for perceived injustices in China every year.[14] The rise of mass actions since the early 1990s, driven by economic and social inequalities, is evidence of the fascinating changes in the Chinese governance landscape.[15] With social inequalities widening, the Chinese State grapples with governance challenges comparable to those of its Occidental counterparts, and this comparability is perhaps more significant than generally recognised.

It should be noted that my purpose in critiquing assumptions and conclusions based on Occidental notions is not to discredit or dismiss Occidental legal and governance traditions and values. However, relying solely on them to explain government-citizen interactions in China is inadequate and can be misleading. It is crucial to avoid assuming a single governance doctrine in China. The next two sections of this chapter critically analyse notions and framings often used to study the Chinese case, which have led to persistent confusion and misunderstanding. The

[11] Gerth and Mills (1946), pp. 219–221.

[12] The Chinese economy was ranked 16th in the 2021 World Competitiveness Rankings by the International Institute for Management Development (up from 20th in 2020). Notably, it achieved a remarkable growth rate of 18.3 percent in the first quarter of 2021 compared to the previous year, marking the highest quarterly year-on-year growth since 1993. See: South China Morning Post (17 June 2021) China climbs list of world's most competitive economies, as Hong Kong and Singapore slide.

[13] The World Justice Project (2011) The World Justice Project Rule of Law Index®2011.

[14] Wu and Cheng (2013), pp. 48 and 66.

[15] Weng (1995), p. 82.

aim here is to propose an alternative line of analysis that can enhance our knowledge of Chinese approaches to dealing with mass actions beyond Eurocentric schemata.

1.2 Eurocentric Notions and Framings and Their Limits

To comprehend Chinese approaches to addressing mass actions, it is essential to understand the continuity and changes in Chinese indigenous traditions of State governance in general and government accountability in particular. A thorough analysis of traditional governance practices and a comprehensive evaluation of contemporary legislative and institutional developments are necessary. In light of the puzzles and misinterpretations identified in the preceding section, this section examines the dominant Eurocentric notions and theories that shape popular assumptions about the central theme of the book (Sect. 1.2.1). It then scrutinises the validity of two commonly used analytical framings, plurality and peculiarity, for explaining Chinese governance measures, and delineates their limitations (Sect. 1.2.2). Finally, this section synthesises the essential elements to formulate a holistic and nuanced account of Chinese rules and procedures for handling mass actions (Sect. 1.2.3).

1.2.1 Liberal Theories on the State and Law

Liberal theories encompass a broad spectrum of topics related to individuals, the State, and their relationships, and represent diverse concerns and claims. Despite their diversity, liberal theories share a fundamental premise: the ultimate purpose of the State is to safeguard and promote individual freedom.[16] This premise often conceptualises the State as a necessary evil that protects individual liberty from threats posed by humans and nature. This part concentrates specifically on liberal concepts and theories of the State and law. The State as a necessary evil and its subsequent claims have had a significant impact on modern political and legal theories in the Occident. However, their compatibility with non-Occidental governance traditions is still a matter of debate.

To summarise a complex debate, liberal theories of law can be divided into two categories: narrow and broad. In the narrow sense, the liberal approach focuses primarily on the formal status of law within the State. This perspective, heavily influenced by selected Occidental histories, finds its most influential expression in the work of Albert Dicey from the 1880s. Dicey's theory underscores the absolute supremacy of law as an essential component of the legitimate mandate of the modern State, positing that laws ought to apply to all, including State powers.[17] While this

[16] Ratnapala (2017), p. 263.

[17] Dicey (1915), pp. 179–180.

emphasis on the formal primacy of law has profoundly shaped Occidental legal theories, its generalisability can be questioned, as it is derived from the legal and constitutional histories of Britain and is therefore more specific to British and comparable systems.[18]

A related thesis, advanced in the early twentieth century by the German sociologist Max Weber, integrates the formal and substantive values of law to explain the rationalised governance of modern States. Although Weber's account of law refers to Oriental legal cases, it primarily describes governance experiences in the Occident. Notably, Weber himself acknowledges that the transformative role of law in shaping modern State governance is nowhere reached outside the Occident.[19] Both Diceyan and Weberian theories of State and law are analytically insightful, and their concepts of the supremacy of law and the formal and substantive values of law in the (modern) State are still frequently cited by contemporary researchers and discussants.

In contrast to the narrow approach, the broad liberal approach to law is more expansive, considering the role and values of law in State governance in relation to its institutional and social contexts. This approach sees the primacy of law as an outcome of, rather than a precondition for, the development of the modern State. It regards other elements, beyond the formal status of law, as crucial to the primacy of law within the State. These include an institutional culture where governing powers routinely base their decisions on legal rules and a social culture where natural and legal persons habitually act in accordance with legal rules.[20] This more nuanced account of law, known as the thick version of the rule of law ideal, signifies a remarkable shift from an isolated view to a holistic perspective that takes into account institutional and social factors in explaining the developments of State governance and law.

The reconciliation of the prevailing dichotomous approach, which posits that law either plays a central role in shaping the decision-making processes of State powers and members of the society or has no role at all, is a significant development in the field of liberal theories of the State and law. This reorientation implies that the development of State governance and that of law are intertwined and mutually affect each other. Both conceptually and empirically, the institutionalisation and socialisation of law are dynamic and multi-faceted processes. The amended approach views law as an evolving force, rather than a static and rigid entity, which is particularly relevant for analysing transitional governance systems such as China, where the role of law in State governance is changing, marked by periods of expansion and regression.

[18] May (2014), p. 34.

[19] Berman and Reid (2012), pp. 231–232.

[20] Shapiro (1994), pp. 328–330.

1.2.2 *Assessing Plurality and Peculiarity Framings*

The relationship between State governance and law in China has been the subject of intense debate, both domestically and internationally. Research and policy discussions on this topic often include the plurality framing and the China-being-peculiar framing. This part examines the contributions and limitations of both framings in explaining and assessing the role of law in Chinese State governance.

The argument for political plurality is that it is essential for maintaining a system of checks and balances between the State's governing powers. The existence of political plurality also allows members of society to express their divergent views on decisions made by those in power and choose a different governing power if they lose confidence in the current leadership.[21] The impact of this framing is evident in both domestic and foreign policy formulations across various Occidental regions. In the EU, for instance, the preservation of political plurality and the promotion of democracy are key policy objectives.[22] However, when this framing is applied to the Chinese context, it encounters two major challenges.

Conceptually, the political plurality framing often simplifies the dynamics of Chinese State governance by reducing it to a single defining factor: its political form. The view disregards other factors that contribute to the complexity of Chinese State governance and fails to consider the multifaceted processes of governance and legal transitions. China has implemented rule of law provisions into its governance practices, and it is reductionist to attribute these developments solely to a means of containing citizen discontent and dissent.[23] In particular, the enactment of government accountability rules to receive and review external complaints about government decisions in China is often seen as an authoritarian strategy to suppress popular resistance,[24] overlooking the institutional and social implications of such measures.

Practically, the theoretical argument of political pluralism is not viable in China due to the constitutional establishment of the CPC as the indispensable leading political party in the country. It is legally prohibited to challenge the political dominance of the CPC,[25] which has maintained its absolute political centrality in China for over seven decades. While Chinese courts have the power to review the lawfulness of specific government decisions and, in certain circumstances, also the general rules permitting specific government decisions,[26] there is no judicial or

[21] Shapiro (1994), pp. 34–35.

[22] The Policy Department of the European Parliament (2015) Good Governance in EU External Relations: What Role for Development Policy in a Changing International Context (EP/EXPO/B/DEVE/2015/02).

[23] Fukuyama (2014), pp. 538–541.

[24] Koesel et al. (2020), pp. 60–61.

[25] Article 1, in the Constitution of the People's Republic of China (2018 amended).

[26] For more details on China's introduction of judicial review on government conduct into its governance system can be found in Chap. 2, in particular Section 4 "The Legal Renaissance since the 1980s".

external procedure through which the lawfulness of CPC decisions can be contested. This means that the concept of political pluralism, which envisages a plurality-oriented transformation of the political system, is at odds with the current reality of China's State governance system.

In recent years, there has been an increasing recognition of the limitations of the plurality account of Chinese measures for addressing citizen disagreements. Although political plurality is absent in China, the significance of the rule of law in several aspects of Chinese State governance is thriving.[27] At the beginning of the twenty-first century, China added the principles of the rule of law and human rights protection to its Constitution in 1997 and 2004, respectively, which was a promising sign of China's transition towards a rule-based governance model. This raises critical questions about whether there is an inherent opposition between political singularity and legal development, and whether it is possible for the State to undergo a rule-based governance development under singular political leadership.

The availability of new empirical data and analytical insights has led to the emergence of an alternative approach that emphasises China's distinctive governance traditions and their relevance for understanding and evaluating government-citizen interactions in contemporary times, as well as Chinese measures for managing citizen grievances. This perspective, referred to as peculiarity framing, posits that political unity and stability are essential for economic growth and social development.[28] In contrast to plurality framing, peculiarity framing provides a critical perspective on the frequent and sometimes tumultuous changes in political leadership that lead to inconsistent and ineffective implementation of the State's governance strategies and plans.[29] The peculiarity framing sheds light on contextual aspects beyond the political form of Chinese State governance.

However, it has limitations in terms of its excessive focus on the distinction between Chinese and Occidental governance traditions and their practical implications. It is conceptually and empirically flawed to attempt to differentiate what is considered 'Chinese' from what is considered 'non-Chinese' given the intertwined influences of both China's indigenous and foreign governance norms on contemporary Chinese governance practices. As will be discussed in Chap. 2, the introduction of administrative procedural law in China, which subjects government conduct to legal control and judicial review, is largely inspired by the Occidental governance principle of checks and balances and has now become a basic norm of the Chinese State governance system.[30] In summary, the contents and outcomes of China's governance developments challenge the validity of the plurality thesis that the divide

[27] Peerenboom (2002), p. 115.

[28] Xu (2017), pp. 24–25, 60 and 151.

[29] Bel (2015), pp. 4–6.

[30] In the National Report submitted by China to the United Nations Human Rights Council in November 2018, it acknowledges that the insufficient implementation of international and domestic law, particularly in terms of law-based governance and the impartiality of judicial bodies, poses a challenge to the governance effectiveness in China. In: China's National Report Submitted in accordance with Paragraph 5 of the Annex to Human Rights Council Resolution 16/21.

between Chinese and Occidental governance models is not as clear-cut as the peculiarity framing suggests. Both the plurality and peculiarity theses need to be amended by a nuanced account to unpack the complexity of Chinese governance rules and practices in general and those specific to the handling of mass actions.

1.2.3 Summary: Seeking A Holistic and Nuanced Account

To enhance the validity of the plurality framing, which primarily focuses on the political form of the State, it is necessary to take a holistic approach to the analysis of the multifaceted governance rules in China and their consequential impact on changing institutional practices and social norms. Additionally, it is crucial to acknowledge that the contemporary rules underlying government-citizen interactions in China are not exclusively Chinese, and the boundaries between indigenous and non-Chinese influences are ambiguous.

To develop a comprehensive account of contentious and confrontational government-citizen interactions in China, a nuanced and holistic study is necessary. Oversimplified theories and framings are inadequate in capturing the ongoing institutional and social changes in China, whereas peculiarist theories and claims can lead to misunderstandings and misinterpretations of the evolving relationship between the State and the law, as well as the dynamic interactions between the government and citizens in China. Using a holistic and nuanced approach will contribute to a more accurate account of Chinese governance rules and measures, particularly those for addressing mass actions, as discussed in the next section.

1.3 Introducing A Juridification Perspective and Its Merits

This section first introduces the concept of juridification and outlines the essential components of a juridification theory of legal, institutional and social developments (Sect. 1.3.1). It then critically examines the existing scholarship on mass actions in China (Sect. 1.3.2). Thereafter, it elucidates the need to incorporate the juridification perspective in order to comprehend the evolving role of government accountability law in Chinese measures for addressing mass actions (Sect. 1.3.3). Finally, it delineates the distinctive contributions that this book offers to readers and identifies the target readership interested in exploring government-citizen relations and interactions in China through a juridification study of mass actions and their resolutions (Sect. 1.3.4).

1.3.1 The Concept of Juridification

A holistic and nuanced approach to understanding Chinese governance and legal evolutions is essential for comprehending the dynamics of Chinese mechanisms for managing mass actions, particularly the evolving role of government accountability law in this area. In contrast to the dichotomous notions and overly simplistic analytical framings discussed in the previous section, this part delves into the concept of juridification and demonstrates how it can provide a useful perspective for addressing the core theme of this book.

The term "juridification" was coined around the 1860s to describe the growing importance of legal rules in confirming family relationships and resolving related disputes, a trend that began among the bourgeoisie and later extended to the working class.[31] In the mid-twentieth century, the scope of the concept expanded from the family sphere to the workplace, where the law became increasingly important in establishing employment relations and settling work-related disputes, known as the juridification of modern labour management.[32] Over time, the concept of juridification has been adapted to take account of social changes in contemporary times, with the law becoming the primary basis for regulating various interpersonal relationships and resolving disputes, a phenomenon that sociologists refer to as the juridification of the "life-world."[33]

The juridification perspective argues that modern States, having gained political power through peaceful means such as elections, or non-peaceful means such as revolutions, tend to entrench their political decisions through the creation of laws to legitimise them as part of the basic norm within the State.[34] As a result, social disputes that were once resolved by political means, either formally in bodies of elected representatives, or socially through strikes, boycotts, protests and demonstrations, are now increasingly managed and addressed through legal means.[35] The juridification perspective provides a somewhat sequential account of legal and governance developments, with each stage contributing to the expansion and consolidation of the power of law. More specifically, the juridification process involves three key stages:

> The first stage, the formalisation of laws, establishes a set of rules that affirm the authority of the State to govern and define the rights and duties of members of society. By creating laws, the State confirms the legal recognition of its governance legitimacy and specifies the basic rights and duties of both individuals and collective entities as legal persons under its rule. Consequently, the conduct of public and private actors is defined as the fulfilment of legal duties or the exercise of legal rights.

[31] The literature search was conducted on the English website of Google Scholar, using "juridification" as the search term in the title, and the time range customised as "between 1850 and 1970". The earliest mention of the term "juridification" is found in U Vedder's work titled "Between Genealogy, Degeneration, and Reproduction: The Figure of the Bachelor in Science and Literature," Part I, "A Broader Conception of Heredity," published in 1868. This information is sourced from the reprinted book Ana Barahona et al. (eds) (2010), p. 129.

[32] Atzeni and Ghigliani (2009), pp. 3–4.

[33] Teubner (1987), pp. 4, 11 and 24.

[34] Eckert et al. (2012), p. 5.

[35] Ibid.

> The second stage, the institutionalisation of the law, builds on the first stage by directing the State's governing powers and their agencies to make decisions and deal with external objections by legal means. This process has the effect of embedding the law more deeply in the governance culture and extending its influence beyond the legislature to the wider institutional sphere.
>
> In the third and final stage, the socialisation of the law culminates in the promotion of a social culture in which the law is pervasive. At this stage, social members habitually view their personal and interpersonal affairs from a legal perspective. The content and spirit of the law are internalised as an integral part of social norms, and natural and legal persons consciously or unconsciously comply with the law when making decisions.[36]

The concept of juridification offers a holistic perspective on the dynamic interplay between legal, institutional and social developments. This perspective recognises that the expansion and consolidation of legal power is not only due to the proactive law-making efforts of the State but also depends on institutional and societal changes that affect the way governing powers and members of society interact with each other. In contrast to the rigid and dichotomous theories of governance and law, juridification theory presents a nuanced framing for analysing and assessing the role of government accountability law within Chinese approaches to addressing citizen objections in general and mass actions in particular.

Specifically, juridification theory focuses on the effect of law upon the institutional development of State governance and the evolution of social norms. Both its analytical scope and focus serve the purpose of this book well. It transcends the sole attention to the primacy of law that is central to Eurocentric accounts of the Chinese governance model. Instead, the juridification theory offers a timely contribution to advancing the knowledge of the dynamic interplay between the State and law and the changing interactions between government and citizens in China, taking into account legislative, institutional and social factors that cannot be meaningfully separated from each other.

1.3.2 Current Research on Mass Actions and Its Limitations

This part reviews the research literature on mass actions and their settlements in China, focusing on English-language and Chinese-language academic articles and research reports published between 1990 and 2018. It summarises the prevailing assumptions, recurring lines of analysis and key limitations of the existing research, setting the stage for a more nuanced and holistic account of Chinese rules and procedures for resolving mass actions in the following part.

At first glance, mass actions in China may seem an unlikely topic, given that the Chinese government is often perceived as systematically hostile to citizen objections. However, mass actions challenging government decisions are widely recorded in China. What is striking is that the number of participants in mass actions has increased substantially, from around 730,000 in 1993 to several million in the first

---

[36] Eckert (2012), pp. 4–5.

decade of this century.[37] Such a counter-intuitive phenomenon has been studied from different theoretical perspectives and with varying assumptions.

Over the years, research on this phenomenon has been shaped by two distinct assumptions, each contributing to different research agendas and findings. The first assumption views mass actions as a form of popular resistance to the governing authorities in China and analyses it through the lens of authority-individual confrontation.[38] In this perspective, the governing authorities are seen as systematically hostile to citizen objections and suppressing mass actions, while those who engage in mass actions are perceived to be pursuing a common objective, namely to confront the parties they believe are responsible for their suffering.[39] This perspective has dominated the field of political sociology of mass actions from the 1990s to the 2010s, with some 670 research papers exposing the normative and procedural flaws within the Chinese governance processes that mass actions confront. The most popular keywords associated with this approach include social unrest,[40] group resistance,[41] and grassroots resistance.[42]

The confrontational approach delves into the tactics used by participants in mass actions to secure a satisfactory settlement of their grievances or the conditions under which they must disband without achieving their intended goals.[43] While this approach has detailed the confrontations between Chinese authorities and mass action participants, it has tended to characterise mass actions and their settlements as a zero-sum game. However, emerging empirical evidence suggests that the resolution of mass actions is not always a win-lose scenario. An alternative perspective has begun to arise, which views the Chinese government as a highly diverse entity, with some practices advocating for the solicitation of dissenting opinions from Chinese citizens while others opposing citizen objections.[44]

As a result, new research questions have emerged that move away from assuming mass actions as confrontations with the Chinese authorities. Instead, they are seen as disputes between specific government decision-makers and affected parties that can

---

[37] The Chinese Public Administration Research Team (eds) (2009) Causes for and Solutions of Mass Spontaneous Incidents in China, p. 16.

[38] Diamant et al. (2005), pp. 7–9.

[39] Jacka et al. (2013), pp. 260–261.

[40] As of 31 December 2019, within the most extensive database of Chinese-language academic sources, the China National Knowledge Infrastructure, there are 503 academic publications whose abstracts include the search term of 'social resistance'(*shehui kangzheng*/社会抗争).

[41] As of 31 December 2019, there are 117 academic publications whose abstracts include the search term of 'group resistance' (*qunti kangzheng*/群体抗争) in the China National Knowledge Infrastructure.

[42] As of 31 December 2019, there are 57 academic publications whose abstracts include the search term of 'grassroots resistance' (*diceng kangzheng*/底层抗争) in the China National Knowledge Infrastructure.

[43] Chen et al. (2016), pp. 396–397.

[44] As an example, numerous studies have illustrated distinct responses from China's central and local governments to collective complainants. The State Council is noted for engaging in a so-called "blame game", often shifting responsibility onto local government officials. In: Heurlin (2016), pp. 206–208.

be resolved peacefully through judicial and administrative channels.[45] As of 2022, some 1300 Chinese-language research articles have examined existing policies and measures relevant to the management of mass actions and identified good management practices therein. This shift has introduced new terms to conceptualise various forms of mass actions, including group litigation,[46] group conflict,[47] mass litigation,[48] and, to a lesser extent, group dispute.[49]

In this context, a subfield of public disputes (*gonggong jiufen*/公共纠纷) has gained popularity, demonstrating that China's administrative and judicial authorities act as dispute adjudicators who are bound by accountability rules, rather than as indifferent oppressors. Mass actions are no longer studied as a zero-sum game, but the analytical focus is shifted to the varying contents, grounds and outcomes of mass action settlements. In particular, it examines the rules and measures in place to manage collective grievances about the government's violation of the affected parties' legitimate interests, such as receiving fair compensation for government-approved land requisition projects, or procedural rights, such as receiving a public hearing before a government sanction is imposed.[50] With this conceptual adjustment, the settlement-centric approach sheds light on the normative and procedural elements that contribute to the efficient resolution of mass actions and identifies best practices that can serve as a useful reference for the relevant authorities in the future settlement of collective grievances.

Meanwhile, this approach's focus on efficient dispute resolution has been criticised for neglecting the fairness of the institutional handling of mass actions in its analyses. In the 2010s, Chinese researchers became interested in studying what is known as mass group incidents (*quntixing shijian*/群体性事件), which is an ambiguous term. The term recognises the collective form of mass actions without explicitly discussing their confrontational elements. The use of mass group incidents is thought to be a deliberate consensus among researchers, allowing them to choose between the conventional confrontation-centred approach and the relatively new settlement-centred approach. The former is politically sensitive, while the latter is considered

[45] Schubert (2008), pp. 198–199.

[46] As of 31 December 2022, there are 555 academic publications whose abstracts include the search term of 'group litigation'(*quntixing susong*/群体诉讼) in the China National Knowledge Infrastructure.

[47] As of 31 December 2022, there are 534 academic publications whose abstracts include the search term of 'group disputes'(*quntixing jiufen*/群体性纠纷 or *qunti jiufen*/群体纠纷) in the China National Knowledge Infrastructure.

[48] As of 31 December 2022, there are 195 academic publications whose abstracts include the search term of 'mass litigation' (*minzhong susong*/民众诉讼) in the China National Knowledge Infrastructure.

[49] As of 31 December 2022, there are 29 academic publications whose abstracts include the search term of 'group disputes' (q*untixing zhengyi*/群体(性)争议) in the China National Knowledge Infrastructure.

[50] Chang and Tian (2013), pp. 63–65.

too distant from the aggrieved complainants.[51] As of 2022, more than 10,750 Chinese-language research articles have listed mass group incidents as a keyword, examining national, central-departmental and regional policies and guidelines for handling mass group incidents and assessing their legality and effectiveness.[52]

In summary, the existing research on mass actions and their resolutions in China is underpinned by two recurring lines of analysis. One views mass actions as the confrontation between the authorities and the complainants, and concludes that the Chinese government develops repressive tactics to systematically contain mass action participants. The other characterises mass actions as a form of dispute between specific decision-making authorities and the affected parties, which can be resolved through appeal procedures, and compares different settlements to identify the most efficient resolution measures. Analytically, neither approach has an inherent superiority over the other. Given the central focus of this book, both the confrontationist and the settlementist approaches fail to capture the dynamics of the different rules and practices for managing mass actions. This weakness can be remedied by a juridification account which links the State's legislative developments to their institutional implementations, outcomes and social impacts.

1.3.3 Analytical Contributions of A Juridification Account

Following a summary review of the research literature on mass actions in China, this part details how a juridification account helps to elucidate (contentious) government-citizen interactions and the evolving importance of (accountability) law in the Chinese management of mass actions. This account integrates an analysis of Chinese acceptance of rules of government accountability, and how these rules develop at the institutional level with an examination of how they are incorporated into social norms. In short, the juridification account informs the formalisation, institutionalisation, and socialisation of government accountability rules in Chinese approaches to dealing with mass actions.

Specifically, my juridification account first explains relevant legislative and regulatory developments in the management of citizen objections, particularly those that hold the government accountable for its duty to protect citizens' rights to appeal government decisions and seek redress for their losses. It then analyses the subsequent implementation by China's administrative, judicial, political and non-governmental bodies, and examines the extent to which these implementing bodies comply with the legislative and regulatory provisions. To assess whether and to what extent Chinese rules and practices for resolving mass actions are perceived as normal and acceptable by society, this account also looks into Chinese news

[51] Xiao (2012), pp. 147–150.

[52] As of 31 December 2021, there are 10759 academic publications whose keyword lists include the search term of 'mass group incident' in the China National Knowledge Infrastructure.

coverage of mass actions produced by both official and commercial media. Through this holistic and nuanced account, I hope to deepen our understanding of Chinese approaches to handling mass actions, their institutional contexts, and their governance and social implications.

This juridification account has much potential to add to existing knowledge. First, it modifies reductionist claims that dismiss the legal development of the right to challenge and appeal government decisions under political singularity in China, and that qualify mass actions as a zero-sum confrontation between the Chinese government and complaining citizens. It avoids the oversimplified thesis that the rule-based model is an all-or-nothing proposition determined by the presence or absence of the primacy of law in State governance. The juridification account refrains from examining the factors through dichotomous lens, whether personal or institutional, that shape Chinese approaches to settling mass actions, as they have been extensively explored elsewhere.[53] Instead, it offers insights into the processes of formal acceptance, institutional compliance and social reactions to government accountability rules in contemporary China.

In short, my juridification account aims to help readers well understand and evaluate the Chinese case by recognising both the contents and effects of the rules and practices for holding the government accountable to citizens, as well as those for managing mass actions in recent decades. Undoubtedly, such an account may be considered controversial. It is important to clarify that my advocacy of an account of indigenous Chinese government accountability traditions and their modern adaptions is not a relativist stance. It is not to posit that the role of law in the Chinese context should be exempt from external scrutiny or criticism, nor is it to argue that any evaluation of the Chinese case should be guided by the standards endorsed or accepted by the Chinese government.

On the contrary, the juridification account aims to modify the currently dominant but poorly grounded schema in the research literature and policy debates on the subject of this book. It provides readers with the amended conceptual and analytical tools to make better sense of the highly dynamic government-citizen interactions and institutional arrangements for managing mass actions in China. By paying deliberate attention to both the legally and socially accepted and unaccepted elements of Chinese measures for addressing mass actions, I hope that readers will approach the book's subject by understanding the relevant legislative developments, their subsequent institutional implementation and outcomes, and the implications for changing social norms in China.

Secondly, in addition to conceptual and analytical modifications, my juridification account draws on a wide range of first-hand data. The data collected for this book include ancient archives (mainly in Chap. 2), official records of the Chinese legislative, judicial and administrative data, and Chinese news data. The primary data consists of relevant State legislations, government regulations and

[53] For an in-depth exploration of personal and institutional factors influencing the settlement of mass actions, readers are encouraged to refer to the book: Wright (2019).

policies, and political resolutions and guidelines adopted between the 1970s and the 2010s. The supplementary data are derived from news reports produced by China's official and commercial media over nearly two decades, spanning from the late 1990s to the 2010s. These news reports are collected from the WiseNews database, the world's largest Chinese news repertoire that monitors and captures news from various outlets, including newspapers, news magazines, and news websites in China.[54]

The availability of computer-assisted qualitative data analysis tools has considerably expanded the scope of research on legal and governance topics, as they facilitate the collection and processing of voluminous data in a multitude of languages and formats. To engage the massive and complex data that involve millions of Chinese characters and cover a wide range of sources, including legislative and policy releases, expert commentary, and responses from mass action participants and their stakeholders, this study conducts a software-assisted corpus analysis of the massive news data. The aim of processing news data on mass actions is to understand whether and in what ways Chinese approaches to dealing with mass actions are commonly depicted as normal and acceptable, and the role of government accountability rules in recurring news narratives, an account not available elsewhere in the existing research literature.

In sum, my account of the juridification of Chinese approaches to handling mass actions corrects existing dichotomous and static assumptions and explanations, both conceptually and empirically. It shifts the focus to the critical question of whether the importance of law is on the rise or on the decline in the Chinese governance model in general and its arrangements for dealing with mass actions in particular. This account provides a detailed examination of the evolution of government accountability rules at the formal, institutional and social levels in the context of mass actions. It is an attempt to capture the dynamic interplay between State governance and law, and between the government and citizens in China, beyond any simplistic or Eurocentric notions. It is hoped that this juridification account will help readers formulate a holistic and nuanced understanding of Chinese rules and procedures for tackling mass actions and their implications for future China and the world.

1.3.4 The Book's Novelty and Readership

This book stands out for its innovative perspective and line of analysis, as well as its extensive research data. It goes beyond traditional analyses by looking not only into Chinese legislative, policy and judicial data related to mass action settlements but also into longitudinal news coverage of the issue. As a result, it unravels the legislative, institutional and social factors that shape Chinese rules and practices for addressing citizens' grievances against the government, particularly in the form

[54] As of 2018, The WiseNews, provided by Wisers Information Limited, covers over 1200 Chinese-language news outlets including newspapers, website news, news magazine and wired news.

of mass actions. It also sheds light on the institutionalisation and socialisation of government accountability law, and its implications for reforming government-citizen interactions and social norms in contemporary China.

Methodologically, the book analyses China's acceptance of government accountability rules and their subsequent implementation that are relevant to the content, form and settlement of mass actions. It conducts a careful reading of relevant legislative, judicial, administrative and political decisions adopted between the 1970s to the present to make sense of key developments of government accountability rules at the normative and institutional levels. The supplementary research data, consisting of over 13 million words of news coverage, are then processed using the software AntConc. The aim of analysing the supplementary news data is to reveal the linguistic features, and discursive and social implications of relevant news coverage, and to uncover the extent to which government accountability rules, in particular those that regulate government conduct and protect citizens' rights to appeal government decisions, play a role in qualifying mass actions and evaluating their outcomes.

Written for a wide readership, this informative and multidisciplinary book is a valuable resource for researchers and policy advisors, as well as an ideal university reference book. Its six chapters cover a wide range of topics, including China's indigenous tradition of government accountability and government-citizen dispute resolution and their modern adaptions, as well as contemporary Chinese approaches to dealing with the selected cases of collective petitions, labour actions and farmers' protests and how they are narrated and evaluated in the news. Presented in clear and accessible language, this book is an excellent choice for intellectually curious readers seeking insights into Chinese governance traditions and modern transitions. It explores and explains the dynamic interplay between the long-standing concern of the Chinese governing powers to be (perceived to be) competent and the emerging importance of government accountability rules in the Chinese institutional and social landscapes.

1.4 The Book's Scope, Foci and Methods with A Note on Chinese News

This section outlines how the juridification perspective is used to analyse Chinese approaches to handling mass action. It begins by specifying the scope of Chinese rules, procedures and social norms studied in this book, and clarifies how the juridification of government accountability helps to better understand Chinese rules and practices for dealing with mass actions (Sect. 1.4.1). It then explains the book's analytical focus and the methods used to collect, process and interpret the relevant archival and official data and the findings of the current research literature, forming a consistent line of analysis in three case studies of collective petitions, labour actions, and farmers' protests and their settlements (Sect. 1.4.2). This is followed by a collection and analysis of official and non-official news reports on mass actions and their resolutions, highlighting the political and market dynamics that shape the operation of Chinese news media and the relevance of Chinese news reports to understanding the socialisation of government accountability law in China (Sect. 1.4.3).

1.4.1 On the Scopes of Chinese Rules, Procedures and Social Norms

The Chinese rules examined in this book include both statutory rules and customary rules that authorise or regulate the conduct of China's governing authorities in dealing with citizens' complaints about government conduct. Specifically, the rules examined in each case study cover laws enacted by the Chinese legislature, administrative regulations and directives issued by the Chinese State Council (which is the Central Government in China) and its departments, and political resolutions adopted by the CPC Central Committee. The procedures studied cover a range of processes by which mass actions are handled by the relevant authorities, including internal procedures such as administrative appeals and external procedures such as judicial review, mediation and arbitration involving the third party. The implementing bodies discussed consist of both State authorities in particular, the government and the court, and non-State actors such as social organisations, which are involved in the management of mass actions either on an *ad hoc* or a regular basis. This book examines the historical antecedents, contemporary reforms and outcomes, and the norm-agency consistency of each of the above elements, focusing on the development of government accountability rules there.

With regard to the social norms that are observed in mass actions and how they change over time, a common approach is to collect responses from individuals who have been involved in a dispute and to examine their feedback. For example, in the area of labour dispute resolution, researchers have asked about the feelings and opinions of the complainants during and after the resolution and assessed whether the process for resolving the dispute is understood as normal and acceptable by the complainants.[55] Similarly, researchers studying public attitudes to judicial review have interviewed litigants who have recently had their dispute resolved by the court and analysed their feedback in the context of their economic and social background.[56]

The survey approach to disputants relies on individual experiences and accounts, which are often time- and context-specific. As a result, the findings provide insights into whether a dispute settlement is considered as acceptable by selected respondents. Alternatively, an analytical approach that looks into a variety of narratives,

[55] Brockner and Wiesenfeld (1996), pp. 204–205.

[56] Tyler and Jackson (2014), pp. 89–91.

such as those found in the news, provides a broader picture of what is generally considered normal and acceptable than individual feedback. Research into the relationship between news content and general perceptions is complex and can take several different directions, including formal (i.e. text-based study), cognitive (e.g. the influence of news framing upon the perceptions of the target audience), and sociological (e.g. the relationship between news discourse and social behaviour). This study takes a textual approach to examining the socialisation of government accountability law throughout the development of mass actions in China, identifying recurring narratives and key framings in the news and their social implications. Given that existing scholarship already focuses heavily on survey-based analyses, the study adopts an alternative approach in the hope of gaining a more holistic understanding of whether mass actions and their settlements are commonly understood as normal and acceptable in China.

1.4.2 On Analytical Foci and Methods

This book focuses on three types of mass actions in its case studies: collective petitions, labour actions and farmers' protests. Each type is selected based on four specific criteria: a. their claims are directed against flaws in government policies, implementing procedures, or the conduct of implementing agencies; b. they take a collective form without being deliberately violent;[57] c. their aim is to get the authorities to pay attention to their grievances, consider their claims and redress their losses; and d. they have been widely reported in the Chinese news over a relatively long period of time and constitute a matter of public concern.

The selected cases of collective petitions, labour actions and farmers' protests are essentially non-violent, and each addresses an inappropriateness or serious injustice in government decisions. Participants in these mass actions seek to engage the relevant authority to resolve their grievances without confronting the government as a whole or challenging its legitimacy. Moreover, these cases have been extensively reported in the Chinese news, reflecting the changing views and diverse

[57] There is no internationally accepted distinction between peaceful and non-peaceful forms of collective actions. For example, with regard to typical forms of mass actions such as demonstrations and rallies, the Organisation for Security and Cooperation in Europe (OSCE) states that the determination often depends on whether organisers and participants have the intention to use violence. The OSCE stresses that the use of violence by a small number of participants or the involvement of passive resistance should not render an assembly as 'non-peaceful.' In: OSCE/ODIHR-Venice Commission Guidelines on Freedom of Peaceful Assembly, second edition, adopted by the Venice Commission on 4 June 2010.

In contrast, under Chinese law, non-peaceful forms of demonstration or assembly are defined as failure to cooperate with government authorities in maintaining or restoring public order and security, which may be punishable by administrative and criminal penalties. Article 27, In: The Law of the People's Republic of China on Assemblies, Processions and Demonstrations (2009 Amended).

attitudes of both State and non-State actors. It's important to stress that this selection of cases is neither exhaustive of all significant categories of mass actions (e.g. environmental protests) nor definitive. There is some overlap between the selected types of mass actions in terms of their complaining form. For example, a labour action may include collective petitioning which will be discussed in more detail in Chap. 4. However, the applicable rules and major procedures for managing each case remain distinct.

In recent decades, whenever there has been a (perceived) injustice in the functioning of the Chinese government, affected citizens have been active in filing complaints and seeking redress. In 2009, for instance, around eighty per cent of all documented mass actions expressed grievances for which the Chinese government was allegedly responsible.[58] To capture the key elements of the formalisation of government accountability rules in China's management of citizen complaints, I look into the statutory rules enacted by the Chinese legislature, which serve as the basis for the decision-making by China's administrative and judicial bodies. I also examine relevant secondary rules promulgated by the State Council and its ministries in the form of administrative regulations and directives, which government authorities are required to follow. I then assess the institutionalisation of these statutory and secondary rules by analysing whether the implementing procedures and agencies adhere to the adopted legal rules in handling collective petitions, labour actions and farmers' protests. In cases where there is a lack of consistency between rules and agencies, I identify the factors that lead to such discrepancies based on first-hand data and literature review findings.

With regard to the socialisation of government accountability rules in the realm of mass actions, I collect all available news reports on collective petitions, labour actions and farmers' protests produced between 1998 and the mid-2010s. During this period, it has become acceptable, and to some extent, desirable, for the Chinese government that news media expose flawed and unlawful government decisions as a means of keeping local authorities in line with central decisions. Critical news reporting was officially recognised in 1998 as "the people's mouthpiece, the government's mirror",[59] which has encouraged an increasing number of news media to develop a reputation for being critical of those in power and helping to maintain the integrity of Chinese governing authorities. Nevertheless, the debate is valid whether Chinese news coverage accurately reflects changes in social norms when it comes to mass actions, which are considered politically sensitive. This point merits a separate discussion in Sect. 1.4.3 below.

---

[58] Yu (2009), p. 115.

[59] China's former Premier Zhu Rong-ji (Head of the government from the year 1998 to 2003) wrote an epigraph for an investigative news program called Focus during his visit to the State-owned China Central Television Broadcasting Company on 7 October 1998 that read "舆论监督，群众喉舌，政府镜鉴，改革尖兵 (meaning: the monitor on the public opinion, the mouthpiece of the people, the mirror for the government, the leading soldier for the reform)". In: The People's News Online(2019): Ten Memorable Moments in the History of the News Reporting in People's Republic of China.

Next, I conduct a corpus analysis of all relevant news reports on the selected types of mass actions and their settlements, focusing on the reference to government accountability rules in the popular narratives and framings in Chinese news. For a corpus analysis, there are two necessary steps in processing the data.[60] One step deals with the natural features of the corpus based on the occurrence of a word or a phrase across the text, which is the wordlist method, and the occurrence of words or phrases in close proximity to a target term, which is the collocation method. The results of the frequency and collocation methods reveal highly frequent words and word collocations in the selected news text, which serves as the first basis for making sense of recurring news narratives about the selected mass actions. The second step is the keyword-in-context method, which looks at how the target terms appear in the text. The results allow the researcher to identify the typical contexts in which target terms occur and to carry out a close reading of these contexts.

Before proceeding any further, it is helpful to explain briefly what the term 'corpus' means and what a good corpus requires. A corpus is generally understood to be a collection of machine-readable texts that provide a reasonable basis for studying a particular domain of discourse.[61] In other words, a good corpus consists of the texts that: a. are produced in a natural way; or put differently, they are produced in a way that is normally done; b. they are representative of a particular discursive domain, which means that they are quantitatively and qualitatively suitable for studying the discourse domain under consideration; and c. they are coded in a machine-readable way since almost all types of corpus analysis depend on professional linguistic software.[62]

In line with the corpus collection steps accepted in the field, I first define a comprehensive set of search terms on collective petitions, labour actions and farmers' protests and their settlements by various governing authorities so as to capture all relevant news reports to form the research corpus for each case study. This set includes both official descriptions and informal synonyms and connotations. I then use these terms to search for relevant news reports in the WiseNews database, which consists of a variety of news reports from official and non-official Chinese news media, as shown in Table 1.1:[63]

As the written Chinese language consists of square block characters (*fangkuai zi*/方块字), which does not contain spaces to separate words like other language systems (e.g. English), the collected Chinese news data cannot be processed directly in the corpus software whose algorithms are sensitive to spaces throughout the text. In order to make the collected reports processable in the corpus software, I use a professional Chinese spacing software called Corpus Word Phraser to add

[60] Gries (2017), pp. 591–592.

[61] Elena Semino (2017), pp. 464–465.

[62] Stefan Th. Gries (2017), p. 591.

[63] The WiseNews (2016) Content List of 'Wisers Information Portal'.

Table 1.1 The scope of news reports studied in this book

News producer	Newspaper			News journal	News agency	Website News		Total
	Official	Commercial	E-news			News page	Web portal	
Amount	29	72	587	16	19	559	21	1,303
Percentage	2.2	5.5	45	1.2	1.5	42.9	1.6	100
	52.8			1.2	1.5	44.5		

Table 1.2 How the spaced news data are processed in the AntConc

Computing method	Controlled condition	Result list
Wordlist	Default	Sort by the frequency of a word or a phrase in the corpus.
Collocate	Search window span: 20 to Left, 20 to Right	Sort by the frequency of a word or a phrase collocated with a target term relative to its own occurrence in the corpus.
Concordance	Search window size: 100 KWIC sort: default	Show how a word or phrase is commonly used in a KWIC(keyword in context) format.
Keyword list	Default	Sort by the keyness of words that are unusually frequent in a target corpus compared to a reference corpus.

linguistically meaningful spaces to the collected data.[64] Thereafter, I process the spaced data in a corpus analysis software called AntConc,[65] which calculates the occurrence, co-occurrence and concordance of words and target terms in the corpus (see Table 1.2).

For each case study, there are four steps in my textual analysis of the news data. First, I search for relevant news reports by using an inclusive list of search terms and test the relevance of the collected reports to the target topic by closely reading randomly selected news samples. I then define the keywords in the news samples that are irrelevant to the topic of the case study, search for similar reports in the corpus, and remove these reports from further analysis. Second, I process the cleaned corpus using the Wordlist and Collocate methods in AntConc, report the results and interpret their implications. Third, I process the corpus using the Concordance method, report its results and interpret their implications. Fourth, where relevant, I process the corpus using the Key-word-list method and investigate whether there are any changes in the news narratives over time and with what implications.

In summary, my analytical focus in this book is on the juridification process of Chinese rules and practices for dealing with mass actions. My analytical methods combine an analysis of the statutory and secondary rules of government

[64] The software is called Corpus Word Phraser, which is an open-source software developed by Dr. Xiao Hang at the Institute of Applied Linguistic Ministry of Education.

[65] Version 3.4.3w, September 2014, developed by Laurence Anthony.

accountability and the compliance of implementing agencies with these rules, with a textual analysis of Chinese news coverage. The intended outcomes are twofold: first, to gain insights into whether implementing agencies function in accordance with government accountability rules when handling collective petitions, labour actions and farmers' protests; and second, to uncover whether these rules and their implementation are introduced and narrated as the, or rather, a fundamental ground for categorising mass actions and assessing their settlements in the news.

1.4.3 On Chinese News: Reflective of Changes in Social Norms?

For my analysis of the socialisation of government accountability law in the context of mass actions in China, readers may question whether the news reports and commentary produced by Chinese official and commercial media are helpful in serving my research objective. The core question is whether the news data collected for this study are duly social, that is, whether it accurately reflects what is socially considered normal and acceptable. This part answers this question from two angles: first, I analyse the general regulatory environment in which Chinese news media expose the flawed or unlawful conduct of China's governing authorities. Then, I examine the specific regulatory environment and professional rules that are relevant to the news coverage of disruptive issues such as mass actions.

To begin with, the development of the Chinese news media is more complex and dynamic than is usually assumed. A common perception is that the Chinese news media are a single, undifferentiated entity and operate at the behest of the Chinese government. Monolithic as they may appear to be, the Chinese news media are in fact diverse in terms of what they cover and how they cover it. In sociological terms, the news media have played an important role in shaping and reshaping what scholars call the public agenda in modern societies. The growing influence of the news media on public and social lives in modern China is no exception. What is special in the history of Chinese media development is the relatively direct influence of the government on how the media organise their production and products.

The almost unprecedented scale and depth of the government-led media development in China makes the operation of the Chinese news media unique in its own way. In particular, during the national socialist transformation in the 1950s, all Chinese news media were integrated into the State governance apparatus. This established the status of the news media as a kind of government agency until the 1990s. Later, after the market-oriented economic reforms of the 1990s, a considerable part of the Chinese news media also underwent marketisation, which shifted their operation from being solely responsible to the government towards being sensitive to the tastes and preferences of the general public.

Indeed, the Chinese news media were once State-owned, as were nearly all the other sectors in the country in the 1950s. China had undergone critical vicissitudes in the first half of the twentieth century, leaving the country's governance framework fragmented and ineffective. When the CPC took over the political leadership in 1949, it saw the unification of the country as the most urgent task, and the solution to accomplish this task was to restore a centrally commanded governance system to minimise coordination costs and maximise production output.[66] By the mid-1950s, the State Council had succeeded in integrating various media, including print, broadcast, political and commercial, into a State-owned regime.[67] Under this regime, media units did not compete for market profit, but relied on government subsidies to cover their operating costs; accordingly, the news media became a *de facto* government agency, following government orders and promoting government policies.

Structurally, the Chinese news media were administered hierarchically, along the lines of the central, provincial, municipal and county levels of the government system, and the relationship between news units at different levels was similar to that of the government: news units at a lower level disseminated what the media at higher levels had reported, and the latter controlled what the former would report.[68] As a result, the Chinese news media primarily covered topics and contents that the government had approved. In 1956, Mao Zedong, the founding father of the People's Republic of China, instructed the then editor-in-chief of the People's Daily (the highest-ranking official newspaper in China) to leave the management of the newspaper to politicians.[69] By the 1960s, politically guided management of news production had been extended to the broadcast media.

From the point of view of State governance, news production under political control facilitated the effective dissemination of government decisions across a vast geographical territory, without which it would be virtually impossible to mobilise a diverse population and a fragmented society to restore the country's economic and military might.[70] The circulation of Chinese newspapers, in particular, rose from around three million in 1950 to over 40 million in 1960 and 164 million in 1980.[71] Apart from connecting government decisions to the general public, the Chinese news media also worked the other way around. News units regularly gathered public opinion and discontent and reported them to senior government officials through a channel known as the internal reference (*neican*/内参). Internally referred reports were categorised as unsuitable for external dissemination and were read only by a limited number of authorised officials who had the power to decide on the matter referred or otherwise refer it to the higher-level authority for consideration.[72] In this sense, the Chinese news media functioned as a public relations agency for the

[66] Li (1987), pp. 188–190.

[67] Li (2004), p. 23.

[68] Lien and Wang (2004), pp. 81–82.

[69] Mao (1983), p. 215.

[70] LI (2004), pp. 68–71.

[71] The National Bureau of Statistics of China: Data on National Post Service, Year 1950, 1960 and 1980.

[72] Wang (2006), pp. 88–89.

government, whose role was to promote government policies to the public and monitor public opinions for the government.

The 1990s saw a decisive change in the organisation of the Chinese news media. As early as 1978, eight news units were selected as pilot projects for the media marketisation reform, in which news production was to be managed by measures sensitive to market profit.[73] The Guangzhou Daily, which had been owned and controlled by the Guangzhou Municipal Committee of the CPC since 1952, began to be "self-responsible for income and expenditure, and self-responsible for profit and loss" in the 1980s,[74] and consequently, the primary goal of its news production shifted the official paper (*jiguan bao*/机关报) to the news paper (*xinwen bao*/新闻报).[75] By the early 1990s, the Guangzhou Daily had successfully commercialised its operations: from the news gathering and editing to the printing and distribution, all costs were covered by the newspaper's advertising revenue.[76]

With the approval of the Publicity Department of the CPC Central Committee and the State Administration of Press, Radio, Film and Television, the Guangzhou Daily News Group was set up on 15 January 1996 and has since served as a model for the marketisation of Chinese news units in other regions. In 2003, the State Council put an end to the mandatory news subscription policy under which all government departments and State-owned Enterprises (hereafter referred to as the "SOEs") were required to subscribe to designated news outlets, with a handful of exceptions for the central-level and provincial-level official newspapers that continued to accept government control in exchange for government subsidies to cover their operating costs.[77] Most regional and local news units had to turn to the market to secure their income. As a result, the implementation of the media marketisation reform saw commercial media emerge and grow, whose primary goal was no longer to promote government policies but to retain as many voluntary subscribers as possible.[78]

Put differently, the saleability of their news products has become a top priority for the majority of the news media in China. Financial independence allows for editorial autonomy, and investigative journalism emerged in the 1990s. News reports exposing the improper conduct of those in power became a selling point in the market, as

[73]It is called *shiye danwei, qiye jingying* (事业单位,企业经营) in Chinese. Shi-ye dan-wei, which literally means "public enterprise unit" and is translated as public institutions in English, refers to the government-owned organisation that provides public services such as education and research, culture, press and publications, radio and television. In: Article 2 of the Interim Regulation on the Registration of Public Institutions (事业单位登记管理暂行条例), promulgated by the State Council of the People's Republic of China on 25 October 1998.

[74]The government directive is called *zichou zizhi, zifu yingkui*(自筹自支,自负盈亏) in Chinese.

[75]Li and Duo (2019), pp. 109–110.

[76]Li and Duo (2019), pp. 109–111.

[77]The Central Publicity Department of the CPC and the State Administration of Press Publication, Radio, Film and Television, and State Post Bureau (2003) Notice on Suspending the Mandatory Subscription within the News Publication Units (关于报刊出版单位暂停征订活动的通知).

[78]Cao (1999), p. 133.

these stories were previously almost inaccessible to the general public.[79] For the managerial boards of the marketised news units, gaining popularity in the marketplace not only ensured that their organisations were financially sustainable, but also that they were resilient to potential political pressure from government officials who were unaccustomed to the government being questioned or challenged from the outside.

On the other hand, investigative news reporting that exposed government wrongdoing was tolerated by liberal officials who believed that critical journalism could make a positive contribution to building law-based governance in China.[80] In his memoirs, Zuo Fang, the founder and former editor-in-chief of the liberal newspaper Southern Weekly, revealed that in 1993, the Weekly was on the verge of being shut down by the order of the Publicity Department of the CPC Central Committee after it published an article criticising police misconduct and provoked protests from the Ministry of Public Security and the Ministry of State Security, which complained that the Weekly had leaked classified information; thanks to the Weekly's sizeable subscription base and excellent sales records (over a million copies per week at the time) as well as its proven credibility (some high-ranking officials regularly read it), Lin Ruo—the former provincial governor of Guangdong—endorsed the Weekly and asked the ministerial officials concerned: "Do you really think that what the public security, procuratorial and judicial officers are doing is flawless? What would be the harm in exposing the police officers' misconduct?" In the end, the political order to close the Southern Weekly was modified to require a statement from Zuo Fang clarifying that the newspaper and the news article had no malicious intent against the government but rather aimed to contribute to China's transformation from the Soviet legacy towards a law-based governance system.[81]

In the 1990s and 2000s, the Chinese news media achieved remarkable commercial success and gained public trust. This led to a rise in the number of university graduates interested in pursuing careers in the news sector. At the same time, Chinese universities began to offer degrees in mass communication and journalism and often adopted a liberal approach to educating a new generation of communication and journalism professionals. These programs emphasised the role of news as a truth provider in a free market of diverse opinions and as a power balancer between public authorities and individual citizens.[82] In 2015, 681 Chinese universities offered mass communication and journalism programs from which 230,000 bachelor students graduated; and approximately seventy-two per cent of these graduates either worked in media companies and media research institutes or continued their studies with related master's degrees.[83] University graduates bring not only their qualifications but also liberal ethics to the profession. This is a departure from the previous

[79]Peter Lorentzen (2014), pp. 403–404.

[80]Zhang (2010), p. 953.

[81]Fang (2014), pp. 238–251.

[82]Li (2010), pp. 7–8.

[83]Hu (2016) Employment Situations and Challenges of University Graduates with the Journalism and Communication Degrees (新闻传播学生就业现状及难点).

generation, most of whom worked for the government. When there is political interference in news production, young news editors and reporters tend to resist as much as they can.[84] Considering the operational changes in the Chinese news media since the marketisation reform and the evolving liberal values within newsrooms, it can be argued that news production in China is generally more aligned with the interests of its readers and audiences than with government agendas.

The following question to consider is whether the Chinese news media are willing and able to report on mass actions in the same manner as they cover other stories. Undoubtedly, mass actions are a topic that China's political authorities are cautious about, while the public is interested in them. It would be too simplistic to conclude that mass actions are simply absent from Chinese news coverage. News editors and reporters weigh news value against political risk when deciding whether and how to cover mass actions. In fact, a significant challenge for this study is not the limited amount of news data on mass actions, but rather that the relevant news reports are so massive that they need to be processed by automated text-processing software for possible human analysis.[85]

Moreover, it is important not to assume that the Chinese news media simply repeat what the government says when reporting on mass actions, thereby compromising their professional autonomy. It should be noted that Chinese news coverage of mass actions does not solely reflect the government's perspective, detached from popular sentiments and attitudes in society. While investigating a large-scale farmers' protest in Guangdong Province, journalists from a leading weekly journal and a major commercial newspaper met with other reporters from various news outlets in the village where the protest had broken out. With the support of experienced editors, the truth-seeking journalists managed to publish their investigative findings, which were widely read and among the most popular news stories about the protest.[86] It is acknowledged that Chinese news reporters and editors face greater political risks when covering mass actions that expose flawed or even unlawful government conduct. However, it must be recognised that the regulatory environment, operational arrangements and newsroom culture of the Chinese news media are indeed diverse. Chinese news coverage of mass actions is not solely to propagate the government's suppressive view, but rather reflective of the diverse stances and opinions of official and non-official actors.

---

[84] Zhao (2004), pp. 179–212.

[85] The news data collected for this study consists of news reports on collective petitions amounting to 3.92 million Chinese characters, labour actions amounting to 8.05 million, and rural demonstrations amounting to 1.35 million.

[86] I conducted several interviews, in person and by email, with journalists from the leading weekly journal and a major commercial newspaper in January-February 2014 and November 2014, respectively. The complete information on the interviews are with the author.

1.4.4 *Summary*

This section outlines the analytical scope, focus and methods for understanding and assessing the juridification of Chinese measures for dealing with mass actions. It details two interrelated parts. First, it examines relevant Chinese rules and implementation procedures for handling three areas of mass actions: collective petitions, labour actions and farmers' protests, with a particular focus on the norm-agency consistency, from the 1970s to the present. Second, it investigates Chinese news coverage of mass actions and their settlements, identifying popular narratives and framings used to qualify mass actions and assess their settlements from the late 1990s and the mid-2010s. By employing a juridification perspective to analyse Chinese measures for addressing mass actions, this book aims to provide a holistic and nuanced account of government-citizen contentious interactions in China, the institutional arrangements for managing these interactions and the evolving role of government accountability rules in them.

1.5 An Overview of Each Chapter of the Book

This book consists of six chapters and aims to provide a comprehensive and nuanced account of Chinese rules and procedures for dealing with mass actions. The first chapter is an introduction that outlines the book's basic concepts and assumptions, analytical foci and methods. Chapter 2, entitled "Indigenous Chinese Tradition for Addressing Grievances against the Government and Its Modern Adaptions", provides a detailed account of China's tradition of government accountability and its procedural arrangements for managing grievances against governing authorities, focusing on key elements of their continuity and changes in the modern and contemporary periods.

Specifically, it begins with an overview of the origins and development of governmental arrangements for receiving and investigating petitions against the ruling class. Moving forward, it delves into the political and conceptual conditions that shaped modern Chinese dispute settlement rules, highlighting the introduction of the people-oriented governance principle by the Republican State in the 1910s, and the incorporation of the mass-line governance doctrine by the Socialist State in the 1940s. It concludes with an analysis of the Chinese legal renaissance of the 1980s, outlining its influences on contemporary Chinese approaches to handling grievances against the government.

Chapter 3, which is titled "Chinese Measures for Managing Collective Petitions: An Unsettled Shift from Political Norms to Legal Rules", scrutinises China's institutional arrangements for handling collective petitions over the past few decades. Although China has enacted legal rules to limit the review and remedial powers of government petition-handling departments, tens of thousands of petitioners continue to seek redress for losses and grievances from government petition handlers, posing a major challenge to the juridification of China's petition management and settlement measures.

Against this backdrop, the chapter examines the changing dynamics between legal rules and political norms in the management of collective petitions and assesses the extent to which legal rules protecting rights to challenge and appeal to the government have been integral to the governmental handling of collective petitions. It then examines Chinese news coverage of collective petitions and their settlements, uncovering the popular narratives and framings for qualifying collective petitions and evaluating their settlements from the 1990s to the 2010s.

Since the 1990s, labour disputes have become a major source of mass action in China. Against this background, Chap. 4, entitled "Chinese Measures for Handling Labour Actions: The Rise of Labour Protection Rules and Its Challenges", looks into Chinese rules and practices for handling labour actions. It first contextualises the emergence of labour disputes as a result of the marketisation of Chinese labour management in the 1980s and the 1990s, which resulted in millions of Chinese workers being laid off from the SOEs while receiving rather limited unemployment and social welfare benefits.[87]

It then outlines the key governance and legal reforms that have shaped Chinese labour dispute settlement measures, focusing on the relevance of labour protection law in this realm. In addition to examining Chinese legal and procedural developments relevant to the protection of labour rights, the chapter also analyses Chinese news reports of labour actions and their settlements published between the late 1990s and the mid-2010s, uncovering the role of labour protection law in qualifying labour actions and assessing their settlements in the leading narratives and framings in the news.

The dissolution of collectivised rural communes in the 1980s posed a significant challenge to the mechanisms of rural governance in China, leading to frequent and sometimes violent disputes between rural residents and local governing authorities. Nearly half of the documented mass actions in 2012 were the result of unresolved grievances over decisions or conduct of rural governing powers.[88] In this context, Chap. 5, which is titled "Sending Law to the Countryside: Local Acceptance and Resistance", examines Chinese measures for dealing with farmers' protests.

In specifics, it explains the introduction of the self-governance principle and its impact on the relationship and interactions between rural residents and their governing powers. It begins by analysing the shift from collectivist rural governance to an autonomous and participatory model. It then investigates the rise of legal assertiveness among rural residents and its influence on the form and content of farmers' protests. In addition, it also examines Chinese news coverage of an influential farmers' protest in Wukan which occurred in 2009 and ended in 2012 and uncovers the relevance of self-governance and rights protection rules to

---

[87] Li and Tian (2014), pp. 270–288.

[88] Public Opinion Monitoring Centre of the Legal Daily (2012) Annual Report on Mass Group Incidents of 2012 (2012年群体性事件研究报告).

recurring news narratives and framings for qualifying the Wukan protests and assessing their outcomes.

Chapter 6, entitled "The Challenged Juridification of Chinese Approaches to Addressing Mass Actions", concludes the book. This final chapter provides a comprehensive synthesis of the conceptual developments and research findings that Chaps. 2 to 5 present: the juridification account of government accountability rules in China that separates administrative and judicial powers, affirms the State's duty to protect labour rights, and recognises the basic political and economic rights of farmers in key areas of mass actions and their resolutions in contemporary China.

The concluding chapter also summarises the trend towards greater legal accountability of public authorities and a stronger legal basis for citizens' grievances against the government, although there are challenges posed by the persistence of political norms and the reluctance of implementing agencies to apply legal rules as the primary basis for their decision-making. Finally, both the content and the outcome of mass actions have shaped what is generally considered normal in the context of government-citizen relations and interactions in recent decades. The growing rights awareness and legal assertiveness of aggrieved parties challenge politically prioritised norms of stability and conformity. The grievance of the complaining parties is gaining more sympathy, while the harsh response of the government is being problematised in the news discourse.

In short, the book finds that the introduction of government accountability rules into Chinese approaches to managing citizens' disagreements has led to significant changes in the way mass actions are handled. The most notable developments include the formal recognition of citizens' rights to challenge and appeal government decisions and the State's obligation to provide accessible and fair review and redress venues, the expanded power of the court in dispute resolution processes, and the establishment of public accountability alongside political accountability of Chinese governing powers. However, challenges remain in achieving systematic consistency between government accountability rules and agency decision-making processes, in reconciling conflicts between legal compliance and political conformity, and in bridging the gap between legal rules and social norms. While the book follows a coherent line of analysis across all chapters, each chapter stands on its own in terms of analytical focus and methods, data sets and research findings. This allows readers with limited time or specific interests to engage with individual chapters and still gain meaningful insights.

1.6 A Final Caveat

In concluding this chapter, it is important to acknowledge the limitations that have been encountered throughout my research journey. While every effort was made to overcome limitations in the design and conduct of my research, three limitations stand out: conceptual, methodological and operational. These limitations are worth mentioning because they highlight common challenges faced in formulating a promised holistic and nuanced account of the juridification of Chinese measures for addressing mass actions, which is relevant to researchers and policy advisors alike interested in advancing the knowledge on the subject.

The first limitation stems from the conceptual postulate that the growing primacy of law in State governance intersects with institutional and social developments. This postulate has its intellectual origin in evolutionary institutional concepts and theories (in particular, the concept and theory of juridification), which have received both considerable popularity and criticism. To this day, some of the fundamental disputes about the primacy of law as a precondition or result of the development of modern State governance have not been convincingly resolved. While this study assumes that the Chinese State follows the general process of juridification with its political form being a secondary factor influencing this trend, I remain open to criticism of the analytical concept and assumption to which I have subscribed in the book.

The methodological limitation arises from the use of textual analysis of Chinese news coverage to understand the socialisation of government accountability rules in the context of mass actions and their settlements. While mining massive news data to make sense of popular perceptions and views is a well-established research approach, any text-based attempt to explain social reality can be challenged as unscientific.[89] Perspective and interpretive biases are undeniably present in my text-based analysis of what is generally considered normal and acceptable in Chinese society by mining longitudinal news reports, however discernible they may appear.[90] Given this more or less inherent limitation of the text-based analysis, I have employed an automated method to uncover the linguistic features of the relevant news data as the basis for my further interpretations. In other words, my analysis of the news data is based on the results generated by the corpus analysis software, which I hope has duly reduced my subjective bias in the processing of the collected news data.

The final caveat is an operational limitation of this study. The extent to which the Chinese news coverage of mass actions reflects the content of social norms and changes in them warrants scrutiny. While the Chinese government is known for its inactive tolerance of a free press, the marketisation of the media sector in the 1990s and 2000s has significantly changed the regulatory environment, organisational structure, newsroom culture and news reporting ethics within the Chinese news media.

A detailed analysis of massive news coverage over eighteen years (from 1998, the earliest date for which the full-text report is available in the WiseNews database) helps understand what is commonly considered normal and acceptable during mass actions and their settlements. However, this timeframe is not ideal, as several legislative and procedural developments relevant to the management of collective citizen complaints against the government had already been introduced before 1998.

---

[89] Karl Popper (2014), p. 266.

[90] Benno Herzog (2016), p. 44.

Nevertheless, this book has examined the largest Chinese-language news data (more than thirteen million characters) on Chinese approaches to dealing with mass actions up to 2022.

Despite these limitations, this book has developed a modified conceptual and analytical approach to formulate a comprehensive and nuanced account of the juridification of Chinese measures for addressing mass actions. The combination of investigations into the formalisation, institutionalisation and socialisation of government accountability rules in the dynamic realm is intended to cover as many relevant aspects of the reality of the subject as possible, and the selection of the key areas of mass actions is intended to be inclusive and stimulating for readers, particularly researchers and policy advisors, interested in deepening their understanding of these fascinating topics. Each chapter is self-contained in terms of its focus, analysis and argument so that readers can read them individually and still navigate through the analytical journey of each chapter.

For non-Chinese and non-academic readers who may be constrained by language barriers, limited reading time or a lack of interest in academic jargon, this book can serve as an interesting and useful entry point to understanding the substance of Chinese legislative, administrative and judicial efforts to manage mass actions in recent decades, their outcomes and their interplay with institutional and social changes in the nature, form and result of mass actions. With an engaging writing style and the vernacularisation of research findings, the book makes a valuable contribution to both the research field and the public debate domain, and readers are encouraged to approach the findings with an open and critical mind and engage them in further discussion and research.

References

Article 2 of the Interim Regulation on the Registration of Public Institutions (事业单位登记管理暂行条例), promulgated by the State Council of the People's Republic of China on 25 October 1998. http://www.lawinfochina.com/display.aspx?lib=law&id=3601&CGid=. Accessed 5 Aug 2017

Article 27, In: The Law of the People's Republic of China on Assemblies, Processions and Demonstrations (2009 Amended), adopted at the Seventh National People's Congress and amended in 2009. http://www.npc.gov.cn/wxzl/gongbao/1989-10/31/content_1481217.htm. Accessed 24 Dec 2021

Articles 1, 57, 58, 85, 93, 125, 132 and 137, in The Constitution of the People's Republic of China (2018) adopted at the Fifth National People's Congress on 4 December 1982 and amended in 1988, 1993, 1999, 2004 and 2018. http://www.hldxc.jcy.gov.cn/art/2019/3/25/art_3916_20469.html (full text in Chinese)

As of 2018, The WiseNews, provided by Wisers Information Limited, covers over 1,200 Chinese-language news outlets including newspapers, website news, news magazine and wired news. https://libw.cuc.edu.cn/2018/1110/c996a19753/page.htm. Accessed 28 July 2019

Atzeni M, Ghigliani P (2009) "Labour movement in Argentina since 1945: the limits of trade union reformism", in the edited book CL Phelan: Trade Unionism since 1945: towards a global history. Peter Lang, pp 3–4

Barahona A et al (eds) (2010) The hereditary hourglass: genetics and epigenetics, 1868–2000. Max Planck Institute for the History of Science, p 129

Bel DA (2015) The China model: political meritocracy and the limits of democracy. Princeton University Press, pp 4–6

Berman HJ, Reid CJ (2012) Max Weber as legal historian. In: Turner S (ed) The Cambridge companion to Weber. Cambridge University Press, pp 231–232

Brockner J, Wiesenfeld BM (1996) An integrative framework for explaining reactions to decisions: interactive effects of outcomes and procedures. Psychol Bull 120(2):204–205

Cao P (1999) A study of newspaper groups in China (中国报业集团发展研究). Xinhua Publishing House, p 133

Chang J, Tian F (2013) Institutional construction for managing public conflicts (公共领域冲突管理的制度建设). J China Natl School Adm 5:63–65

Chen J, Pan J, el. al. (2016) Sources of authoritarian responsiveness: a field experiment in China. Am J Polit Sci 60(2):396–397

China's National Report Submitted by Paragraph 5 of the Annex to Human Rights Council Resolution 16/21. documents-dds-ny.un.org/doc/UNDOC/GEN/G18/254/62/PDF/G1825462.pdf?OpenElement. Accessed 2 Dec 2021

Diamant NJ, Lubman SB et al (eds) (2005) Engaging the law in China: state, society, and possibilities for justice. Stanford University Press, pp 7–9

Dicey AV (1915) Introduction to the study of the law of the constitution, 8th edn. Macmillan and Co., pp 179–180

Eckert J et al (eds) (2012) Law against the state: ethnographic forays into law's transformations. Cambridge University Press, pp 4–5

Fang Z (2014) Oral narratives by the founder of the Southern Weekly (钢铁是怎样炼不成的——<南方周末>创始人左方口述历史). Cosmos Books Ltd, pp 238–251

Fukuyama F (2014) Political order and political decay: from the industrial revolution to the globalisation of democracy. Profile Books, pp 538–541

Gerth HH, Mills CW (eds) (1946) From Max Weber: essays in sociology. Oxford University Press 1946:19–22

Gries ST (2017) Corpus approaches. In: Dancygier B (ed) The Cambridge handbook of cognitive linguistics. Cambridge University Press, pp 591–592

Herzog B (2016) Discourse analysis as social critique: discursive and non-discursive realities in critical social research. Palgrave Macmillan, p 44

Heurlin C (2016) Responsive authoritarianism in China. Cambridge University Press, pp 206–208

Hu Z (2016) Employment Situations and Challenges of University Graduates with the Journalism and Communication Degrees (新闻传播学生就业现状及难点). People's Opinion. http://www.xinhuanet.com/zgjx/2016-06/26/c_135466456.htm. Accessed 6 Aug 2017

Jacka T, Kipnis AB et al (2013) Contemporary China: society and social change. Cambridge University Press, pp 260–261

Koesel K et al (eds) (2020) Citizens and the state in authoritarian regimes: comparing China and Russia. Oxford University Press, pp 60–61

Li H (1987) The history of modern Chinese thoughts (中国现代思想史论), 1st edn. Eastern Publishing Company, pp 188–190

Li L (2004) Selected works of LI Liangrong: exploring news reforms (李良荣自选集:新闻改革的探索). 1st edn. Fudan University Press, pp 23 and 68–71

Li L, Duo F (2019) The 40 years of reform and opening-up in China: an investigation cantered on marketisation, a case study of Guangzhou Daily (中国新闻改革40年: 以市场化为中心的考察——基于《广州日报》的个案研究). J Commun Rev 72(3):109–111

Li L, Tian H (eds) (2014) China's legal development yearbook (No. 12) (中国法治发展报告No.12). The Social Sciences Academic Press, pp 270–288

Li X (ed) (2010) The future of journalism education (新闻教育未来之路). Tsinghua University Press, pp 7–8

Lien B, Wang J (eds) (2004) Twenty-five selected lectures on mass media (媒介二十五讲). Tsinghua University Press, pp 81–82

Lorentzen P (2014) China's strategic censorship. Am J Polit Sci 58(2):403–404

Ma H, Wang J (2018) Building a government based on the rule of law: history and development, 1st edn. Springer, pp 220–222
Mao Z (1983) Selected works on journalistic management by Mao Zedong (要政治家办报, 载于《毛泽东新闻工作文选》). The Xinhua Publishing House, p 215
May C (2014) The rule of law: the common sense of global politics. Edward Elgar, p 34
OSCE/ODIHR-Venice Commission Guidelines on Freedom of Peaceful Assembly, second edition, adopted by the Venice Commission on 4 June 2010. www.venice.coe.int/webforms/documents/default.aspx?pdffile=CDL-AD(2010)020-e/. Accessed 21 Sept 2016
Peerenboom R (2002) China's long March toward rule of law. Cambridge University Press, p 115
Popper K (2014) Conjectures and refutations: the growth of scientific knowledge. Routledge, p 266
Public Opinion Monitoring Centre of the Legal Daily (2012) Annual Report on Mass Group Incidents of 2012 (2012年群体性事件研究报告). https://www.163.com/news/article/8KGUC63B0001124J.html. Accessed 25 Feb 2017
Ratnapala S (2017) Jurisprudence, 3rd edn. Cambridge University Press, p 263
Schubert G (2008) One-party rule and the question of legitimacy in contemporary China: preliminary thoughts on setting up a new research Agenda. J Contemp China 17(54):198–199
Semino E (2017) Corpus linguistics and metaphor. In: Dancygier B (ed) The Cambridge handbook of cognitive linguistics. Cambridge University Press, pp 464–465
Shapiro I (ed) (1994) The rule of law. New York University Press, pp 328–330
South China Morning Post (17 June 2021) China climbs the list of the world's most competitive economies, as Hong Kong and Singapore slide. https://www.scmp.com/economy/china-economy/article/3137658/china-climbs-list-worlds-most-competitive-economies-hong-kong. Accessed 1 Dec 2021
Standard Eurobarometer 86 (2016) Public Opinion in the European Union (in the "Trust in Political Institutions"), the European Commission. europa.eu/eurobarometer/api/deliverable/download/file?deliverableId=59418. Accessed 1 Mar 2019
Teubner G (ed) (1987) Juridification of social spheres: a comparative analysis in the areas of labour, corporate, antitrust and social welfare law. Walter de Gruyter. pp 4, 11 and 24
The Central Publicity Department of the CPC and the State Administration of Press Publication, Radio, Film and Television, and State Post Bureau (2003) Notice on Suspending the Mandatory Subscription within the News Publication Units (关于报刊出版单位暂停征订活动的通知). https://www.chinacourt.org/article/detail/2003/07/id/67640.shtml. Accessed 5 Aug 2017
The Chinese Public Administration Research Team (ed) (2009) Causes for and Solutions of Mass Spontaneous Incidents in China (中国群体性突发事件成因及对策, 第二章"群体性突发事件成因"), 1st edn. Chinese Academy of Governance Press, p 16
The European Commission (2006) EU-China relations: commission sets out its strategy. https://ec.europa.eu/commission/presscorner/detail/en/IP_06_1454. Accessed 17 Mar 2019
The European Commission (2019) Joint Communication to the European Parliament, the European Council and the Council: EU-China – A Strategic Outlook". https://ec.europa.eu/info/sites/default/files/communication-eu-china-a-strategic-outlook.pdf. Accessed 10 Jan 2021
The European Parliament (2021) The European Parliament Resolution on A New EU-China Strategy (2021/2037(INI)): A New EU-China Strategy. https://www.europarl.europa.eu/doceo/document/TA-9-2021-0382_EN.pdf. Accessed 1 Dec 2021
The National Bureau of Statistics of China: Data on National Post Service. http://data.stats.gov.cn/easyquery.htm?cn=C01&zb=A0G0T&sj=2016. Accessed 17 Jan 2016
The People's News Online (2019) Ten Memorable Moments in the History of the News Reporting in People's Republic of China (新中国新闻报道史上的十大难忘记忆5). http://media.people.com.cn/n1/2019/0708/c14677-31219127-5.html. Accessed 10 July 2019
The Policy Department of the European Parliament (2015) Good Governance in EU external relations: what role for development policy in a changing international context. (EP/EXPO/B/DEVE/2015/02).www.europarl.europa.eu/RegData/etudes/STUD/2016/578012/EXPO_STU(2016)578012_EN.pdf. Accessed 2 Dec 2021

The software is called Corpus Word Phraser, which is an open-source software developed by Dr. Xiao Hang at the Institute of Applied Linguistic Ministry of Education. http://www.cncorpus.org/index.aspx. Accessed 21 January 2015. It detects and segments linguistically divisible components in the text, including nouns (e.g. words that refer to a person, substance, place, timing, direction, region, organisation, surname, and given name), verbs (e.g. words that describe an ongoing action, auxiliary, directional complement, linking complement, and a state of being), adjective (including normal adjectives, distinguishing adjectives such as male/female and single/double, numerals, and quantifiers), pronoun, preposition, particle, interjection, onomatopoeia, idiom, abbreviation, punctuation and a special symbol

The WiseNews (2016) Content List of 'Wisers Information Portal', updated on 28 July 2016. http://libwisesearch.wisers.net.eproxy2.lib.hku.hk/WISENEWS-SHARED/wortal/docs/content.pdf. Accessed 3 Aug 2018

The World Justice Project (2011) The World Justice Project Rule of Law Index®2011. worldjusticeproject.org/sites/default/files/documents/WJP_Rule_of_Law_Index_2011_Report.pdf. Accessed 1 Dec 2021

Tyler TR, Jackson J (2014) Popular legitimacy and the exercise of legal authority: motivating compliance, cooperation and engagement. Psychol Public Policy Law 20(1):89–91

Version 3.4.3w, September 2014, developed by Laurence Anthony, Faculty of Science and Engineering, Waseda University, Japan. Downloaded 1 Jan 2015

Wang S (2006) Models of Agenda setting in public policies in China (中国公共政策议程设置的模式). Soc Sci China 2006(5):88–89

Weatherall M, Huang MH (2017) Perceptions of corruption and institutional trust in Asia. ABS: www.asianbarometer.org/FileServlet?method=DOWNLOAD&fileId=1668754649529.pdf. Accessed 5 Mar 2018

Weng J (ed) (1995) Developmental Status and trend in China (中国发展状况与趋势), 1st edn. China Social Sciences Press, p 82

Wright T (2019) Handbook of protest and resistance in China. Edward Elgar Publishing

Wu X, Cheng J (2013) The emerging new middle class and the rule of law in China. China Rev 13(1):48 and 66

Xiao T (2012) Conceptualising, categorising and identifying mass group incidents in contemporary China (当代中国的 "群体性事件":概念、类型与性质辨析). J Human 4:147–150

Xu Z (2017) The Confucian misgivings: Liang Shu-ming's narrative about law. Springer. pp 24–25, 60 and 151

Yu J (2009) Types and features of mass group incidents in China (当前我国群体性事件的类型与特征). J Chinese Univ Polit Sci Law 6:115

Zhang Q (2010) A constitution without constitutionalism? The paths of constitutional development in China. Int J Const Law 8(4):953

Zhang X (2017) Rule of law within the Chinese party-state and its recent tendencies. Hague J Rule Law 9(2):394–396

Zhao Y (2004) The state, the market, and media control in China. In: Thomas P, Nain Z (eds) . Southbound Press, Who owns the media: global trends and local resistance, pp 179–212

Chapter 2
Indigenous Chinese Tradition of Addressing Grievances Against the Government and Its Modem Adaptions

2.1 Governance Norms and Arrangements in Ancient China

The development of indigenous Chinese norms and practices for dispute resolution is always contingent on broader institutional and social contexts. What is generally considered a reasonable dispute resolution practice in one context may raise eyebrows in another. To make sense of the governance and social contexts in which ancient notions and practices of government accountability evolved, the following parts first introduce the normative grounds based on which the ancient Chinese governments developed a procedure for receiving and resolving complaints from the ruled about the ruling class—an appeal mechanism that has survived many dynastic changes in ancient China (Sect. 2.1.1), and then analyses the specific practices and agencies for handling petitions from the aggrieved, their merits and weaknesses (Sect. 2.1.2).

2.1.1 Principle of Reciprocity and Introduction of Petition-Handling Practices

The basic means of production in ancient China was plough farming, and the constituent units of ancient Chinese society were the family and the family-related lineage (the latter consisting of multi-generational families, usually with the same surname).[1] The general norms for regulating social interactions and interpersonal

[1] Ancient China was (partially) conquered by powers whose economy was not based on plough farming but on seasonally mobile and pastoral activities, such as Khitan that ruled China from the year 916 to 1125 AD, Jurchen from 1115 to 1234 AD, Mongolian from 1271 to 1368 AD, and Manchu from 1644 to 1912 AD. After gaining control of agriculturally dominated territories in

C.-r. Qiao, *Chinese Rules and Procedures for Addressing Mass Actions*,
https://doi.org/10.1007/978-3-031-62201-4_2

relationships reflect what is known as the society of the well-acquainted (*shuren shehui*/熟人社会).[2] The relationship between the Chinese ruler and the ruled is traditionally abstracted as an extended form of the family relationship, and accordingly, the governance ideal is typically construed as comparable to the management of family interactions—the ruled ought to respect and obey the ruling superiors in the same way as they would their parents and lineage elders.[3]

Taken as a whole, the Chinese governance tradition treats government as a necessary good to ensure the welfare of the governed, which differs greatly from the Occidental governance tradition which deems government to be a necessary evil to safeguard the security and freedom of the governed.[4] This does not mean, however, that the influential governance ethics in ancient China blindly justified however the governing power treated the governed. In fact, the governing power was bound by the governance principle of reciprocity, whereby the governing class should limit its exercise of the power to the limits permitted by the Will of Heaven (*tianming*/天命). To summarise a highly complex and complicated concept, the Will of Heaven attributes the ultimate source of the ruler's legitimacy to the Law of Heaven (*tiandao*/天道). A legitimate ruler is supposed to substantiate his status as a son of heaven through his supreme wisdom and competence to maintain the harmony between human society and nature—in other words, a ruler's ability to rule well is seen as the basic proof of his legitimate rule.[5]

This competence-based justification for the legitimacy of the government is also reflected in Confucianism, which was accepted as the official ideology for regulating human behaviour and governing society during the Han Dynasty (from about 200 BC to 220 AD).[6] Classic Confucianism holds that members of society should fulfil their duties determined by their social status and role.[7] The ruling class, well-educated and qualified, should run a civilised government whereas the ordinary people, referred to as the Hundred Surnames (*baixing*/百姓), are regarded as the ignorant people (*min*/民) who must be guided by the ruling elites.[8] Hence, the conduct of the ruled to challenge the ruling members was usually considered abnormal, if not deplorable, in society. On the other hand, this does not mean that the ruling class was allowed to do as it pleased. The respect and obedience of the

China, these ruling powers inherited the indigenous governance principles and mechanisms that supported the agricultural economy and the social norms that accompanied it. See: Bertrand Russel (1922) The Problem of China.

[2]Huang (2010), pp. 31–32.

[3]Chen (2016), p. 763.

[4]Xu (2017), pp. 24–25, 60, and 151.

[5]It should be noted that attributing ruling legitimacy to the Will of Heaven is not exclusive to ancient China. The belief that earthly rulers have some divine supremacy was also popular in other traditional societies. For example, kings in the Roman States were viewed as human agents of a supernatural power. See: Maine (1870), pp. 4–6.

[6]Loewe (2008), p. 652.

[7]Ying-shih (1987), pp. 33–35.

[8]Ung-bing (1914), p. 48.

ruled to the ruler was reciprocal to the benevolence and competence of the ruling class.

The principle of reciprocity was binding on the members of the ruling class, including the emperor as the supreme earthly ruler, who had to demonstrate their governing integrity and ability to the ruled.[9] In particular, the ruling class was expected to be able to maintain the economic and social well-being of the ruled, mitigate the damage of natural disasters, such as floods and droughts, to agricultural production, and resist attacks and invasions by nomadic tribes.[10] The failure of the ruling class to fulfil these expectations of the ruled was seen as an indication of the illegitimacy of the ruling power.[11] When the legitimacy of the ruling class was questioned, the emperor would claim responsibility and announce positive actions to alleviate the suffering of the ruled. As the ancient archives show, several emperors, when faced with widespread popular discontent, issued the self-denunciation edict (*zuiji zhao*/罪己诏), in which they criticised themselves for wrongfully formulated policies and promulgated remedial policies to correct the harm done to the people.[12] If a ruler overlooked or ignored the suffering of the ruled, it meant that the ruler had violated the principle of reciprocity and therefore, the people's resistance to the ruler and his ruling dynasty was rightful.[13]

To maintain a competent governance apparatus over a vast territory, the central ruling body had devised several mechanisms to train its governors and officials. From the late sixth century, candidates for government office—regardless of social class, wealth and ethnicity—were educated and trained through subject-specific examinations (*keju*/科举). Candidates were tested by written exams and interviews on subjects relevant to State governance, including Chinese literature and classics, social and political history, economic and military management, and cultural traditions and rituals.[14] The best-performing candidates were appointed by the Central Government and formed an influential governing class in ancient China, known as the scholar gentry (*shi*/士). Although the Chinese emperor appeared to be at the apex of the entire governance system, he usually sanctioned co-governance with the scholar gentry by granting them considerable discretion in interpreting and implementing imperial orders at the local level.[15]

[9] Qianfang (2012), pp. 5–6.

[10] Genpan (2015).

[11] Loewe (2008), pp. 654–657.

[12] The Luntai Edict (*luntai zhai*/轮台诏) made and promulgated by Emperor Wudi of the Han Dynasty in 89 BC is the earliest fully kept self-denouncing edict. It stated that the abolition of the law and policy that granted excessive power to local governors to impose exploitative duties and taxes on the people was the most critical task.See: Yu-qing (1984), pp. 3–20.

[13] Peerenboom (2002), p. 10.

[14] In the Tang Dynasty, the Keju system included seventy-seven subjects. See: Lizhu (2005), pp. 11–12.

[15] Johnston (2014), pp. 64–67.

The expansion of China's territory and population presented a major challenge to the quality and therefore legitimacy of its monarchical government. By the year 1500, the population under monarchical rule had reached fifty-one million, and by 1851, it had surged to over 431 million.[16] Chinese emperors faced increasing difficulty in maintaining the integrity of the widely spread governance apparatus and staying informed about the implementation of central decisions by local governors and officials. The history of the central-local mistrust, and sometimes even conflicts, is complex and continues to pose challenges to the quality and integrity of present-day Chinese State governance. To summarise this complex topic, the central governing power remained concerned about the malfunctioning of local governing agencies which could undermine its governance legitimacy. This concern incentivised the central government to explore measures through which people could report complaints about local governing bodies or officials directly to central authorities.[17]

Autobiographical records from the last Qing dynasty reveal that Chinese local officials habitually coerced detainees into paying a reconsideration fee by threatening them with severe punishment.[18] In an effort to reform internal oversight practices, Emperor Hongli (reign: 1711 to 1799) sent trusted commissioners to inspect the work of local officials on an irregular basis and without prior notice.[19] However, the reform attempt ultimately failed due to the resilient shield practices employed by central and provincial officials to protect their loyal subordinates from central inspection.[20]

In summary, it is generally not socially acceptable for the Chinese population to disobey the decision of the ruling class or challenge the conduct of the ruling members under the guiding governance principle of reciprocity.[21] However, the central rulers did make exceptions to allow aggrieved individuals to present their complaints and claims against members of the ruling class.[22] As early as in the Han dynasty, Emperor Wendi (reign: 180 to 157 BC) established a reception office near his palace to provide an external check on his bureaucracy. This office allowed petitioners to express critical opinions about government decisions and the conduct of government officials.[23] The practice of receiving petitions was inherited by succeeding dynasties in ancient China, with some variations in the form of receipt practices and the scope of admissible complaints. The basic idea persisted that the

---

[16] Table 59 "Population of Xiaozong Reign in Ming Dynasty (明孝宗朝户数)" and Table 77 "Population of Xianfeng and Tongzhi Reigns in Qing Dynasty (清咸丰、同治两朝的人口数)", See: Fangzhong (2008), pp. 266 and 348.

[17] Ying-shih (1987), p. 38.

[18] Tung-tsu (2003), pp. 79–82 and 85.

[19] Kuhn (1992), p. 200.

[20] Tung-tsu (2003), pp. 91–94.

[21] Simon (1991), pp. 532–533.

[22] Tung-tsu (1998), pp. 4–5.

[23] Fang (2009), p 1107.

central authority should address damages to the petitioners caused by the wrongful conduct of the ruling class.[24]

2.1.2 The Development of Petition-Handling Practices

The ancient Chinese government archives do not commonly use the exact term petition, the Chinese translation of which means to make an appeal through speaking aloud or speaking upward.[25] Meanwhile, related terms can be found in historical records. The lung-shaped stone (*fei-shi*/肺石) is the earliest recorded instance, dating back to the third century BC. It was a stepping stone placed in front of the imperial palace, where complainants could voice their grievances to the central government; and the lung shape symbolised that both complaints voiced and government responses rendered should be as sincere as a human heart (the ancient belief took human lung and heart as the same organ).[26] The governments in ancient times made changes to their practices for receiving and reviewing complaint petitions. Below are some of the significant amendments.

A major procedural amendment was the introduction of different forms of identity protection. In the second half of the first century BC, the government began using bamboo and tile cases (*xiang*/缿) that resembled present-day post boxes where petitioners could put or send complaint letters to protect their identity compared to the earlier practice where petitioners had to voice complaints in public.[27] In the fifth century, government petition receivers started categorising petitions based on their urgency and confidentiality: complaints about the content of the government policy were deposited into a wooden case, while complaints about the conduct of government officials or the ruling elite were placed into a red-coloured stone case.[28]

During the period from the seventh to the tenth centuries, a pigeonhole cabinet was used to further refine the government practice of receiving petitions. The cabinet is composed of four distinct compartments. The blue compartment, which symbolises fairness due to its resemblance to the colour of the sky, is designated for complaints concerning the appointment of government officials and the content of government policies; the red compartment, symbolising good intention, for complaints about the conduct of government officials; the white compartment, symbolising innocence, for appeals to rectify wrongful convictions; and the black compartment, symbolising wisdom, for proposals to improve government policies.[29]

[24] Fang (2009), pp. 1121–1122.

[25] The most relevant terms for petition in Chinese are *shen-su* (申诉) and *shang-su* (上诉).

[26] Yifan and Ducai (1998), pp. 79–80.

[27] Yifan and Ducai (1998), p. 79.

[28] Yifan and Ducai (1998), p. 80.

[29] Fu (1961).

Between the eleventh and thirteenth centuries, various types of envelopes were used to channel petitions of varying degrees of severity to the relevant government authority. A petition against a central or provincial official would be submitted in two sealed envelopes with the smaller one enclosed within the larger one, each of which is stamped with an official seal to prevent any unwarranted intervention before it reaches the intended reviewer;[30] in contrast, a petition letter against an official below the provincial level would be sealed in a single envelope and will be reviewed by a competent petition handler at the provincial level, and depending on the petition handler's assessment of the case, the complaint may be transferred to the central authority.[31]

In addition to refining the practices of receiving petitions, ancient Chinese governments also developed admissibility criteria over time. Petitions concerning family disputes, such as inheritance or property division, and minor crimes such as non-severe bodily injury, were generally not admissible to the government petition office.[32] Petitioners were responsible for the validity of the evidence presented to the petition handler and had to include the name of a guarantor who owned a certain amount of wealth and was able to pay the false petition penalty, without which the petition could be rejected by the handler.[33] Besides that, certain forms of presenting a petition were considered to undermine the integrity of society and were therefore prohibited; for instance, displaying bodily harm in public was morally forbidden under Confucianism, which values bodily integrity as a blessing from one's ancestors and parents and therefore should not be deliberately damaged.[34]

After a petition was accepted, the handler would review the factual basis of the petitioned matter; if the case was deemed severe or urgent, it should be presented to the provincial or central authority, and for extraordinary cases, to the emperor's office.[35] During the review process, the petitioner would be provided with government protection and could stay in the designated place until the relevant authority decided on the case.[36] In cases where a petition revealed severe misconduct by a government official, an investigator appointed by the emperor's office would cross-examine the evidence and, if necessary, travel to the location of the complaint to collect additional evidence.[37] While there are no undisputed records of how appointed investigators collected and verified the evidence, the ancient government archives on criminal investigation can render some reference for understanding their work methods.

---

[30] The petitioner was required to sign a consent form acknowledging that corporal penalties could be applied if the presented claims were found to be ungrounded. See: Yifan and Ducai (1998), p. 90.

[31] Yifan and Ducai (1998), p. 90.

[32] Xianjue (1986), pp. 37, 60 and 69.

[33] Yifan and Ducai (1998), pp. 88–89.

[34] Zhongxin (1997), p. 89.

[35] Yifan and Ducai (1998), pp. 88–89.

[36] Yifan and Ducai (1998), p. 87.

[37] Xianjue (1986), pp. 60–61.

The archival records indicate that testimonies played a significant role in the criminal investigation. Investigators generally adopted an inquisitorial approach to obtain testimonies from the suspected wrongdoers.[38] In cases of major crimes, investigators may be authorised to use physical coercion on the suspect after receiving approval from a competent government office; during the interrogation, the use of torturous measures should be limited to specific body areas, such as the thigh or buttocks, and should not exceed one hundred beatings with a bamboo cane or eighty slaps to the face.[39] After collecting and assessing the evidence, the investigators presented their findings to their superiors, taking into account the relevant statute (*lv*/律), imperial decree (*ling*/令), interpretive and supplementary rules (*ge*/格) and analogous precedents (*bi*/比).[40]

To summarise, the government's handling of petitions as special measures complemented the general justice system, which was responsible for dealing with the majority of civil and criminal cases. The central ruling power allowed the aggrieved people to petition government officials and ruling elites on their misconduct or wrongful decisions. If these grievances of the ruled were not addressed, the ruling power would be seen as violating the principle of reciprocity and lose its governance legitimacy. Practically, petition cases helped the central ruler stay informed of the malfunctioning of local governors and officials. Ancient governments had developed measures for receiving and reviewing petitions over more than two thousand years, with various procedural and decisional improvements. However, these measures were not institutionalised as a permanent and regular procedure. The receipt, investigation and decision of petition cases often proceeded on an *ad hoc* basis, subject to the discretion of individual petition handlers and investigators.

2.1.3 Summary

In ancient China, the guiding governance principle was based on reciprocity. The governing power had a duty to govern society well, and in return, the governed were expected to respect and obey the decisions of the ruling power. The legitimacy of the ruling power was considered to rely on the governance competence of the ruling class. The absence of effective oversight methods made it challenging to guarantee the fair functioning of the governance bureaucracy. The central rulers received petitions submitted by the public, especially from aggrieved individuals. The handling of petitions became a long-standing governmental practice that allowed the general public to seek redress for government misconduct. However, in ancient China, these practices were not institutionalised as a permanent and regular mechanism. Instead, their outcomes depended on the discretion of specific handlers,

[38] Haiqing (2005), pp. 20–22.

[39] Jinfan (1992), p. 474.

[40] Liyan (2008), pp. 65–67.

investigators and decision-makers. In modern times, governance principles have significantly changed. A new set of rules for addressing complaints about governing bodies has emerged, which are detailed in the following section.

2.2 China's Acceptance of Government Accountability Law

During the second half of the nineteenth century, the Chinese government was unable to resist the military and geopolitical domination of European and Japanese States over China. Consequently, Chinese ruling elites developed a series of reform strategies to cope with external interventions and internal uprisings. The implementation of these reforms inadvertently weakened the normative, institutional and social grounds for the monarchical governance system that had been in operation in China for more than two millennia. The following parts discuss significant changes to Chinese governance notions and norms between the late nineteenth century and the early 1940s (Sect 2.2.1), as well as the legislative progress confirming government's duty to be accountable to the people from the 1910s to the 1940s (Sect. 2.2.2).

2.2.1 The Rise of People-Oriented Governance Concept and Principle

By the 1850s, a growing number of senior officials in the Chinese imperial government had publicly advocated "opening one's eyes and observing the world", lobbying the Chinese emperor to learn from the Occident to strengthen his governance competence. The Chinese imperial family initially supported the self-strengthening reforms (known in the English academic literature as the Western Affairs Movement) and financed the import of modern technology (especially military and defence equipment) from the Occidental States.[41] After some three decades of advancing Chinese technological competence, the self-strengthening reformers could not save China from European and Japanese military domination, the message of which became devastatingly clear when the Chinese navy was ruinously defeated by its Japanese counterpart in 1894 and 1895.

By the end of the nineteenth century, technology-focused reform attempts were widely regarded as unsuccessful. At the dawn of the twentieth century, the influence of republican ideas grew. Chinese republicans wanted to completely abolish the centuries-old monarchy as a necessary step to revive the strength of the Chinese State.[42] As British and French legal and political theories of popular sovereignty

---

[41] Ting-yee and Kwang-Ching (1978), pp. 528–529.

[42] Shenzhi and Jiadong (2000), pp. 124–126.

were translated into Chinese,[43] the notions of natural rights, social contract and checks and balances became attractive to revolution-minded elites.[44] Sun Yat-sen, the founding father of the Republic of China that replaced the monarchical government in 1912, marvelled at the American governance system during his visits to America between the late 1870s and the early 1910s. Sun vigorously promoted his idea in the Chinese press that a democratically elected and legally accountable government was the key to a prosperous economy and a well-managed society.[45]

Sun's essay published in the People's Newspaper (*minbao*/民报) in 1906 was widely discussed, in which he argued that "our country must enact . . .a series of democratic and progressive laws. . .that reflect what the people demand and facilitate what the development of a modern society requires".[46] Republican reformers promoted the normative and instrumental values of holding the exercise of State powers accountable to the wishes and demands of the people.[47] The Chinese monarchical government, unable to deal with the internal resistance movements that permeated seventeen (out of twenty-five) provinces, adopted the Outline of the Imperial Constitution in 1908, which was intended to cater to the popular demand for recognising the fundamental rights of the people.[48]

Despite its conservative elements, such as the article upholding the principle of maintaining the supremacy of the "Great Qing Emperor. . .for all generations",[49] the 1908 Imperial Constitution recognised a range of rights and freedoms of the ordinary people, which was unprecedented in Chinese history. These included the right to be free from arbitrary arrest, detention and punishment, and the right to freedom of expression.[50] However, the final efforts of the monarchical government could not save itself from an ultimate downfall. On 12 February 1912, the last Chinese Emperor Xuan-tong announced his decision to abdicate: "Seeing my people suffering every day, knowing that my people are in favour of a republican government, . . .it would be too selfish not to listen to what my people want, whose wish is the

[43] Yan Fu (1854–1921) was a Chinese thinker and translator who played a significant role in making Occidental political and legal theories accessible to Chinese intellectuals. His most influential translation works include Tian Yan Lun (On Evolution), which was translated from Thomas Henry Huxley's Evolution and Ethics in 1898, Yuan Fu (On Wealth), which was translated from Adam Smith's The Wealth of Nations in 1901, and Qun Ji Quan Jie Lun (On Boundary between Self and Group), which was translated from John Stuart Mill's On Liberty in 1903.

[44] Jinfan (2014), p. 495.

[45] Lum and Lum (1999), pp. 22–23.

[46] Jinfan (2014), p. 534.

[47] Jinfan (2014), p. 683.

[48] Jinfan (2014), pp. 601–603.

[49] Article 1, in the Outline of the Imperial Constitution 1908, promulgated by the Qing Government on 27 August 1908.

[50] Article 14: "The rights and obligations of subjects", in the Outline of the Imperial Constitution 1908.

message from Heaven.... I now announce that I am resigning (as Head of the Chinese State)."[51]

The succeeding Republican government promulgated a new governance principle known as the "Three Principles of the People" (*sanmin zhuyi*/三民主义). The principle was coined by Sun around 1905 as an abridged expression of his promotion of people-oriented State governance: a. the principle of building an independent nation (*minzu*/民族) that the Chinese people have the right to live in an independent and unified country; b. the principle of people's power (*minquan*/民权) that the Chinese people are the ultimate source from which the Chinese State derives its power, and that the people are entitled to elect, question and challenge State officials; and c. the principle of people's well-being (*minsheng*/民生) that the Chinese people are entitled to a decent standard of living in which agriculture and industry are fairly developed, and basic needs such as food, clothing, housing and transportation are met.[52]

This people-oriented principle was enshrined in the Provisional Constitution of the Republic of China in 1912, which stated that "the sovereignty of the Republic of China is vested in the people", and that Chinese citizens had the right to petition the parliament and the government and the right to sue State officials for breaking the law in the administrative court.[53] The constitutional recognition of the right to challenge the government in court marked a turning point in the notion of the government-citizen relationship, and the governing power was no longer deemed as the supreme guardian of the governed and it was no longer deemed as a favour but as an obligation of the State to address people's complaints about the government.[54]

2.2.2 The Introduction of Government Accountability Rules and Its Challenges

It requires a separate study to analyse the legacies of the Chinese Republican State governance in contemporary China. For analytical purposes here, this part focuses on two republican governance innovations that are closely related to the modernisation of Chinese rules for handling complaints against the government. Generally speaking, traditional Chinese dispute resolution practices had two functions: first, to review the dispute and determine liability, and second, to defuse tension between the

[51] The Edict of Abdication of Qing Emperor Puyi (大清帝国皇帝爱新觉罗·溥仪(奉隆裕皇太后懿旨):清室退位诏书), issued on 12 February 1912.

[52] Yat-Sen (1915).

[53] Articles 2, 7, 8 and 10, in the Provisional Constitution of the Republic of China, adopted by the Provisional Senate (临时参议院) on 8 May 1912.

[54] Wei-fang (2012), p. 27.

disputing parties so that their social and economic interaction could continue as usual after the dispute was resolved.[55]

Traditional dispute resolution practices were problematic when it came to addressing a complaint about the government where the disputing parties were not equal, as would be the case in a civil dispute. The Constitutional Drafting Committee was commissioned by the Republican Government to advise the establishment of a new appeal procedure for managing citizens' complaints about the government. On 7 September 1913, the Committee, comprising forty-seven members, deliberated on the advantages and disadvantages of two models: one from America where the ordinary court had jurisdiction over both civil and administrative disputes, and the other from Japan where a special court located in the capital heard and decided complaints about the government.[56]

Thirty-five out of forty-seven members of the Committee voted against the Japanese model, who argued that China's vast territory and underdeveloped public transportation network made it meaningless to introduce a special administrative court in the capital.[57] The Committee decided to adopt the American model, allowing existing courts to receive and review complaints about the government, provided that the presidents of the courts would be held accountable to the National Assembly, namely the then national legislature.[58] However, the Committee's proposal was not supposed by Yuan Shi-kai, Commander-in-Chief of the Northern Army and the most powerful leader of the Republican Government. Instead, as Great President of the Republican State from 1912 to 1916, Yuan exerted pressure on the National Assembly to hold court presidents accountable to the government and allow the government to review court decisions concerning complaints about the government before they were finalised.[59]

Yuan obtained the authority to approve the appointment of court judges and presidents, thereby consolidating the government's control over the court.[60] The government led by Yuan held the power to receive complaints about official misconduct, such as the abuse of power, misuse of public resources, negligence of public duty, or intimidation of citizens, and refer the accepted complaints to the court for review.[61] After the court made its decision, it was sent to the Office of the Great President for review and accreditation.[62] In other words, the court's review of government misconduct did not align with the Constitutional Drafting Committee's original proposal to separate the review and decision work of the court from the government, which ended up being futile under Yuan's rule.

---

[55] Huang (2010), p. 31.

[56] Jin (2015), pp. 184–187.

[57] Ibid.

[58] Ibid.

[59] Qian (1999), p. 122.

[60] Jin (2015), p. 189.

[61] Chuangxin (2005), pp. 422–423.

[62] Yuansheng (2000), p. 500.

The proposal to separate the judiciary from the government, which had been suspended by Yuan, was resumed after he died in 1916. Several legislative proposals for separating State powers survived political pressure in the 1920s and 1930s. In October 1928, the National Assembly passed the Organisational Law of the Republic of China, which divided State powers into five separate branches: the House of Legislation (the highest legislature), the State Council (the highest executive), the Court of Justice (the highest court), the House of Examination (the highest authority for selecting and appointing government officials), and the House of Supervision (the highest supervisory body).[63] The Administrative Litigation Law, which came into effect in November 1932 (amended in July 1942), specified the procedure for the court to assess the admissibility of a complaint about the government, investigate the admissible case, and make a decision.[64]

The establishment of the House of Supervision embodied the aspiration of liberal legislators to institute a regular mechanism that would, on the one hand, monitor the work of government bodies, and, on the other hand, hear citizens' complaints against State officials.[65] From 1930 to 1946, the House of Supervision reviewed 1509 administrative cases and referred them to the court, and conducted investigation into 2678 cases of official misconduct involving both high-level officials such as ministers and provincial governors and local officials at the municipal and town levels; from 1938 to 1947, it submitted 884 requests to the State Council to launch internal investigations into the misconduct of 1539 government officials; and in the year 1947 alone, it reviewed 2109 external complaints of official misconduct.[66]

Apart from internal monitoring and appeal measures, the Republican Government also set up the Department of Administrative Justice in 1930, the purpose of which was to oversee the fairness of court proceedings in deciding administrative cases and to facilitate the enforcement of court decisions. Initially directly answerable to the Central Government, the Department of Administrative Justice was integrated into the court system in 1934 as an intra-court supervisory body, and then re-organised as an intra-government supervisory body in 1942.[67] The Chinese Republican State brought about some remarkable changes (in particular, the confirmation of the right of citizens to sue the government and the duty of the government to be accountable to the people) to the modern Chinese State governance system. It also devised internal and external appeal procedures for dealing with complaints about the government, albeit only at the central level and in a fragmented manner.

On the other hand, although the Chinese Republican State recognised the primacy of law in its governance, it never prioritised the institutional promotion of government accountability rules for addressing the harm caused to citizens by the government. In April 1924, the top decision-makers adopted a three-step strategy for

63 Wilbur (1983), pp. 190–191.

64 Qing-yuan and Hua (2005), p. 664.

65 Qing-yuan and Hua (2005), pp. 650–651.

66 Qing-yuan and Hua (2005), p. 681.

67 Jin (2015), p. 189.

modernising State governance in China.[68] The first step was to focus on strengthening military power under the command of the Central Government to defeat internal warlords and unify the fragmented country.[69] Once all the provinces had been unified, the second step started—the government educated the general public to become familiar with the basic political rights of suffrage, impeachment, the making and review of law and made the public exercise these rights at the town level in preparation for the third step.[70]

When half the country had completed the second step, the Central Government was to organise a general election through which the general eligible population would elect a national congress to decide on national matters, while leaving local matters (i.e. at and below the provincial level) to be discussed and decided by the local residents.[71] Throughout the republican era, the Central Government barely managed to end the internal military division and unify the whole country, let alone achieve the second and third steps as envisaged in the 1920s.

2.2.3 *Summary*

The republican governance principle as well as government accountability rules adopted by the Chinese Republican State were ground-breaking in several aspects. It established the principle of people-oriented governance, confirmed the State's duty to handle citizens' complaints about the government, and recognised the separation of the judiciary from the government. Yet, the statutory rules of appeal and their subsequent implementation were never a top concern of republican leaders. From the early 1910s to the mid-1940s, the republican government faced several major political and military crises, both domestically and internationally. Nonetheless, the notions of accountable government and judicial review of administrative procedures, introduced by the republicans, shifted the traditional principle of reciprocal governance where the duties of the ruler and the ruled were understood in moral terms, towards a modern one where they were confirmed in legal terms.

2.3 The Marginalisation of Law During the Revolutionary Era

The preceding section has analysed the transition from monarchical State governance to a republican one in China, and the resulting changes in normative grounds, formal rules and correspondent arrangements for handling citizens' complaints about

---

[68] Article 5, in the Outline of Constructing the State by the Republican Government (国民政府建国大纲), drafted by Sun Yat-Sen and reviewed at the first National Conference of the Chinese Nationalist Party in January 1924, promulgated on 12 April 1924.

[69] Article 6 in the Outline of Constructing the State by the Republican Government in 1924.

[70] Articles 7–22 in the Outline of Constructing the State by the Republican Government in 1924.

[71] Articles 23–25 in the Outline of Constructing the State by the Republican Government in 1924.

the government. This section discusses another important development of Chinese rules and procedures for dealing with citizen complaints, focusing on the period between the 1940s and the 1970s during which the revolutionary doctrine of mass line played an influential role. It first examines the domestic and international catalysts for the growing popularity of socialist ideas in China (Sect. 2.3.1). It then deals in detail with the application of the mass line doctrine to dispute resolution and justice delivery under the leadership of the Communist Party of China (hereafter referred to as the "CPC"), initially regionally and ultimately nationally (Sect. 2.3.2). Thereafter, it presents some characteristic elements of contemporary Chinese procedure for managing petitions and complaints about the government (Sect. 2.3.3).

2.3.1 The Rising Popularity of Socialist Thoughts

To understand the impact of socialism on the modernisation of governance norms and measures in China, it is essential to understand the major social and political transitions that took place in the first half of the twentieth century. Both the Nationalist Party of China (known as "Kuomintang" in English literature), which was the then leading political power in China and the CPC, which was an opposition political party before 1949, concurred that it was necessary to liberate China from external colonisation and internal feudal oppression to democratise Chinese society.[72] However, the CPC's approach to realising this goal differed from that of the Kuomintang due to their different views on how to address China's domestic and diplomatic issues at the time.

Intellectual discussions on socialism materialised in China around the 1900s. Chinese intellectuals were concerned about the countless misfortunes in Chinese society and found the narrative appealing that property ownership was the fundamental contributor to social inequality. Jiang Kang-hu (born 1883, died 1954), a founding member of one of the first socialist associations in China, advocated that property-less labourers could in fact form a powerful class if they were unified, and could transform the oppressive governance structure if they were guided by the right ideas.[73] Jiang put forward three fundamental conditions for ending structural exploitation by the property-owning class: first, introducing collective ownership of properties and means of production, which was a necessary condition for eliminating structural inequality between property owners and labourers; second, setting up a universal labour regime where workers could access non-exploitative job opportunities and receive fair labour reimbursement; and third, providing an accessible education system that could properly teach and prepare individuals for suitable employment at an appropriate age.[74]

---

[72] Mao (1940), pp. 689–692.

[73] Liangyu (1989), pp. 77–79.

[74] Liangyu (1989), pp. 101–102.

Mao Zedong (born 1893, died 1976) found himself inspired by socialist notions, particularly the belief in the power of the working mass to combat oppressive forces at home and abroad.[75] Mao cited the French Revolution of 1789 and the Russian Revolution of 1917 as evidence that any compromise reached between the bourgeoisie and the proletariat would be temporary, conditional and ultimately unsustainable due to the inherent contradiction of interest between the two classes.[76] While serving as editor-in-chief of a news journal called Xiang-jiang Weekly Review, Mao published over forty essays (until the then provincial governor Zhang Jing-yao banned the circulation of this journal), promoting the idea that China's political and social crises could only be tackled by mobilising the long-suppressed working masses to resist the Japanese invasion and overthrow the corrupt domestic rule by capitalist elites.[77]

Mao expanded the scope of the working class, which doctrinally referred to industrial labourers who earned their living through trading their labour force, to include peasants, which was necessary because the number of Chinese industrial workers was considerably smaller than that of Chinese rural labour force who accounted for more than eighty-six per cent of the entire Chinese population.[78] Mao proposed the Three New Principles of the People, as a new governance principle to distinguish their political aspiration and vision from Sun's Three Principles of the People upheld by the republican government.

While agreeing with the governance goals of the republican government, namely, liberating the Chinese nation from internal and external oppressions, and protecting the fundamental rights and welfare of the Chinese people, Mao argued for three different conditions for achieving those goals. These were: first, to mobilise the Chinese proletariat and peasants in the liberation revolution; second, to accept the political leadership of the CPC during the revolution, and third, to form an alliance with the Union of Soviet Socialist Republics (hereafter referred to as the "USSR") to deal with international affairs.[79] In 1935, Mao was elected as the top leader of the CPC at the enlarged meeting of the CPC politburo. This gave Mao the necessary authority to make his idea the dominant political thought of the CPC.[80] In the late 1940s, the CPC became the leading political party in China, and Mao's thought was confirmed as a leading theory on social revolution across the country.[81]

The popularity of socialism in China cannot be solely explained by theoretical and ideological developments at the time. International and domestic political changes also play a crucial role. Since the mid-nineteenth century, China had

[75] Wakeman (1973), pp. 201–207.

[76] Literature Research Office of the Central Committee of CPC (ed.) (1988), pp. 91–92.

[77] Wakeman (1973), p. 99.

[78] The Communique on the Census Results of the Chinese Population (全国人口调查登记结果的公报), issued on 1 November 1954 by the National Bureau of Statistics of China.

[79] Mao (1940), pp. 689–692.

[80] Mao (1940), pp. 662–709.

[81] Mao (1925), pp. 7–9.

criticised the inequality and unfairness of its diplomatic relations with Occidental States. Following the victory of the Allied Power (to which China was a member) in World War One, the Chinese delegation at the Paris Peace Conference lobbied the United States, France and the United Kingdom to return the Jiaozhou Bay area in China's Shandong Province, which had been 'rented' by Germany since 6 March 1898; the delegation demanded that China's full sovereign rights over the area be recognised and respected.[82] The Occidental State's draft resolution on the so-called 'Shandong Problem' soon disappointed the Chinese delegation as their requests were not accepted.

The Versailles Treaty concluded on 28 June 1919 stated that the "rights, title and privileges, particularly those concerning the Jiaozhou Bay, railways, mines, and submarine cables,... all other arrangements relative to the Province of Shandong" and the right to the railway including "branch lines together with its subsidiary property of all kinds, stations, shops, fixed and rolling stock, mines, plant and material for the exploitation of the mines, ... together with all rights and privileges attaching thereto," which had been formerly exclusive to Germany, were to be transferred to Japan.[83] The unsuccessful diplomatic effort of the Chinese delegation caused a surge in nationalist sentiments in China, with widespread accusations that the Occidental nations were hypocritical and had betrayed China's trust.[84]

In contrast, the USSR supported China's efforts to rectify the unfair international agreements that had exploited China's interests. Shortly after the Paris Peace Conference, Leo P. Karakhan, the People's Commissariat for Foreign Affairs of the USSR, stated in July 1919 that all the unequal Sino-Russian treaties secretly signed under the Tsarist regime, together with privileges and special interests granted to Russian entities on Chinese territory, were renounced.[85] In July 1920, the leader of the USSR, Vladimir Lenin, expressed sympathy for the Chinese nation which he believed was being treated unfairly, and criticised the capitalist powers for ignoring the requests of underdeveloped nations, such as China, to enhance their say in international affairs.[86] It was in these domestic and diplomatic contexts that socialist ideas and political powers gained increasing popularity in China.

---

[82] Yongjin (1991), pp. 66–67.

[83] Article 156 in the Treaty of Versailles, that reads "Germany renounces, in favour of Japan, all her rights, title and privileges particularly those concerning the territory of Jiaozhou, railways, mines and submarine cables [in Shandong]." adopted on 28 June 1919 and came into force on 20 January 1920.

[84] Schwartz (1983), pp. 407–408.

[85] Tse-Tsung (1960), p. 210.

[86] Lenin (1920).

2.3.2 The Doctrine of Mass Line and Its Implementation

The Three New Principles of the People, advocated by the CPC, were enshrined in China's new constitution. The preparatory body for drafting the new constitution, the Chinese People's Political Consultative Conference, consisted of 662 representatives from various regions, classes and professions across China and approved an interim constitution on 29 September 1949. The interim constitution established the fundamental governance principles of the People's Republic of China to be founded on 1 October 1949, which were to uphold a people's democratic dictatorship led by the working class of workers and peasants, to oppose imperialism, feudalism and bureaucratic capitalism, and to unite with "all peace-loving and freedom-loving countries and peoples throughout the world, first and foremost, with the USSR".[87]

The Organisational Law on the Chinese Central Government was adopted by the Chinese People's Political Consultative Conference before passing the interim constitution. This law specified the constituting organs of the Central Government, their powers and duties. As per this law, the People's Inspection Committee was established to oversee the conduct of government bodies and officials.[88] The interim constitution established the structure and powers of the Socialist State and recognised the fundamental rights of citizens, including the right to challenge State organs and officials who violated the law or failed to perform their duties.[89] Following 1 October 1949, the National People's Congress, China's highest legislature, amended the interim constitution and passed the Chinese Constitution on 20 September 1954.

The Chinese Constitution consists of a preface, General Principles (with twenty articles) in Chapter One, the State Structure (with sixty-four articles) in Chapter Two, Fundamental Rights and Duties of Citizens (with nineteen articles) in Chapter Three, and National Flag, Emblem and Capital (with three articles) in Chapter Four.[90] The chapter on fundamental rights of citizens covers several rights related to the relationship and interaction between the government and citizens, including equality before the law, the right to assembly, association and demonstration and the right to complain, in writing or verbally, about unlawful conduct or negligence of State organs and officials and request compensation for any resulting

---

[87] Articles 1 and 11, in the Common Program of the Chinese People's Political Consultative Conference, adopted by the Chinese People's Political Consultative Conference on 29 September 1949.

[88] Article 18, in the Organisational Law of the Central Government of the People's Republic of China (中华人民共和国中央人民政府组织法), adopted by the Chinese People's Political Consultative Conference on 27 September 1949.

[89] Article 19, in the Common Program of the Chinese People's Political Consultative Conference in 1949.

[90] Constitution of the People's Republic of China, adopted on 20 September 1954 by the First National People's Congress and invalidated on 17 January 1975 by Fourth National People's Congress.

loss or harm, while the State is obliged to provide material facilities to facilitate citizens in exercising these rights reasonably easily.[91]

Although the right to challenge State organs and officials was constitutionally confirmed and protected, it was not practically exercisable under the revolutionary governance system. The CPC considered the governance measures developed by the Shaan-gan-ning border region government (hereafter referred to as the "border region government") as an advanced exemplar and decided to apply those measures nationwide after it became the leading political party in China.[92] From 1937 to 1949, the CPC controlled the border region while the then-legitimate Chinese government was led by Kuomindang. The border region government administered the areas of Northern Shaanxi, North-Western Gansu and South-Eastern Ningxia provinces and administered a population of around two million.[93]

The border region government implemented the Mass Line (*qunzhong luxian*/群众路线) doctrine as the basic principle for establishing its governance structure and measures.[94] The Department of Justice, staffed by the CPC cadres and government officials, served as the highest judicial authority to which the court had to submit its adjudicative decisions before they were finalised.[95] Xie Jue-zai, a senior jurist who later served as President of the Chinese Supreme People's Court between 1959 and 1965, argued that the administration of justice could not be separated from political power. According to Xie, the capitalist class advocated for the principle of judicial independence, but in fact, it only meant the independence of trial only because the prosecution and investigation were conducted by prosecution officers who represented the State and after the judicial procedure, the government still had the power to grant immunity or leniency.[96]

As the political significance of the Mass Line doctrine increased, Xie also proposed that the new Chinese State, which now represented the interests of the working class, should use vernacular language in its legal and judicial work to make it more accessible to the working masses. The proposal advocated for the use of the plain language of the working class in legal and judicial procedures and documents, avoiding lengthy and literal terms; it also recommended that the court maintain a close relationship with the government and consider the demands and preferences of the working masses in its decision-making.[97] Xie's proposal to apply the mass line doctrine to the judiciary received mixed reactions from jurists and judicial officials.

During his service as Interim President of the Higher Court from May 1942 to December 1943, Li Mu-an advocated for judicial professionalism and urged the CPC leaders to free the judiciary from political guidance to ensure professional and

[91] Articles 85, 87 and 97, in the 1954 Constitution of the People's Republic of China.

[92] Mao (1945).

[93] Nie (2022).

[94] Yaotong (2013), pp. 6–7.

[95] Xinyi (2005), p. 4.

[96] Xinyi (2019).

[97] Long and Xiang-ning (2012), p. 139.

impartial decision-making. However, Li's campaign was halted in December 1943 when he was forced to resign, following the decision of the CPC leaders that his initiative was "unbearably distancing the work of the judiciary from the practical needs of the people".[98] During the Yan'an Rectification Movement, over 15,000 individual supporters and sympathisers of Li's judicial professionalism campaign were accused of being capitalist thinkers for their "arbitrary, bureaucratic and dogmatic conducts".[99]

Ma Xi-wu, a senior judge born into poverty, prioritised a mass-alignment approach to court work. When handling cases, Ma frequently sought input from local CPC cadres and villagers who were familiar with the dispute situation; after drafting his decision, he mediated the dispute by explaining the contents of his proposed settlement and its rationale to the disputing parties, with the presence of their fellow villagers.[100] Ma discovered that the involvement of local villagers and cadres in case hearings and decision-making improved the enforceability of dispute settlements, and also helped the working mass become familiar with the spirit and contents of judicial work that had previously been commonly perceived as too formal or elitist.[101] In June 1944, the border region government endorsed Ma's dispute resolution concept and approach as a model for administering people's justice (*renmin sifa*/人民司法).[102]

Although Ma's dispute resolution model was controversial, the core methods of his mass engagement were introduced into Chinese dispute resolution practices in the following decades. The border region government announced its goal of resolving approximately ninety per cent of all types of disputes in the border region through mediation, preferably with the involvement of the masses in the dispute resolution procedures.[103] Four types of mediation were commonly used: community mediation by lineage members and fellow villagers, social mediation by a panel appointed by the people's association to which the disputing parties belonged, public mediation by government officials, and judicial mediation by judges.[104]

Procedurally, a complainant could seek a judicial remedy before the court after going through one or more of the above-listed mediations; even after the court proceeding started, the disputing parties could still resort to mediation, with or without the judge's presence.[105] Mediation settlements typically include either a verbal or written apology and material compensation for the victim; in some cases, non-material forms of compensation such as providing labour assistance during the

[98] Xinyi (2004), pp. 132–133.
[99] Xinyi (2004), pp. 137–138.
[100] Cong (2014), p. 30.
[101] Cong (2014), pp. 34–35.
[102] Xibo (2009).
[103] Juezai (1996), p. 137.
[104] Juezai (1996), p. 284.
[105] Xinyi (2007a), pp. 104–105.

busy harvest period to the victim's family, could also be accepted due to the limited availability of currency in the border region.[106]

Mediation-centred dispute resolution, which developed in the border region between the late 1930s and the mid-1940s, involved consulting local villagers and cadres to settle disputes and engaging them in the case hearing and decision-making processes.[107] The judge's work was evaluated based on the frequency of villagers' involvement in the trial and the extent to which their input was reflected in the court's decision.[108] The implementation of the mass line doctrine in dispute resolution rules and practices led to a reduction in the number of legal professionals employed by the court. In 1942, a census of judicial staff found that the Higher Court in the border region had only five legally trained staff members - one president, two judges, and two registrars, while the remaining one hundred and seventy-three staff members received little or no legal education.[109]

Furthermore, the Department of Justice required court staff to perform manual labour on farms in the region, the purpose of which was to gain a better understanding of the lives of the working masses and to win their trust.[110] In 1959, about ninety-seven per cent of court staff in Shanxi Province spent forty-nine days carrying out farming activities to meet the performance assessment standards set by the Supreme People's Court in January 1958.[111]

2.3.3 *The Revival of the Petition-handling Procedure*

After assuming power as the leading political party in 1949, the CPC set up political and government agencies to handle complaint letters and visits (*xinfang*/信访) from the public.[112] In 1950, the General Office of the CPC Central Committee started receiving complaint letters and visits intended to petition senior cadres of the CPC.[113] On 29 October 1950, the CPC adopted a political resolution mandating government organs at all levels to set up a specialised department responsible for registering, reviewing and transferring complained matters to the relevant official or

---

[106]Ibid.

[107]Cong (2014), pp. 34–35.

[108]Xinyi (2007a), p. 104.

[109]Xinyi (2004), p. 130.

[110]Xinyi (2007b), p. 118.

[111]Ibid.

[112]The term 'letter and visit' refers to two common methods of filing a petition: sending a letter or paying a visit to the government petition office. In this chapter, the terms petition, letter and visit, and complaint letter are used interchangeably.

[113]Chao (2009), pp. 46–47.

office, and overseeing the handling of the matters to ensure them to be dealt with appropriately.[114]

In 1950, the Secretariat of the State Council,[115] the Central Government of the Chinese Socialist State, along with the Premier Office, began accepting complaint letters and visits. The staff at these offices summarised the complaints and the supporting evidence presented by petitioners and then submitted a summary to the relevant officials.[116] In 1951, after reflecting on several sporadic petition-handling measures in various regions, the Central Government decided to make the petition-handling work a regular task of local governments, the aim of which was to keep officials informed about the suffering and demands of the public.[117] By 1953, local governments across China had set up departments for receiving and reviewing complaint letters and visits from the public.[118]

As government offices dealing with complaint letters and visits expanded to a national scale, the Central Government issued guidelines to regulate their work. In June 1951, the first regulatory policy was adopted, specifying the registration, referral and oversight duties of government petition-handling offices.[119] Two years later, a special procedure called the leader's reception day was introduced. On this day, senior officials would meet with petitioners to learn about their complaints and requests.[120] The officials who received the petitioners would assign the most relevant office or official to further investigate the cases and resolve any reasonable requests, and such assignments were made based on the judgement and authority of the receiving officials who were usually in senior government positions.[121]

The government department for handling complaint letters and visits had the power to decide whether or not the petitioned case had sufficient merit to be referred to a relevant office or official for resolution. In other words, once the petition office examined the case and referred it to the relevant authority, it had fulfilled its core duty. As there was often no clear guideline on how the competent authority should deal with a petition received, a considerable number of cases were not concluded, a problem that was officially recognised in the late 1950s. In response, the first National Conference on People's Letters and Visits was convened in May 1957,

---

[114]Mao (1950), p. 691.

[115]The State Council is the highest administrative authority in China and is synonymous with the Central Government in the Chinese governance framework.

[116]Mao (1950), p. 691.

[117]The State Council (1957) Guiding Opinions on Improving the Handling of People's Letters and Visits (国务院关于加强处理人民来信和接待人民来访工作的指示). Issued on 19 November 1957.

[118]Chengjie (1996), p. 332.

[119]Articles 3 and 5, in the Decision of the State Council on the Handling of Letters from the People and the Receiving of Visits of the People (政务院关于处理人民来信和接见人民工作的决定), issued by the State Council on 7 June 1951.

[120]Chao (2009), p. 48.

[121]Yujie (2011), p. 29.

and in November 1957, the State Council issued a guidance to standardise the procedures for examining and concluding petitions.[122]

However, these guidelines did not help to improve the effectiveness of government petition departments in addressing public complaints. Instead, throughout the 1950s, these departments focused on supporting political movements rather than facilitating citizens' exercise of their constitutional right to challenge State powers. In particular, during the large-scale Three Anti Campaign and Five Anti Campaign of 1951 to 1953, the petition departments received a rapidly increased number of complaint letters and visits accusing government officials and businessmen of politically condemned conducts, such as embezzlement and bribery, waste or theft of public resources, and tax evasion.[123] In January 1953, for example, the government called on the public to expose so-called 'capitalist malpractice' in the State-owned enterprises; in 1953 alone, the petition departments received more than 70,000 exposure letters.[124] Later, in the 1960s and the 1970s when the revolutionary governance rules and practices were at their height, a significant number of government agencies were dysfunctional and the rules governing the petition-handling processes were not implemented.[125]

2.3.4 *Summary*

This section has analysed the normative basis and procedural arrangements for resolving disputes in general and for dealing with complaints about the government in particular, focusing on the period between the 1940s and the 1970s. The mass line doctrine was the leading principle in shaping the State governance framework, and statutory rules and legal professionals were marginalised during this period. The administration of Chinese courts was subject to political guidance and the involvement of the working masses in the mediation-centred dispute resolution was promoted. In addition, the petition-handling procedure was revived in the 1950s to manage complaint letters and visits on the one hand and to facilitate a range of political campaigns and movements on the other. Overall, between the 1940s and the 1970s, China's rules for addressing general disputes and disputes over government conduct lacked legal ground and procedural regularity, which was widely seen as problematic by the end of the 1970s.

[122] The State Council (1957) Guiding Opinions on Improving the Handling of People's Letters and Visits.

[123] Yujie (2011), p. 29.

[124] Mao (1953), pp. 72–73.

[125] Chao (2009), p. 48.

2.4 Legal Renaissance Since the 1980s

By the mid-1970s, critical reflections and dissenting views on the revolutionary governance principles and practices had emerged in China, leading to the (re-) introduction of a set of statutory rules to regulate public powers and protect citizens' rights, which is referred to as the legal renaissance in contemporary China. The first part of this section focuses on the normative impact of the new Chinese Constitution adopted in 1982, which marked a departure from the revolutionary State governance framework (Sect. 2.4.1). Thereafter, it examines the key legislative reforms that affirmed the government's legal and public accountability and instituted the law-based review and redress procedures for managing complaints about the government (Sect. 2.4.2). Then it analyses some of the major challenges to the development of government accountability law in the Chinese dispute resolution system (Sect. 2.4.3).

2.4.1 The Normalisation of Chinese State Governance

China's revolutionary State governance framework prioritised ideological and political matters over economic and social developments and was based on central commands, such as political decisions of the CPC or the guidelines issued by the State Council, rather than on statutory rules and customary norms. The widespread malfunction and dysfunction of the government led Chinese leaders, including Mao himself, to discuss and debate the instrumental value of the revolutionary approach to managing the Chinese population and society in 1974 and 1975; Mao's death on 9 September 1976 provided the window of opportunity for the succeeding leaders to embark on a pragmatic approach to governing economic and social affairs, ushering in a new phase of Chinese State governance known as the Chinese Reform Era.[126]

Hua Guo-feng, the successor Chairman of the CPC Central Committee chosen by Mao in his last days, announced the successful end of the Cultural Revolution at the 11th National Congress of the CPC on 12 August 1977.[127] The government had to deal with numerous complaints about the now officially acknowledged wrongs of the previous revolutionary government. In January 1978 alone, the Organisation Department[128] of the CPC Central Committee received thousands of complaint

[126]Vogel (2012), pp. 78–84.

[127]Guo-feng (1977) Report to the Eleventh National Congress of the CPC, delivered on 12 August 1977 and approved by the CPC Central Committee on 18 August 1977.

[128]The Organisation Department of the CPC (*zuzhibu*/组织部) administers the organisational and personnel matters of the party. The Organisational Department of the CPC Central Committee is responsible for tasks such as organisational integrity (e.g. the management of local CPC organs), cadre management (e.g. suggesting appointments, position adjustments, or removals of central cadres), cadre education (e.g. organising national cadre educational trainings), and cadre

letters, enough to fill six human-size sacks, in which the complainants demanded that the government restore their political reputations and entitlements that had been unfairly damaged during the Cultural Revolution, that they be given official permission to leave the labour farms and return to their places of origin, and that they reclaim the ownership of their property, which had been confiscated by the government.[129]

In the absence of a well-functioning court system and with the number of complaints from all walks of life soaring, the State Council decided to restore the petition-handling procedure to address massive injustices that needed to be redressed. The Second National Conference on People's Letters and Visits was held in September and October 1978, after which the State Council assigned some 200,000 officials to handle complaints about unfounded political charges and wrongful punishment.[130] In September 1980, the legislative and administrative organs at the central, provisional, municipal and town levels opened offices to receive and review such complaints. The petition-handling procedure operated based on immediate territorial jurisdiction. A petitioner should submit his or her case to the petition office of the place where he or she was registered as a resident, namely, a petitioner living in a town should go to the petition office of the town rather than to the next higher municipal petition office, and a petitioner living in a city should go to the municipal petition office rather than to a provincial petition office.[131]

The petition-handling offices did not hold the power to decide on the settlement of the petitioner's claim, while the government authority that did have the power to settle the petitioner's claim was generally neither accessible nor accountable to the petitioner. Due to the top-down accountability mechanism of Chinese governing powers, a referral from the highest possible authority to settle a petition was usually the most effective. Hence, the central-level authority was seen as the most meaningful venue for redressing petitioners' grievances and many travelled to Beijing to petition the central authority, despite the jurisdictional limitations. In 1981, the Chinese central-level offices reported being overwhelmed by an influx of thousands of petitioners waiting outside their doors, severely disrupting the normal functioning of these offices.[132]

In May 1982, the State Council authorised the Ministry of Public Security and Civil Affairs to identify individuals without valid travel and residence permits to stay in cities, particularly, Beijing, and to repatriate them to their registered places of residence, to prevent petitioners from taking their cases to higher authorities located

---

supervision (e.g. reviewing track records of senior cadres). See: Duties of the Organisation Department of the CPC.

[129]Chengjie (1996), pp. 236–238.

[130]Chao (2011a).

[131]The General Office of the CPC Central Committee (1986), p. 6.

[132]Chao (2011b), pp. 53–55.

in cities while bypassing local juridification.[133] If the government petition office concluded that a petitioner had failed to comply with procedural requirements (in particular, not bypassing the local petition handler or behaving unreasonably, such as causing an interruption to the work of public offices), it could request the public security and civil affairs departments to initiate the detention and repatriation process to help maintain what was officially termed 'normal petitioning order'.[134]

In August 1982, the People's Daily, the highest-ranking official newspaper in China, published an editorial stating that complaints revealing the government's "historical mistakes" had been reviewed and rectified by the government, marking the de facto closure of the officially sanctioned ad hoc procedure for redressing massive injustices and grievances for which the government was responsible.[135] After this People's Daily editorial, a petition seeking redress for harm or loss caused by the government during the Cultural Revolution was generally inadmissible to the petition office. The government petition office, on the other hand, was open to complaints about decisions or conduct of current government authorities.

The 1980s saw several legislative reforms that were instrumental in shifting Chinese governance norms from ideological towards rational. The Chinese Constitution was substantially amended at the 5th National People's Congress in 1982, which moved the ideological primacy of Marxism-Leninism and Mao Zedong Thought as a general principle[136] to the background statement in the preface;[137] and expanded the section on protecting the fundamental rights of Chinese citizens from four articles[138] to eighteen articles. In particular, the constitutional amendment of 1982 has added Article 33, which recognises equality before the law and Article 37, which prohibits police detention of citizens without the approval of the people's procuratorate or a decision by the people's court.[139]

Furthermore, at the end of the 1980s, after a series of academic debates and political negotiations, China introduced the administrative procedural law. For the doctrinal theorists, the Chinese Socialist State was fundamentally more advanced than its Occidental counterparts, which represented the interests of the bourgeoisie and were explorative of the working masses; and there was no need for China to introduce legal control of the Chinese government since its personnel came from the

[133] Article 1 and Article 2, in the Implementing Rules for Administrative Custody and Repatriation of Vagrant Beggars in Cities, adopted in 1982 and annulled in 2003 by the State Council.

[134] Chao (2011b), p. 49.

[135] Chao (2011a), pp. 45–46.

[136] Article 2, in the Constitution of the People's Republic of China, adopted on 17 January 1975 by the Fourth National People's Congress at its First Session.

[137] Paragraph 5, in the Preface to the Constitution of the People's Republic of China, adopted on 4 December 1982 by the Fifth National People's Congress.

[138] Articles 26–29, in the 1975 Constitution of the People's Republic of China.

[139] In comparison, the 1975 Constitution permitted police arrests at the discretion of the police, whereas the 1982 Constitution prohibits any police arrest of citizens without the approval or decision of the procuratorate or the decision of the court (Article 37, in the 1982 Chinese Constitution).

working class and could not go against the interests of the working masses.[140] The content of the new administrative procedural law should be drafted in such a way that the courts would help improve the functioning of the government. Such notions and arguments are collectively referred to as the administration-facilitating theory (*guanli lun*/管理论) of Chinese administrative law.[141]

Liberal theorists, on the other hand, argued that properly regulated public powers and well-protected individual rights were the inseparable prerequisites for a just governance framework.[142] Arguments that assumed the fallibility of government agencies and advocated the need for accountability of the government are collectively known as the power-regulating theory (*kongquan lun*/控权论).[143] The power-regulating theorists proposed that the new administrative law should be as restrictive of public powers and as protective of individual rights as possible. Faced with the sharp theoretical divide that hindered progress in finalising the draft administrative law, Luo Haocai, together with some like-minded scholars, proposed the balanced theory (*pingheng lun*/平衡论) as a reconciliatory theory on the basis of which political and legislative debaters could reach the minimum consensus needed to pass the new law.

The balanced theory assumes a dual nature of socialist administrative law: on the one hand, to support the functioning of State organs and, on the other, to safeguard the legitimate rights of individuals; after all, "every State organ, public unit and individual is equal before the law", and those who violate the law should be punished by the law.[144] By 1989, the legal community had largely accepted that administrative law should hold accountable three elements of the government conduct: a. its motive must be in accordance with the law; b. its formulation process must be based on legitimate considerations; and c. its content(s) must be legitimate.[145] The tripartite structure (i.e. motive-process-content) for judging government conduct was incorporated in the Chinese Administrative Litigation Law (hereafter referred to as the "ALL"), which was enacted in 1989.[146]

2.4.2 *The Legalisation of the Complaint-handling Procedures*

The lack of accessible and effective venues for redressing grievances against the government led to academic criticism and public discontent in the 1980s. In

[140] Min-an (2019).

[141] Haocai (2014), pp. 14–23.

[142] Brooks and Nussbaum (2015), p. 65.

[143] Haocai (2014), pp. 14–23.

[144] Haocai et al. (1993), pp. 53–54.

[145] Deng-feng (2016), pp. 88–89.

[146] The Administrative Litigation Law of the People's Republic of China, adopted at the Seventh National People's Congress on 4 April 1989.

response, the Chinese State instituted new appeal procedures for challenging government conduct and reformed existing procedures. This part analyses the main reforms of three appeal procedures, namely, the government petition, administrative reconsideration, and administrative litigation. In October 1995, China passed the National Regulation on Complaint Letters and Visits (hereafter the "Regulation of 1995"), which aimed to legalise the government petition-handling procedure (discussed in more detail in Chap. 3).

In general terms, the Regulation of 1995 addressed two main obstacles to the effectiveness of the government petition-handling procedure: the insufficiently defined power of the government petition office (with the consequent lack of specified responsibility), and the insufficiently regulated appeal procedure (which led to procedural irregularities). Under the Regulation of 1995, complaints to the government petition office were admissible if they concern: flawed performance by a government organ or its staff, unlawful or negligent conduct by a government organ or its staff, or, conduct of a government body or its staff that violated the petitioner's legitimate rights or interests.[147] The petition could also be admissible to the petition office: if it concerned a private enterprise or a non-governmental organisation authorised by the government to manage public affairs or provide public services, or, if it concerned the conduct of self-governing bodies, such as the villagers' committee in rural areas and the residents' committee in urban areas, it could be admissible to the government petition office.[148]

The Regulation of 1995 set out the duties of government petition offices as: first, to receive petitions from natural and legal persons; second, to forward the accepted petition to the relevant government department; and third, to oversee the review and conclusion of the forwarded case.[149] In February 2000, under the supervision of the State Council and the CPC Central Committee, the National Bureau for Complaint Letters and Visits[150] was established in Beijing to supervise the implementation of the Regulation of 1995 at the central and local levels and to coordinate the handling of petition cases between government departments and other public authorities such as the court.[151] In short, the promulgation of the Regulation of 1995 and its subsequent implementation mark the transition to specified and standardised procedures for receiving, reviewing and concluding petition cases.

In parallel with the reform to standardise the government petition-handling procedure, two appeal procedures were introduced to the Chinese dispute resolution system: administrative litigation and administrative reconsideration, respectively.

---

[147] Articles 8, 26 and 32, in the Regulation on Complaint Letters and Visits, adopted by the State Council on 28 October 1995 and effective on 1 January1996 (invalidated by the adoption of the amended Regulation on Complaint Letters and Visits in 2005).

[148] Articles 4 and 5, in the 1995 Regulation on Complaint Letters and Visits.

[149] Articles 2, 3, 26 and 30-32, in the 1995 Regulation on Complaint Letters and Visits.

[150] The National Bureau for Complaint Letters and Visits has been officially renamed as the National Public Complaints and Proposals Administration in English translation.

[151] The National Bureau for Complaint Letters and Visits (2009) Duties of the National Bureau for Complaint Letters and Visits.

Referring to the 1982 Constitution that China shall "strengthen the socialist rule of law, … to build China into a strong modern socialist country",[152] the National People's Congress passed the ALL in 1989 and then the Administrative Reconsideration Law (hereafter referred to as the "ARL") in 1999.[153] Since the ARL came into force in 1999, citizens and legal persons can appeal against a government decision to an administrative reconsideration office internal to the government; and if the appeal concerns an administrative sanction, such as an administrative warning or an administrative order to suspend one's business, or a failure by the government to protect one's personal or property rights, the applicant can request the reconsideration body to review not only the lawfulness but also the properness of the government decision appealed against.[154]

If an applicant believes that the government has violated her or his rights or interests or both, s/he can request the court to review the government's decision in question.[155] After accepting the case, the court examines whether there is an incorrect or inappropriate application of the law in the formulation or implementation of the questioned government decision.[156] It is prohibited to submit the same complaint to both the administrative reconsideration body and the court, that is to say, once the reconsideration body has accepted a complaint, the same case cannot be brought to the court, and *vice versa*.[157] An applicant is, however, not obliged to go through the reconsideration procedure prior to initiating an administrative litigation. Yet, the court often advises the applicant to apply for an internal reconsideration first if s/he has not done so, except in situations involving the disputed ownership of natural resources, such as land, mineral resources, rivers, forests, mountains, grasslands, beaches, maritime waters, where the law expressly requires the reconsideration procedure to precede court review.[158]

2.4.3 Challenges to the Law-Based Appeal Procedures

Despite legislative reforms to introduce legal accountability of the government, Chinese procedures through which the public can appeal the government decision have been challenged on several fronts. The first challenge comes from the governance context in which the primacy of law is not yet in place, which is

[152] Preamble, in the 1982 Constitution of the People's Republic of China.

[153] The Administrative Reconsideration Law of the People's Republic of China, adopted in 1999, effective in 1999 and revised in 2017.

[154] Articles 1, 2, 3 and 6, in the Administrative Reconsideration Law of the People's Republic of China.

[155] Article 2 in the Administrative Litigation Law of the People's Republic of China.

[156] Article 6 in the Administrative Litigation Law of the People's Republic of China.

[157] Article 16 in the Administrative Reconsideration Law of the People's Republic of China.

[158] Article 30 in the Administrative Reconsideration Law of the People's Republic of China.

complicated by an institutional structure where the government has been much more powerful than its judicial counterpart. Formally, the government petition-handling procedure is supplementary to the law-based appeal procedures, meaning that a complaint that shall be handled through administrative litigation, arbitration and reconsideration is inadmissible to the government petition office.[159] Practically, complainants reported that it was not easy to have their complaints about the government accepted by the court, and that was precisely why they bypassed the court and petitioned the government authority.[160]

What's more, there is often procedural overlap between administrative and judicial decision-making when it comes to the settlement of complaints about the government. The enforceability of court decisions was, and to a large extent still is, weak.[161] The government department is more likely to comply with an order from a higher government official than to enforce the court decision.[162] The involvement of government officials in the handling of administrative complaints is a double-edged sword (which will be analysed in detail in Chap. 3). In short, while political involvement increases procedural efficiency and decisional enforceability in resolving complaints against the government, it also creates incentives for the complainant to bypass legal appeal and review procedures, which complicates the institutional and social contexts for building socialist rule-of-law governance in China.[163]

The second challenge stems from the weak financial independence of Chinese courts from the government. They used to be funded by governments at the same administrative level, and the court's financial dependence on the government became a structural hindrance to staying impartial in dealing with cases against the government. In 2002, the Supreme People's Court, with the support of the State Council, initiated court budgetary reform, whereby the administration, material and personnel costs of the court at the town and municipal levels (where the majority of cases are handled each year) are largely covered by the central and provincial budgets.[164] Since then, local courts have become less financially dependent upon local governments, thereby rectifying their operational subordination to the government.

Third, public awareness of the right to challenge the government as a legitimate and effective exercise is still developing in China. The behaviour of citizens, either collectively or individually, seeking judicial support for redressing their grievances against government decisions was often considered to be akin to 'hitting the stone with an egg'.[165] A survey of lawyers' involvement in administrative cases shows that only a fraction of around three per cent of the lawyers had worked on

[159]Article 14, in the Regulation on Complaint Letters and Visits, adopted by the State Council on 10 January 2005 and effective on 1 May 2005.

[160]Yanying (2011), p. 56.

[161]Jianqiu (2009), pp. 81–83.

[162]Zhe (2009), p. 89.

[163]Rong (2007), pp. 48–49.

[164]Jinwen (2010), pp. 17–18.

[165]O'Brien and Lianjiang (2004), pp. 76–77.

administrative litigation, either as paid legal representatives in court or as voluntary legal advisors outside the court; these lawyers tended to advise their clients to settle with the challenged government department, as this was seen as a more meaningful way of redressing the applicant's loss than waiting for the court to decide.[166]

Furthermore, during the court review, the judge is likely to advise the applicant to withdraw the case and to participate in a mediation settlement, while the applicant may feel insufficiently heard during the formulation of the mediation settlement.[167] Between 1994 and 2000, more than half of the accepted administrative cases were withdrawn from the court after both parties agreed to resolve the dispute through mediation; in 2006, the courts reported 32,146 voluntary withdrawals of accepted administrative cases, amounting to thirty-four per cent of all the unheard cases.[168]

Lastly, there are inconsistencies in the statutory rules on how to present a complaint against the government. While the right to challenge the government in court has become exercisable since 1990, other forms of challenging the government, such as assembly, procession and demonstration as recognised in the 1982 Constitution,[169] are generally restricted. The Chinese Law on Assemblies, Processions and Demonstrations, enacted in October 1989 in the aftermath of mass demonstrations in the spring of that year, stipulates that before the start of an assembly (defined as an activity in which people gather in a public place to express their views or present their petitions),[170] or a demonstration (defined as an activity in which people express their demand in the form of protest, assembly, procession or sit-in in a public place),[171] the organiser(s) must submit an application to the relevant government department that has the power to approve the assembly and demonstration after assessing whether the location, number of participants and starting and the finishing times would cause a disproportionate disturbance to social and public order.[172]

An unapproved assembly or demonstration would expose its organiser(s) and participants to administrative sanction or even criminal charges. As will be discussed in Chaps. 3–5, mass actions are spontaneous and sometimes interruptive, and

---

[166] Ji (2013), p. 837.

[167] Although mediation is generally not allowed during administrative litigation procedures, except in cases involving administrative compensation, subsidies, or other types of administrative discretionary decisions, it is often used in practice. This will be further explained in Chaps. 3 and 4, in particular the parts on the "grand mediation mechanism".

[168] Taigao (2008), p. 110.

[169] Article 35, in the 1982 Constitution of the People's Republic of China.

[170] Article 2 in the Law of the People's Republic of China on Assemblies, Processions and Demonstrations, adopted at the Seventh National People's Congress in 1989 and amended in 2009.

[171] Ibid.

[172] The competent authority is usually the public security bureau at or above the town level. See: Articles 6 and 7 in the Law of the People's Republic of China on Assemblies, Processions and Demonstrations.

therefore in principle not permitted by the law. Nevertheless, mass actions do occur with varying intensity throughout China. The State Council decided in 2001 that local governments should pursue two goals in handling what are officially termed 'mass group incidents', a euphemism for mass actions: to maintain public order and to pacify the participants.[173] Over the past decade, the Chinese State has been promoting what is known as Diversified Dispute Resolution Mechanisms (*duoyuanhua jiufen jiejue jizhi*/多元化纠纷解决机制) to more effectively resolve complaints against the government. These mechanisms consist of court-assisted mediation, lawyer-assisted mediation, administrative arbitration, administrative reconsideration, and court review.[174]

2.4.4 Summary

After ending the revolutionary governance norms and measures in 1977, the Chinese State introduced government accountability rules and public appeal procedures. The Chinese administrative procedural law, in particular, has confirmed the motive-process-content-lawfulness requirement for government decision-making, the failure of which provides sufficient grounds for affected citizens to challenge the government either through the internal appeal procedure or in court. The passage of Chinese regulation on the complaint letter and visit in 1995 and the enactment of the Chinese administrative reconsideration law in 1999 have specified the duties and liabilities of the government petition office and administrative reconsideration body. Despite these progressive reforms, the settlement of complaints against the government, be they in the form of petition, reconsideration request or administrative litigation, is not solely—or rather primarily—based on the law. The top-down political accountability of the Chinese government and the nascent public confidence in legal remedies are challenging the present rules and procedures for addressing complaints about the government.

2.5 Conclusion: Four Phases of Transitions

This chapter examines the historical development of Chinese rules and practices for handling grievances against the government, which provides a detailed account of the major changes in the fundamental governance principles and the corresponding institutional arrangements for managing citizen-government relations and disputes. It identifies four phases of transitions, namely, from a monarchical governance

---

[173] Baogang (2008), p. 555.

[174] The Supreme People's Court (2016) Guiding Opinions on How to Further Deepen the Reform of the Diversified Dispute Resolution Mechanism (Policy No. 4).

framework to a republican one in 1912, to a revolutionary one in 1949, and ultimately to a progressive governance model in the late 1970s.

The chapter begins by examining the traditional governance principle of reciprocity, which requires the ruling class to demonstrate its governing competence and integrity in exchange for popular acceptance of its rulership. In line with this principle, the ruling power in ancient China developed practices that allowed ordinary people to voice their grievances against the government and the ruling class, which became a long-standing mechanism for the government to receive petitions and grant ad hoc redress to petitioners.

Moving on to the modern era, the chapter analyses the theoretical, political and social contexts for the emergence of the people-oriented governance principle introduced by the republican government between the 1910s and 1940s. For the first time in Chinese history, it recognised the legal duty of the government to be accountable to the people and the right of the people to complain about the harm caused by government conduct and to seek judicial review. The popularity of socialism and its localisation between the 1920s and 1940s had a lasting impact on Chinese dispute resolution rules and procedures, in which the governance principle of the mass line doctrine justified political guidance and promoted mass participation in dispute resolution while marginalising the status of statutory rules and role of legal professionals.

Finally, the chapter focuses on the legal renaissance that began in the late 1970s and analyses its impact on Chinese dispute resolution rules and procedures. It highlights the merits of the reformed government petition-handling procedure, the government's internal reconsideration procedure, and court review for addressing complaints about government decisions, as well as the major challenges to the effectiveness of these procedures.

To conclude, this chapter sheds light on the historical, institutional and social contexts for China's acceptance of government accountability rules in general and their implementation in dealing with complaints about the government in particular, as well as their progresses and limitations in recent decades. Understanding the transitions from reciprocal principle, to people-oriented principle, to mass line doctrine and to law-based principle is crucial to understanding the content and rationale of contemporary Chinese approaches to addressing mass actions, which are examined in detail in three case studies in Chaps. 3–5. By providing a holistic account of indigenous Chinese governance principles and dispute resolution practices and their modern and contemporary transitions, this chapter aims to make the following case studies accessible to readers with limited prior knowledge of the subject.

References

Article 1 and Article 2, in the Implementing Rules for Administrative Custody and Repatriation of Vagrant Beggars in Cities, adopted in 1982 and annulled in 2003 by the State Council. http://www.people.com.cn/GB/shizheng/1026/1923232.html. Accessed 20 May 2016

Article 156 in Section VIII of Part IV "German Rights and Interests Outside Germany", in the Treaty of Versailles, adopted on 28 June 1919 and came into force on 20 January 1920, full text accessed 7 January 2017 at: http://avalon.law.yale.edu/imt/partiv.asp

Article 18, in the Organisational Law of the Central Government of the People's Republic of China (中华人民共和国中央人民政府组织法), adopted by the Chinese People's Political Consultative Conference on 27 September 1949.https://zcfg.cs.com.cn/chl/52992.html?libraryCurrent=law. Accessed 18 Mar 2016

Articles 1, 11, and 19 in the Common Program of the Chinese People's Political Consultative Conference, adopted by the Chinese People's Political Consultative Conference on 29 September 1949 and invalidated with the adoption of the Constitution of the People's Republic of China by the National People's Congress on 20 September 1954. https://sourcebooks.fordham.edu/mod/1949-ccp-program.asp. Accessed 18 Mar 2016

Articles 1, 2, 3, 6, 16 and 30 in the Administrative Reconsideration Law of the People's Republic of China, adopted in 1999, effective in 1999 and revised in 2017. Available at: http://en.pkulaw.cn/display.aspx?cgid=497d709c9225b1e3bdfb&lib=law

Articles 1 and 14 in the Outline of the Imperial Constitution 1908, promulgated by the Qing Government on 27 August 1908. Available at http://ctext.org/wiki.pl?if=gb&chapter=177805&remap=gb. Accessed 11 Mar 2016

Articles 2, 6 and 7, in the Law of the People's Republic of China on Assemblies, Processions and Demonstrations, adopted at the Seventh National People's Congress in 1989 and amended in 2009. Available at: https://www.12371.cn/2020/06/22/ARTI1592759118350546.shtml

Articles 2, 7, 8 and 10, in the Provisional Constitution of the Republic of China, adopted by the Provisional Senate (临时参议院) on 8 May 1912, Online archive available at: https://archive.org/stream/jstor-2212590/2212590_djvu.txt. Accessed 20 Mar 2016

Articles 2, and 26–29 in the Constitution of the People's Republic of China, adopted on 17 January 1975 by the Fourth National People's Congress at its First Session. https://china.usc.edu/sites/default/files/article/attachments/peoples-republic-of-china-constitution-1975.pdf. Accessed 20 May 2016

Articles 2 and 6, in the Administrative Litigation Law of the People's Republic of China, adopted at the Seventh National People's Congress on 4 April 1989. Available at: www.npc.gov.cn/zgrdw/englishnpc/Law/2007-12/12/content_1383912.htm

Articles 2–3, 4–5, 8, 14, 26 and 30–32, in the Regulation on Complaint Letters and Visits, adopted by the State Council on 28 October 1995 and effective on 1 January 1996 (invalidated by the adoption of the amended Regulation on Complaint Letters and Visits in 2005). Available at: https://www.gov.cn/flfg/2005-08/06/content_21025.htm

Articles 3 and 5, in the Decision of the State Council on the Handling of Letters from the People and the Receiving of Visits of the People (政务院关于处理人民来信和接见人民工作的决定), issued by the State Council on 7 June 1951. https://www.chinacourt.org/law/detail/1951/06/id/44.shtml. Accessed 10 May 2016

Articles 5, 6, and 7–25, in the Outline of Constructing the State by the Republican Government (国民政府建国大纲), drafted by Sun Yat-Sen and reviewed at the first National Conference of the Chinese Nationalist Party in January 1924, promulgated on 12 April 1924. Online version available at: https://zh.m.wikisource.org/zh/%E5%9C%8B%E6%B0%91%E6%94%BF%E5%BA%9C%E5%BB%BA%E5%9C%8B%E5%A4%A7%E7%B6%B1. Accessed 2 Apr 2016

Articles 85, 87 and 97, in the Constitution of the People's Republic of China, adopted on 20 September 1954 by the First National People's Congress and invalidated on 17 January 1975 by the Fourth National People's Congress. http://www.lawinfochina.com/display.aspx?lib=law&id=14754&CGid. Accessed 22 Mar 2016

Baogang Z (2008) Strategies on preventing and processing mass group incidents during social transformation (社会转型期群体性事件预防、处置工作方略). 1st edn. China's Public Security University Press (internal edition), p 555

Bertrand Russel (1922) Chinese Character. In: The Problem of China. Online version available: https://www.gutenberg.org/files/59391/59391-h/59391-h.htm

Brooks T, Nussbaum MC (2015) Rawls's political liberalism. Columbia University Press, p 65

Chao W (2009) A historical account of the sixty years' development of the letter and visit system in China (新中国六十年信访制度的历史考察). CPC Hist Stud 11:46–48

Chao W (2011a) Reflecting on the 60-year history of the petition system (信访制度60年发展历程的回顾与展望). Soc Sci Manage Rev 03. http://www.hprc.org.cn/gsyj/shs/shbzs/201303/t20130302_4044765.html. Accessed 15 May 2016

Chao W (2011b) Transformation of modern Chinese society and transition of letter-and-visit system (当代中国社会转型与信访治理). Stud Mao Zedong Deng Xiaoping Theor 11:49–55

Chen J (2016) Petitioning Beijing: sub-national variation. J Contemp China 25(101):763

Chengjie D (ed) (1996) A brief history of People's Letter and Visits: 1949 to 1995 (人民信访史略:1949–1995). Capital University of Economics and Business Press, pp 236–238, and 332

Chuangxin Z (2005) History of Chinese political institutions (中国政治制度史). Tsinghua University Press, pp 422–423

Cong X (2014) Ma Xiwu's way of judging: villages, the masses and legal construction in revolutionary China in the 1940s. China J 72:30–35

Deng-feng Y (2016) Shifting from reasonableness to proportionality principles (从合理原则走向统一的比例原则). China Leg Stud 3:88–89

Duties of the Organisation Department of the CPC. http://www.qstheory.cn/yaowen/2021-06/02/c_1127523546.htm. Accessed 15 May 2016

Fang Q (2009) Hot potatoes: Chinese complaint systems from early times to the late Qing (1898). J Asian Stud 68(4):1107, and 1121–1122

Fangzhong L (ed) (2008) Statistics on households, farm lands and taxes in Ancient China (中国历代户口、田地、田赋统计). Zhonghua Book Company, pp 266 and 348

Fu W (1961) Institutional History of Tang Dynasty (Vol. 55) (唐会要, 卷 五 十 五). Online version available at: http://gj.zdic.net/archive.php?aid=5695. Accessed 7 Mar 2016

Genpan L (2015) On periods and features of China's ancient agriculture (试论中国古代农业史的分期和特点). In: Economic History Team (ed) Some major topics of the history of China's ancient economy (中国古代经济史诸问题). Fujian People's Publisher. Available at: http://agri-history.ihns.ac.cn/scholars/lgp/lgp18.htm. Accessed 2 Mar 2016

Guo-feng H (1977) Report to the Eleventh National Congress of the CPC, delivered on 12 August 1977 and approved by the CPC Central Committee on 18 August 1977. https://fuwu.12371.cn/2012/09/25/ARTI1348541192153839.shtml. 11 May 2016

Haiqing P (2005) A study of procedural arrangements for criminal justice (刑事诉讼程序设置研究). China Legal Publishing House, pp 20–22

Haocai L (2014) On balancing rights with powers (为了权利与权力的平衡). China Law Rev 1: 14–23. Online version available at: http://www.aisixiang.com/data/76223.html

Haocai L et al (1993) The theoretical basis for modern administrative law: balancing the rights and duties of administrative organs and parties to be affected by administrative decisions (现代行政法的理论基础——论行政机关与相对一方的权利义务平). China Legal Stud 1:53–54

Huang PC (2010) Chinese civil justice, past and present. Rowman & Littlefield, pp 31–32

Ji L (2013) Suing the Leatthan: an empirical analysis of the changing rate of administrative litigation in China. J Empir Leg Stud 10(4):837

Jianqiu H (2009) On the relationship between administrative remedial and administrative reconsideration roles played by petition handlers (论信访的行政救济功能及其与行政复议的关系). Democr Legal Syst 8:81–83

Jin X (2015) On the establishment of administrative litigation system in the Republic of China (论民国初年行政诉讼体制的确立). J Suzhou Univ 3:184–189

Jinfan Z (1992) The ancient Chinese legal system (中国古代法律制度). China Broadcast Film and Television Publishing House, p 474

Jinfan Z (2014) The tradition and modern transition of Chinese law. Springer, pp 495–683

Jinwen X (2010) Achievements, problems and solutions of judicial reforms in contemporary China (当代中国的司法改革:成就、问题与出路——以人民法院为中心的分析). China Leg Stud 1:17–18

Johnston RF (2014) Confucianism and modern China. Cambridge University Press, pp 64–67
Juezai X (1996) On democracy and rule by law (谢觉哉论民主与法制). Law Press China, p 137, 284
Kuhn PA (1992) Soulstealers: the Chinese sorcery scare of 1768. Harvard University Press, p 200
Lenin V (1920) National and colonial questions for the second congress of the communist international (published in 1920 and reprinted in 1965). In: Lenin's collected works (Vol. 31), 2nd English edn. Progress Publishers, pp 144–151. https://www.marxists.org/chinese/lenin/marxist.org-chinese-lenin-19200726.htm
Liangyu L (1989) On early political thoughts of Jiang Kang-hu (江亢虎早期政治思想研究). Soc Sci Stud 1:77–79 and 101–102
Literature Research Office of the Central Committee of CPC (ed) (1988) Philosophical Notes of Mao Zedong (毛泽东哲学批注集). 1st edn. Central Literature Publisher, pp 91–92
Liyan L (ed) (2008) A new approach to Chinese history: Vol. of Law (中国史新论:法律史分册). Linking Publishing Company, pp 65–67
Lizhu L (2005) On extensiveness of Keju on the basis of its subjects and contents (从考试科目与内容看"科举学"的广博性). J China Univ Geosci (Soc Sci Edn) 5(5):11–12
Loewe M (2008) The religious and intellectual background. In: Twitchett D, Loewe M (eds) The Cambridge history of China, Vol. 1. "The Ch'in and Han Empires, 221 BC–AD 220". Cambridge University Press, pp 652, 654–657
Long Y, Xiang-ning L (2012) The revolutionary logic of Chinese justice administration: a reading of Pan Han-nian case (中國司法的革命邏輯——釋讀彭樹華<潘漢年案審判前後>). Twenty-first Century J 134(12):139
Lum YM, Lum RMK (1999) Sun Yat-Sen in Hawaii: activities and supporters. University of Hawaii Press, pp 22–23
Maine HS (1870) Ancient law: its connection with the early history of society, and its relation to modern ideas, 4th edn. John Murray, London, pp 4–6
Mao Z (1925) An analysis of social classes in China (中国社会各阶级的分析). Published 1 December 1925, and reprinted in 1991 in The Selected Works of Mao Zedong (Vol. 1). 2nd edn., The People's Publishing House, pp 7–9
Mao Z (1940) On new democracy (published 9 January 1940), Reprint: the Selected Works of Mao Zedong (Vol. 2). 2nd edn. The People's Publishing House, pp 662–692
Mao Z (1945) On coalition government. In: Selected Works of Mao Zedong, Vol. 3. https://www.marxists.org/chinese/maozedong/marxist.org-chinese-mao-19450424.htm. Accessed 15 Mar 2016
Mao Z (1950) Remarks on handling people's complaint letters (中央转发关于处理群众来信问题报告的批语) (circulated on 30 November 1950 and reprint in 1987). In: Selected writings of Mao Zedong since 1949 (Vol. 1). Central Literature Publishing House, p 691
Mao Z (1953) Countering Bureaucracy, command Doctrine, and administrative offences (反对官僚主义、命令主义和违法乱纪) (circulated on 1 January 1953 and reprint 1991). In: Selected works of Mao Zedong, Vol 5. 2nd edn. People's Publishing House, pp 72–73
Min-an J (2019) A refined 70-year old system for commons to sue officials (七十年不断探索"民告官"制度日臻完善). Legal Daily, http://legal.people.com.cn/n1/2019/0722/c42510-31247382.html
Nie W (2022) Shan-Gang-Ning Border Region - the Ending Point of Long March and the Starting Point of Sino-Japanese War (陕甘宁边区:从长征落脚点到抗战出发点). Study Times. https://dangjian.gmw.cn/2022-04/28/content_35697556.htm. Accessed 27 Aug 2016
O'Brien K, Lianjiang L (2004) Suing the local state: administrative litigation in rural China. China J 51:76–77
Peerenboom R (2002) China's long march toward rule of law. Cambridge University Press, p 10
Preamble, Articles 35 and 37, in the Constitution of the People's Republic of China, adopted on 4 December 1982 by the Fifth National People's Congress. http://www.npc.gov.cn/zgrdw/npc/zt/qt/gjxfz/2014-12/03/content_1888093.htm. Accessed 20 May 2016
Preamble, in the 1982 Constitution of the People's Republic of China

Qian W (1999) An analysis of administrative proceedings of the Northern Warlords Governments (论北洋政府的行政诉讼制度). China Leg Sci 5:122
Qianfang Z (2012) The constitution of China: a contextual analysis. Oxford Hart Publishing Ltd., pp 5–6
Qing-yuan W, Hua B (eds) (2005) History of Chinese political institutions (中国政治制度史), 2nd edn. Renmin University Press, pp 650–681
Rong H (2007) Peasants' petitioning experiences and decline of their political trust (农民上访与政治信任的流失). Sociol Stud 3:48–49
Schwartz BI (1983) Themes in intellectual history: may fourth and after. In: Fairbank JK (ed) The Cambridge history of China (Volume 12: Republican China, 1912–1949, Part I). Cambridge University Press, pp 407–408
Shenzhi L, Jiadong H (2000) Road of China (中国的道路). Nanfang Daily Press, pp 124–126
Simon HA (1991) Public administration, 1st edn. Routledge, pp 532–533
Taigao W (2008) Judiciary-centred management of administrative litigations in China (司法主导下的中国行政诉讼法制发展). ECUPL J 60(5):110
The Communique on the Census Results of the Chinese Population (全国人口调查登记结果的公报), issued on 1 November 1954 by the National Bureau of Statistics of China, Accessed 10 Mar 2016: http://www.stats.gov.cn/tjsj/tjgb/rkpcgb/qgrkpcgb/200204/t20020404_30316.html
The competent authority is usually the public security bureau at or above the town level. See: Articles 6 and 7 in the Law of the People's Republic of China on Assemblies, Processions and Demonstrations
The Edict of Abdication of Qing Emperor Puyi (大清帝国皇帝爱新觉罗·溥仪(奉隆裕皇太后懿旨):清室退位诏书), issued on 12 February 1912. Available at https://zh.m.wikisource.org/zh/%E6%B8%85%E5%AE%A4%E9%80%80%E4%BD%8D%E8%A9%94%E6%9B%B8
The General Office of the CPC Central Committee (1986) Guiding opinions on handling complaint letters and visits (policy No. 8). In: Selected policies on complaint letters and visits (internal edition) (信访工作政策选编,内部发行), p 6
The National Bureau for Complaint Letters and Visits (2009) Duties of the National Bureau for Complaint Letters and Visits. https://www.gjxfj.gov.cn/gjxfj/xxgk/jgzn/gzzz/A09010201 index_1.htm. Accessed 7 Aug 2017
The State Council (1957) Guiding Opinions on Improving the Handling of People's Letters and Visits (国务院关于加强处理人民来信和接待人民来访工作的指示). Issued on 19 November 1957 http://www.pkulaw.cn/fulltext_form.aspx?Gid=161718&Db=chl
The Supreme People's Court (2016) Guiding opinions on how to further Deepen the reform of the diversified dispute resolution mechanism (Policy No. 4) (最高人民法院关于人民法院进一步深化多元化纠纷解决机制改革的意见). http://www.court.gov.cn/zixun-xiangqing-22742.html Accessed 4 June 2019
Ting-yee K, Kwang-Ching L (1978) Self-strengthening: the Pursuit of Western technology. In: Fairbank JK (ed) The Cambridge history of China (Vol 10: Late Ch'ing 1800–1911, Part I). Cambridge University Press, pp 528–529
Tse-Tsung C (1960) The may fourth movement: intellectual revolution in modern China. Harvard University Press, p 210
Tung-tsu C (1998) Function of law in Chinese society: a historical perspective (法律在中国社会中的作用——历史的考察). Peking Univ Law J 4:4–5
Tung-tsu C (2003) Local Government in Qing Dynasty (清代地方政府). English edn. in 1962 and Chinese edn. in 2003, Law Press, pp 79–82, 85, 91–94
Ung-bing L (1914) Outlines of Chinese history (in Chapter X "Ancient Society, Law and Customs"). Shanghai Commercial Press, p 48
Vogel EF (2012) Deng Xiaoping and transformation of China (鄧小平時代). Chinese University Press, pp 78–84
Wakeman FE (1973) History and will: philosophical perspectives of Mao Tse-tung's thought. University of California Press, pp 99 and 201–207

Wei-fang H (2012) In the name of justice: striving for the Fazhi in China. Brookings Institution, p 27

Wilbur CM (1983) The nationalist revolution in China: 1923-1928. Cambridge University Press, pp 190–191

Xianjue X (1986) A brief history of Chinese judicial system (中国司法制度简史). Shanxi People's Press, pp 37, 60–61 and 69

Xibo Z (2009) Adjudicative work of Ma Xiwu as a reference for the work of the People's Courts (马锡五审判方式是人民司法工作的一面旗帜). People's Court Daily, https://www.chinacourt.org/article/detail/2009/08/id/369772.shtml. Accessed 7 May 2016

Xinyi H (2004) Judicial reforms of Supreme Court in Shaan-Gan-Ning border region (陕甘宁边区高等法院司法制度改革研究). Chinese J Law 5:132–138

Xinyi H (2005) Formation of judicial institutions, conceptions and mechanisms in Shaan-Gan-Ning border region government (陕甘宁边区司法制度、理念及技术的形成与确立). The Jurist 4: 4

Xinyi H (2007a) People's mediation system in Shaan-Gan-Ning border region (陕甘宁边区人民调解制度研究). Chinese Leg Stud 4:104–105 and 129–130

Xinyi H (2007b) Features of mass justice in Shaan-Gan-Ning border region (陕甘宁边区司法制度的大众化特点). Chinese J Law 4:118

Xinyi H (2019) Thoughts and conducts of Xie Juezai during the regime change: an analysis based on Xie's diaries (政权更迭时谢觉哉的所思所为——以日记为中心的考察). Tsinghua Univ Law J 2. https://www.aisixiang.com/data/116017.html

Xu Z (2017) The confucian misgivings: Liang Shu-ming's narrative about law. Springer, pp 24–25, 60, and 151

Yanying Z (2011) The causes for, institutional limitations to and solutions of litigation-related petitions (涉诉信访之案件成因、制度困局与破解之道). Forum Polit Sci Law 1:56

Yaotong X (2013) Understanding the formation and development of the Mass Line Doctrine of the party (关于党的群众路线形成和发展的认识). Theor Explorat 202(4):6–7

Yat-Sen S (1915) Anthology of Sun Yat-sen, the Second Lecture on People's Livelihood. The online archive is available at: http://wx.cclawnet.com/sunzhongshan/zsxj000.htm. Accessed 20 Mar 2016

Yifan Y, Ducai L (1998) An introduction to opinion box mechanism in ancient China (中国古代匭函制度考略). Chinese J Law (1):79–80, and 87–90

Ying-shih Y (1987) Chinese intellectuals and Chinese culture (士与中国文化), 1st edn. Shanghai People's Press, pp 33–35, 38

Yongjin Z (1991) China in the international system, 1918–20: the middle kingdom at the periphery. Springer, pp 66–67

Yuansheng H (2000) A revised and preliminary study of administrative Judgement of Ping-Cheng-Yuan during 1914-1928 (民初平政院裁决书整编与初探). Natl Sci Council (Human Soc Sci) 10(4):500

Yujie N (2011) Examining letters and visits system in China: history and Status Quo (我国信访制度的历史回顾与现状审视). Chinese Public Adm 11:29

Yu-qing T (1984) On Luntai Self-denouncing Edict (论轮台诏). Hist Stud 2:3–20

Zhe L (2009) Function, status and reforming trend of the letter-and-visit system (信访制度的功能、属性及其发展趋势). J Party School Central Committee CPC 1:89

Zhongxin F (1997) Principle of relatives' concealment in Chinese and Western jurisprudence (中西法律传统中的"亲亲相隐"). Soc Sci China 3:89

Chapter 3
Chinese Measures for Managing Collective Petitions: An Unsettled Shift from Political Norms to Legal Rules

3.1 Mismatch Between Petition Rules and Petitioners' Choices

The procedure for receiving, reviewing and concluding petitions has been a long-standing element of the indigenous Chinese governance tradition. The exact Chinese term for petitions, xinfang(信访), can be translated as complaint letters and visits.[1] In the late 1970s, China re-instituted the petition-handling procedure as an alternative to the then-deficient court system for addressing millions of wrongful charges and mistreatments perpetrated by the governing powers during the Cultural Revolution. The procedure was a popular appeal channel for complainants to seek a remedy for the damage that they claimed was caused by the government until the 2000s when the court gained the necessary power and competence to hear cases against the government.

In China, there are three main appeal procedures through which a complainant, or a group of complainants, can request a review of the allegedly wrongful conduct of the Chinese government and seek an appropriate remedy: administrative reconsideration within the government, administrative litigation in court, and petition to the government. Despite its subsidiary nature, the government petition procedure remains a popular choice for complainants, while the other two procedures are less trusted or favoured by the public, an issue recognised as the "big petition, moderate litigation and small reconsideration (*da xinfnag, zhong susong, xiao fuyi*/大信访、中诉讼、小复议)".[2] The number of petitions filed with the National Bureau for

[1]The term 'complaint letter and visit' refers to two common ways for filing a petition with the petition office in China, i.e. sending a complaint letter and paying a visit. The terms of petition and complaint letter and visit are used interchangeably in this chapter.

[2]Dong-yu (2013), p. 28.

C.-r. Qiao, *Chinese Rules and Procedures for Addressing Mass Actions*,
https://doi.org/10.1007/978-3-031-62201-4_3

Complaint Letters and Visits[3] increased consecutively from 1994 to 2006.[4] In 2013 alone, the central authorities received more than 58,000 petition cases, an increase of seven per cent over the preceding year.[5]

Since the 1990s, Chinese decision-makers have sought to narrow the scope of cases admissible to the government petition office. A major amendment to the National Regulation on Complaint Letters and Visits (hereafter referred to as the "National Regulation") in 2005 reaffirmed that a petition claim that can be addressed by a reconsideration body or a court is inadmissible to the government.[6] The specified supplementary scope of admissible petitions does not correspond well with the choice of many petitioners who consider an inadmissibility decision of the petition office to be unfair and opt for conspicuous actions, such as public protests, in the hope that the office would reverse its decision.[7]

The mismatch between the regulatory rules binding the government petition office and the expectations of petitioners is particularly evident in the case of collective petitions. Currently, there is no bright-line threshold above which a jointly submitted petition qualifies as a collective petition. The National Regulation provides that a petition submitted by five or more petitioners must have one person representing the entire group,[8] and this representative will act as a correspondent petitioner during the review and hearing process that may follow. In some regions, a petition submitted by fifty or more petitioners is categorised as a collective petition and is given priority by the petition office over non-collective petitions.[9] Petitioners with the same or related claims prefer to submit their complaints collectively rather than individually, on the assumption that collective petitions are more likely to be taken seriously by the petition office and therefore their claims are more likely to be resolved.[10]

The research literature that takes a confrontational analytical approach tends to explain the disconnect problem as a result of the systematic irresponsiveness of China's governing powers to the dissenting views of the public and assumes that China's management of collective petitions is based solely on political considerations.[11] The lack of attention given to the evolving regulatory rules, their

[3]The National Bureau for Complaint Letters and Visits is now officially renamed as the National Public Complaints and Proposals Administration. This chapter will continue to use the original name to avoid any confusion.

[4]The People's Daily (29 April 2006), p. 5.

[5]Xinhua News (11 September 2014).

[6]Article 14, in the 1995 National Regulation on Complaint Letters and Visit.

[7]Yi (2013), pp. 238–239.

[8]Article 18, the 1995 Regulation on Complaint Letters and Visits.

[9]Xiucheng (2007), p. 150.

[10]Chinese Public Administration Research Team (ed.) (2009), pp. 93–94.

[11]For a detailed analysis of the strengths and weaknesses of the current research on mass actions in China, please refer to the part "3.2. Current Research on Mass Actions and Its Limitations" in Section 3 in Chap. 1.

implementation by various governing agencies and the outcomes limits our understanding of the nuances of Chinese measures for addressing collective petitions.

This chapter analyses the mismatch problem in the petitioning process in light of its institutional and social cultures. The petition office has both political and legal duties to fulfil; in cases where there is a conflict between the two, it is usually the political duty that takes priority. Collective petitions are a sensitive issue for the petition office, as they can result in disciplinary or even legal consequences for the office and its staff if the collective petitioners become confrontational with the government.[12] If a collective confrontation arises, the petition office must promptly diffuse the petitioners' confronting emotions and behaviours, failing which the petition handler(s) could face job demerit, demotion or even dismissal.[13]

In response to this political pressure, the petition office devised rather controversial measures to prevent so-called abnormal (*fei zhengchang*/非正常) petitions, which typically include collective, repetitive and jurisdiction-jumping petitions.[14] One such measure is the imposition of travel restrictions on 'abnormal' petitioners to discourage them from petitioning higher levels of government authorities.[15] Local petition handles have been accused of bribing central petition offices to reject 'abnormal' petitions from their jurisdiction, or to falsify central records to minimise the amount of 'abnormal' petitions that the local authority should have resolved.[16] The political duty to avoid conflict with petitioners proves to be more important to the petition office than the legal duty to review and resolve petition cases, which has caused and continues to cause much friction with petitioners.

To enhance our understanding of the issue discussed above, this chapter provides insight into the juridification of government accountability rules in the practices for addressing collective petitions as well as in news narratives and framings of the topic. It starts with analysing the legalisation of procedural regularity and legal accountability of the government petition office; and after that, it identifies some main obstacles to implementing these rules, both generally and in the specific context of settling collective petitions (Sect. 3.2). Then, it investigates Chinese news reports on collective petitions and their settlements and examines the relevance of government accountability law in the recurrent narratives and framings of collective petitions in the news (Sect. 3.3). The conclusion consists of a summary of the chapter's findings and suggestions that may be useful to academics and policy advisers interested in Chinese rules and procedures for dealing with collective petitions and their potential development (Sect. 3.4).

---

[12] Chinese Public Administration Research Team (ed.) (2009), pp. 34–36.

[13] Articles 5 and 6, in the Interim Provisions on the Violation of Disciplinary Measures in Handling Complaint Letters and Visits (关于违反信访工作纪律处分暂行规定).

[14] The term 'jurisdiction-jumping (*kua diqu*/跨地区) refers to petitions that bypass the directly competent petition office and go to the next higher or central authority.

[15] Qing-hua (2018), pp. 51–52.

[16] Ibid.

3.2 Legalisation of Chinese Petition Procedure and Its Problems

3.2.1 Introducing Legal Accountability to the Government Petition Procedure

The contemporary Chinese petition procedure shares similarities with its predecessors in terms of the purpose of the central power to monitor the functioning of local powers and a supplementary remedial function fulfilled by the petition office.[17] However, the current procedure has adopted certain procedural and decisional accountability rules, and there are several operational differences from the preceding practices, as summarised in Table 3.1.

Prior to 1995, there were few legal rules regulating the power, process and accountability of Chinese petition handlers. Initially, the government petition office served as an extension of the sporadic petition-hearing work of senior officials in accordance with the mass line doctrine. In the 1920s, Mao Zedong, a founding father of the People's Republic of China, listened to the complaints of petitioners, learned

Table 3.1 The constituting elements of the Chinese government petition procedure

	The Present	Predecessors
Normative ground(s)	National Regulation on Complaint Letters and Visits (adopted in 1995, amended in 2005 and repealed in 2022); (Arguably) the constitutional right to challenge State organs and government officials.	Reciprocity governance principle; Mass-line doctrine.
Jurisdiction	A complaint about the conduct of a government organ, or an organ authorised by the government to fulfil public services, or a villagers' committee and urban residential committee.	Not specified
Objective (s)	Protect legitimate rights and interests of petitioners; Maintain an orderly petition procedure.	Demonstrate governance competence of the government; Keep the government in close contact with the public.
Duties	Accept petitions and refer them to the responsible department; Coordinate the handling of major petitions; Submit advisory reports to the government.	Accept and refer petitions to the competent handler; Investigate petition cases and suggest settlement decisions.
Operating Agency	Government petition offices (at and above the town level).	Not specified.

[17] For more information on the acceptance of legal principles and regulations to govern the government petition process and promote statutory appeal procedures for addressing citizens' grievances against the government, please see Section 4 "Legal Renaissance since the 1980s" in Chap. 2.

about their sufferings and suggested redresses, with the aim of maintaining a close tie with the working masses.[18] With Mao's increasing power within the Communist Party of China (hereafter referred to as the "CPC") in the late 1930s, his political advocacy to ally with the working masses became a leading governance doctrine, which later guided the governing practices of the CPC-led government in China.

In June 1951, the State Council,[19] which is the Central Government in China, passed the Decision on How to Deal with People's Letters and Receive Visitors.[20] In July 1951, the Chinese National Political Consultative Committee, the national advisory body to the CPC and government bodies, adopted the Provisional Measures for Handling People's Opinions.[21] The First National Conference on Handling Complaint Letters and Visits was held in May 1957, the purpose of which was to familiarise senior officials with the work of handling complaints and remedial requests submitted by petitioners.[22] From the early 1950s to the late 1970s, Chinese petition offices operated without legal rules regulating their decision-making process. In fact, they functioned primarily as a whistleblowing channel, allowing the public to report suspicions of misconduct related to the government's efforts to combat various types of anti-socialism conducts.[23]

The function of Chinese petition offices as whistleblowing channels became obsolete in the 1980s. After a hiatus of more than two decades, the second National Conference on Handling Complaint Letters and Visits was held in 1978, followed by the third in 1982; subsequently, in April 1982, the Interim Regulation on Handling Complaint Letters and Visits by the CPC and Government Organs was passed, confirming the petition-handling procedure as a review venue to protect the people's right to suggest, criticise, challenge and petition the CPC office and the government organ at the central and local levels.[24] The interim regulation of 1982 is the earliest example of the government petition-handling procedure being established to protect the right to petition.[25]

The recognition and protection of the right to petition and the right to restitution is a recurring theme in China. Under the Chinese Constitution, Chinese citizens have the right to make to relevant State organs complaints or charges against, or exposures of, any State organ or its personnel for violation of law or failure to fulfil its duty, and

[18] Bing-yi (2010), p. 154.

[19] For those who are not familiar with Chinese State Governance, the Chinese State Council is the Central Government that holds the highest administrative power in China.

[20] The Decision of the State Council on the Work of Handling People's Letters and Visits (政务院关于处理人民来信和接见人民工作的决定).

[21] Working Rules on the Handling of People's Petitions (中国人民政治协商会议全国委员会暨省、市协商委员会关于处理人民意见的试行办法).

[22] Chao (2018), pp. 165–167.

[23] Chao (2018), p. 164.

[24] Interim Rules on the Handling of Petitions by the CPC and Government Organs [Draft] (党政机关信访工作暂行条例(草案)).

[25] Chao (2018), pp. 171–172.

citizens who suffered losses as a result of the infringement upon their lawful rights by any State organ or personnel have the right to claim compensation.[26] Legal academics argue that the National Regulation should acknowledge the objective of the government petition procedure to protect the rights to complain about State organs and to request State compensation for harm caused by the government.[27] The National Regulation contains only a general provision that the petition procedure is to protect legitimate rights and interests of natural and legal persons, without specifying which rights fall under its protection. Besides that, it is unclear whether the petition office operates independently of the government, as is the case with the Ombuds procedure in the Occident that enjoys operational independence from government intervention.

Due to the ambiguous power of the petition office, it was unclear for many years whether its decision could be challenged in court. However, in 2005, the Supreme People's Court clarified this issue in response to a question from the provincial court in *Hubei* Province, stating that the decision of the government petition office has an advisory nature and therefore cannot be the subject of an admissible administrative complaint to be adjudicated by the court.[28] This opinion from China's highest court confirms that the decision of the government petition office is not subject to judicial review, which has been the case since then.

The National Regulation of 1995 specifies three tasks that government petition offices shall fulfil: a. to maintain close contact between the public and government organs at all levels; b. to protect the legitimate rights and interests of petitioners; and c. to keep an orderly environment in which petitions are submitted and handled.[29] In 2005, the State Council made substantive amendments to the National Regulation of 1995. The original text was expanded from around 3500 to 7000 characters in the new version. In 2014, Chinese decision-makers announced that the government's handling of complaint letters and visits would be further subject to legal regulation.[30] The following year, a commissioned group began drafting a proposal to be submitted to the National People's Congress, which is the highest legislature in China, in preparation for the passage of the country's first petition law.[31]

As of 2021, there was no indication that the National People's Congress would adopt the petition law anytime soon.[32] On the contrary, the legislative plan is now

---

[26] Article 41, in the Constitution of the People's Republic of China (2018 Amendment).

[27] Zhe (2009), p. 89.

[28] Guiding Opinion on the Admissibility of Protests Against the Decision of the Letter-and-visit Bureau before the People's Court (最高人民法院关于不服县级以上人民政府信访行政管理部门、负责受理信访事项的行政管理机关以及镇(乡)人民政府作出的处理意见或者不再受理决定而提起的行政诉讼人民法院是否受理的批复).

[29] Article 1, in the 1995 National Regulation on Complaint Letters and Visits.

[30] The CPC Central Committee's Decision on Major Issues for Comprehensively Building the Rule-of-law Country (中共中央关于全面推进依法治国若干重大问题的决定).

[31] Xinhua News (13 May 2015).

[32] The State Council listed an item of 'drafting a petition law' in its work plan in 2016, which has not been shown on the list of its new work plans since 2017.

suspended. The National Regulation was repealed in May 2022 when the Rules on the Petitioning Work became effective.[33] The new rules are designed to uphold and enhance the comprehensive guidance of the CPC over the petition-handling process, which applies to a wide range of State bodies including the government, the court and the procuratorate.[34] The repeal of the National Regulation and the implementation of the petition-handling rules suggest that political accountability is now prioritised over legal accountability of the petition offices. This complicates the co-existence of political and legal considerations in the petition settlement process.

3.2.2 Jurisdictional and Functional Reform of the Petition Office

Following an analysis of the major changes to the rules regulating the petition office, this part focuses on the significant legislative and procedural developments related to the settlement of petitions. For more than three decades, China has been promoting law-based appeal procedures to settle various sorts of complaints, including those about government decisions and conduct. The petition procedure served as an alternative forum when Chinese courts were unable or unwilling to settle complaints about the government in the 1980s and 1990s.[35] This remedial power of the petition office has been reduced with the set-up of the statutory appeal procedures for reviewing complaints about the government.

Before the enforcement of the Chinese Administrative Litigation Law in 1990 and the Chinese Administrative Reconsideration Law in 1999, the petition office was the only entity responsible for receiving and reviewing complaints about losses or damages caused by the government.[36] Petition cases resolved through the petition procedure usually involve the government's land expropriation and requisition plans, property demolition projects, environmental hazards, and the restructuring and bankruptcy of State-owned enterprises.[37] The National Regulation of 1995 already required petitioners to submit cases with litigious and prosecutorial claims to, respectively, the court and the procuratorate.[38] To appeal against the conduct of the government, one should bring the case to either the reconsideration body within the government or the court for judicial review. Procedurally, only requests that have exhausted the applicable statutory appeal venues may be presented to the government petition office.

[33] The Rules on the Petitioning Work, adopted by the Central Committee of the CPC on 24 January 2022.

[34] Articles 1, 2 and 5, in the Rules on the Petitioning Work.

[35] Xing (2004), pp. 58–61.

[36] Article 8, in the 1995 National Regulation on Complaint Letters and Visits.

[37] The Advisory Opinions on Improving the Handling of Complaint Letters and Visits in the New Era, jointly issued by the Central Committee of the CPC and the State Council on 10 March 2007.

[38] Article 9, in the 1995 National Regulation on Complaint Letters and Visits.

However, the legislative effort to separate different appeal procedures is challenged by the overlapping jurisdiction of administrative and juridical powers in reviewing and resolving petition cases. The co-existence and lack of coordination between different appeal procedures can lead to what is commonly referred to as forum shopping by petitioners. Lodging a petition is generally easier than submitting a reconsideration request or initiating a litigation action, and the government petition-handling process is known for being user-friendly. A petitioner can submit a complaint in the form of a letter, email or telegraph, or can orally explain the case to the petition handler over the phone or during a visit.[39] Besides that, forum shopping of complainants also results from the lack of public trust in court review, stemming from the perception that the court is unable to protect the substantive and procedural rights of complainants, an issue officially recognised in the 2010s.[40]

Litigation-related petitions (*shesu xinfang*/涉诉信访) are a common example of forum shopping, where petitioners request government intervention in court decision-making; however, such petitions can have a negative effect on the finality of decisions made by various review bodies.[41] From the year 1994 to 1999, the number of litigation-related petitions filed through the government petition procedure doubled nationwide.[42] In Shandong Province, which is the third largest provincial economy ranked by GDP and the second most populous province in China in 2021, around one-fifth of petition cases handled by the petition office in the 1990s and the 2000s contained complaints about the lawsuit procedure or result; of these cases, over thirty per cent appealed against the court decision and around twenty-five per cent against non-enforcement of the court decision.[43]

The Chinese government has acknowledged that litigation-related petitions fall outside the scope of the government petition procedure, which serves as a supplementary complaint venue.[44] In 2013, the State Council issued Advisory Opinions on Handling Petitions with Litigious Claims to separate litigious claims from the government petition-handling procedure; in 2014, the Central Political and Legal

[39] According to a survey conducted in 2006 in a medium-developed region, over fifty-four percent of complainants found petitioning to be more convenient than other methods of making a complaint. See: The Centre for Education and Study of Human Rights of the South West University of Political Science and Law (2008), p. 37 (Table 21).

[40] Paragraph 5, in the Advisory Opinions on Innovating Measures for Resolving Major Problems in Petitions.

[41] The people's court has a procedure for receiving appeal petitions from applicants. In 2014, local courts received 582,890 petitions requesting an appeal due to claimed incorrectness in the court decision. However, this procedure is not within the scope of this analysis as it does not pertain to the overlap between statutory and petition-handling rules.

[42] Tables of "Statistics of Complaint, Appeal and Letter-and-visit Handled by Courts" and "Cases of Reporting, Accusation and Petition Handled by People's Procuratorate", in the Law Yearbook of China 1995–2000.

[43] Xiucheng (2007), p. 150.

[44] The Guiding Opinions for Handling Litigation-related Petitions in Accordance with Law (关于依法处理涉法涉诉信访问题的意见).

Affairs Committee of the CPC[45] issued three guiding opinions, respectively, on the referral of petitions with litigious claims to the court, the handling of petitions concerning an error in the court decision, and the handling of petitions about enforcing the court decision.[46] As a result, the government petition office must conduct a more rigorous test to determine the admissibility of petition cases. It shall either reject petitions that should be reviewed by a statutory appeal body or refer the petitioners to a relevant appeal procedure.[47] In short, the remedial function of the petition office is significantly reduced while its advisory function is enhanced. Its primary task is now confirmed as producing advisory reports for the government to improve its decision-making process and identify controversial elements before a government decision is made definite.[48]

Apart from efforts to separate the petition procedure from statutory appeal procedures, the Chinese government has also sought to tackle the co-existence of political and legal accountabilities of the petition office. In 2000, the State Council instituted the National Public Complaints Commission (hereafter referred to as the "National Bureau for Complaint Letters and Visits") to manage the work of local petition offices.[49] The National Bureau for Complaint Letters and Visits is an administrative organ answerable to the State Council, and its immediate predecessor is the Central Bureau for Complaint Letters and Visits of the CPC which was answerable to the Central Committee of the CPC. Although the government petition procedure has been legally regulated since 1995, political considerations by petition handlers to maintain social stability and disperse disruptive actions may override legal rules.[50] In 2013, the National Bureau for Complaint Letters and Visits removed a rather controversial criterion for assessing the work of petition handlers based on the recorded number of 'abnormal' petitions, which used to deduct the performance score of petition offices when they failed to prevent the occurrence of 'abnormal' petitions.[51]

Although the amount of recorded 'abnormal' petitions is no longer relevant to assessing the work of petition handlers,[52] the petition office still adheres to political norms that value social stability and continues to involve senior officials in handling

[45] The Central Political and Legal Affairs Committee of the CPC oversees the work of Chinese courts, procuratorates and public security organs.

[46] People's Court Daily (12 September 2014).

[47] The explanatory notes on the Working Rules on the Handling of Complaint Letters and Visits, issued by the National Bureau for Complaint Letters and Visits on 2 August 2017.

[48] Xiao-yong (2011), p. 125.

[49] The Regulation on the Function, Structure and Personnel of the State Bureau for Complaint Letters and Visits, jointly issued by the General Office of the CPC and the General Office of the State Council on 13 February 2000.

[50] HOU (2020), p. 638.

[51] The National Bureau for Complaint Letters and Visits (2015b).

[52] Qinghua (2018).

major petition cases.[53] Generally speaking, the involvement of senior officials in dispute resolution is not uncommon in the Occident. What may be peculiar to China is the habitual prioritisation of political engagement over legal compliance during the settlement of collective petitions. The 1995 National Regulation did not require the government petition office to be accountable to the law or the public in their procedures and decisions. However, the 2005 amendment to the National Regulation now holds government authorities accountable to relevant laws and regulatory rules.[54]

In particular, the 2005 amendment prohibits the petition office from making decisions beyond its supplementary and advisory powers and subjects any incorrect application of the law by the petition handler to disciplinary or even administrative punishments.[55] In 2008, the Interim Regulation on Punishing the Non-compliance with Disciplinary Rules in Handling Complaint Letters and Visits was passed, under which the official responsible for settling the accepted petition may be held liable if one of the following facts can be established: if they make a decision in violation of the law, regulation or policy, resulting in an abnormal petition or other forms of mass actions; or if they fail to consider important facts presented in the petition, resulting in antagonising petitioners and leading to their unrest.[56] In summary, the Chinese petition-handling procedure now has significantly reduced the power to render remedial decisions, and its working processes and decisions are legally accountable.

3.2.3 Subsidiarity of the Petition-Handling Procedure

First and foremost, the Chinese petition-handling procedure is legally confirmed as a subsidiary mechanism to statutory appeal procedures. In other words, it is only intended for complaints that cannot be dealt with elsewhere, and if that is the case, complainants can seek relief or remedy from the government by submitting their complaint and evidence to the petition office. To reinforce the subsidiary status of the government petition-handling procedure, the Chinese government has required the petition office to direct complaints about damage caused by the government to one's property or personality rights to statutory appeal procedures. The petition office shall reject any petition that has already been heard before statutory appeal venues or that should be heard before them.[57]

---

[53] Xiao-yong (2011), pp. 125–127.

[54] Article 32, in the 2005 National Regulation on Complaint Letters and Visits.

[55] Article 40, in the 2005 National Regulation on Complaint Letters and Visits.

[56] Article 5 in the Interim Regulation on Sanctioning the Non-compliance of Complaint Letter and Visit Working Disciplines, adopted by the Ministry of Supervision, the Ministry of Human Recourses and Social Security, and the National Public Complaint Commission in June 2008.

[57] Article 21, in the 2005 National Regulation on Complaint Letters and Visits.

In 2007, the National Bureau for Complaint Letters and Visits reformed the core duty of the government petition office from settling petition cases to identifying common factors that lead to petitioners' complaints and helping the government take those factors into account in its decision-making. Government petition offices are now responsible for collecting public concerns regarding government decisions before they are finalised, and in particular, filtering out the unwelcomed decisions during the drafting stage; and overseeing the settlement of accepted petition cases by the relevant government department and ensuring the petitioners are satisfied with the treatment they receive.[58]

Secondly, the Chinese government has also reduced the punitive power of the petition office as part of its efforts to reform its duties. The power of petition handlers to dissolve prohibited forms of petitions has been a topic of debate in China for years. Petitions that skip the local petition office are generally rejected by petition handlers at higher levels of the government.[59] With the help of an administrative penalty procedure applicable to the person with no legal permit and stable income to stay in urban areas, the petition office used to have the power to request public security to detain or repatriate petitioners who resorted to prohibited forms of petitioning, or to request the employer of petitioners to return them to their places of origin.[60]

In 2005, the power of the government petition office to (co-)impose administrative punishments on petitioners was outlawed. Government petition offices no longer hold the power to disperse 'abnormal' petitions on their initiative. If petitioners organise their petitioning action in a way that is prohibited by the 2005 National Regulation,[61] and the petition office is unable to dissuade 'abnormal' petitioners, it may request the public security department to warn the petitioners to stop the 'abnormal' action.[62] If the public security department concludes that the

[58] The National Bureau for Complaint Letters and Visits (2006) regarding the implementing measures for the Guiding Opinion of the Central Committee of the CPC and the State Council on Improving the Petition Work (中共中央、国务院关于进一步加强新时期信访工作的意见).

[59] Article 16, in the 2005 National Regulation on Complaint Letters and Visits.

[60] Articles 21 and 22, in the 1995 National Regulation on Complaint Letters and Visits. The administrative detention and repatriation imposed on persons with no legal permit and stable income to stay in urban areas was adopted in 1982 and abolished in 2003.

[61] A petition action that causes the damage to the interests of the State, the society and the public or to the lawful rights of other citizens is prohibited, such as: (1). "illegally assembling around offices of State organs or public places, encircling and attacking State organs, intercepting official vehicles, or jamming and obstructing traffic;" (2) carrying dangerous articles or tools that are regulated by law; (3) humiliating, beating up or threatening personnel of State organs or illegally restricting other people's individual freedom; (4) staying and making trouble at the reception places of the petition-handling body; (5) inciting, colluding with, coercing or deceiving petitioners to present their letter and visits with an intention to accumulate wealth; and (6) committing other acts that disrupt public order or threat national or public security. See: Article 20, in the 2005 National Regulation on Complaint Letters and Visits.

[62] Article 47, in the 2005 National Regulation on Complaint Letters and Visits.

'abnormal' petitioning action constitutes a violation of the law, it may impose a restraining order or an administrative penalty on the petitioner(s).[63]

Thirdly, statutory appeal procedures, such as administrative reconsideration and court review, are established by law as preceding the government petition-handling procedure.[64] The petition office will check, based on the information available to it, whether the claim and the request presented in the petition are being considered by a statutory appeal body or have been concluded by such a body. If a petition submission passes this test, the petition office shall, within fifteen working days, refer it to the competent and relevant government department for further consideration and remedy of the matters petitioned.[65] The reviewing department may make two types of decisions: a. if it considers that the redress of the case is beyond its power, it will contact the most relevant government department and discuss with that department a plan for settling the case; and b. if the case falls within its power and duty, the reviewing department will notify the petitioner within fifteen working days that it will decide on the claims and requests made in the petition.[66]

In the early 2000s, the Chinese government experimented with a cross-departmental mechanism for reviewing and redressing major petition cases, including collective petitions, which was joined by twenty-eight administrative, political and judicial authorities at the central level, hoping that the centrally coordinated settlement would speed up the process of investigating petition cases and redressing the legitimate claims in them.[67] The cross-departmental coordination mechanism has received mixed reactions since its inception. The participating authorities do not necessarily share the same view of what counts as a successful petition settlement.[68] In the absence of procedural and accountability rules, the cross-departmental coordination mechanism has de facto reverted to the traditional decision-making pattern where the representative with the highest political authority decides on the petition settlement.[69]

To sum up, the Chinese government has limited the scope of admissible petitions to the government, reduced the remedial and punitive powers of the petition office, and increased its legal accountability. At the same time, reform efforts to make the petition-handling procedure subsidiary to statutory appeal procedures have not resolved the conflict between political and legal considerations, a typical example of which will be analysed in Part 2.4 below.

---

[63] Ibid.

[64] Guiding Opinion of the National Public Complaints and Proposals Administration on the Cross-departmental and Separated Procedures for Handling Complaint Letters and Visits (国家信访局协调"三跨三分离"信访事项工作规范(国信办发〔2013〕29 号).

[65] Articles 2 and 3, in the Working Rules on Handling Petitions in Accordance with Law, adopted by the National Bureau for Complaint Letters and Visits and effective on 12 July 2017.

[66] Articles 7 and 8, in the Working Rules on Handling Petitions in Accordance with Law.

[67] Sina News (3 December 2004).

[68] Heurlin et al. (2017), p. 90.

[69] Benney (2016), pp. 389–392.

3.2.4 The Dilemmatic Political Intervention

The involvement of senior officials, or the leading cadre (*lingdao ganbu*/领导干部) in Chinese, is a common practice for resolving major petition cases in China. Government petition offices are not prohibited from involving political authorities in petition settlement and in fact, they tend to seek political support when dealing with collective petitions.[70] If the petition handler faces difficulties in involving different government departments in the examination of evidence or the formulation of a solution, a supporting opinion from the senior official can make the involvement by the relevant government departments more likely.[71] In the case of litigation-related petitions, a senior official's supporting opinion could make a difference in how the court deals with a petitioner's request for an appeal, which would otherwise have had to wait for a long time due to the court's heavy workload.[72]

Senior officials in charge of major central and local government departments are required to regularly receive petitioners, learn about their complaints and propose a feasible way to settle their cases (usually in the form of a written notice signed by the senior official).[73] In 2010, the cross-departmental coordination mechanism for settling major petitions made it a standard requirement for senior officials to make themselves available to petitioners on a regular basis.[74] Specifically, senior officials at the provincial level shall be present at the petition office and receive petitioners at least one day every six months, those at the city level shall do so at least one day every three months, and those at the town level shall do so at least one day every month; and senior officials shall, based on their judgement and political authority, assign an appropriate body to handle the petition case on or after their reception day.[75]

Political intervention in the petition settlement, when taking place behind the scenes, raises many concerns about potential conflict with procedural regulatory rules.[76] Granting government officials some discretion to rectify inappropriate elements of government decisions is not unique to China.[77] However, political intervention in a non-transparent manner is creating a legal conundrum after the Regulation on the Disclosure of Government Information came into effect on 1 May

[70] Minzner (2006), p. 105.

[71] Suli (2006), pp. 45–46.

[72] Yongtao and Peng (2015), pp. 18–19.

[73] Lin et al. (2008), p. 290.

[74] The summary of the petition-handling work at the Sixth National Conference on Handling Complaint Letters and Visits (第六次全国信访工作会议以来信访工作成就综述), published by the National Bureau for Complaint Letters and Visits 13 July 2012.

[75] Paragraph 6 in the in the Advisory Opinions on Innovating Measures for Resolving Major Problems in Petitions.

[76] Min'an (2005), p. 22.

[77] Xi-xin (2003), p. 71.

2008. Government bodies are legally obliged to make their work records accessible to the public. The National Bureau for Complaint Letters and Visits disclosure rules, on the other hand, stipulate that procedural records of petition settlement, such as the consultation and advisory letters from officials concerned, can be exempted from mandatory disclosure.[78]

The confidentiality of petition settlement is argued to be instrumentally necessary. A retired petition handler who worked for the provincial petition office for about four decades explains that the confidentiality of the settlement of major petition cases ensures the proper functioning of the petition office: "If all successful settlements were made public, petitioners would have rather high expectations of what we could deliver, so high that we could never meet them, and they would end up being disappointed".[79] There is a lack of consensus among policymakers and implementers as to whether political intervention in the petition settlement should be avoided altogether, and to what extent records of political intervention should be made public.

In summary, while political intervention is known to improve the efficiency of petition settlement, it is widely acknowledged that political intervention reinforces the outdated dispute resolution pattern where political support is necessary to obtain relief or remedy for one's loss. It is a delicate balance for the petition office to strike, between complying with procedural rules on the one hand and achieving efficient settlement of petition cases on the other.

3.2.5 The Involvement of Non-Governmental Advisers

The National Bureau for Complaint Letters and Visits encourages the petition office to engage non-governmental advisers, such as lawyers and retired officials, who are experienced in advising collective petitioners on how to formulate a realistic request and choose an appropriate appeal venue.[80] Collective petitioners who are advised by lawyers tend to lower their demands than those who are not.[81] The local pilot projects show that the number of litigation-related petitions decreases after the involvement of lawyers, and several local courts began to hire part-time lawyers to provide explanatory and advisory services to litigants who intend to initiate a

[78] Article 11, in the Rules on Disclosing the Petition-handling Records (国家信访局政府信息公开管理办法), issued by the National Bureau for Complaint Letters and Visits on 2 August 2019.

[79] Author's interview was conducted at the Petition Department of a major municipal government in Central China, dated on 20–22 January 2011. The complete information on the interviews are with the author.

[80] Guiding Opinions on Establishing the System for Lawyers to Participate in Resolving and Representing Petitioned Cases (关于建立律师参与化解和代理涉法涉诉信访案件制度的意见(试行)), issued by the CPC Central Committee of Political and Legal Affairs on 9 November 2015.

[81] Liu and Stern (2020), p. 10.

petitioning action.[82] Lawyers are required by the Chinese Ministry of Justice to provide no fewer than fifty hours of *pro bono* legal services each year in the public interest, such as providing advice to petitioners who need legal guidance and suggestions.[83]

Research shows that when a locally trusted mediator is involved in the petition settlement, petitioners are more likely to opt for a non-confrontational approach to seeking redress of their grievances.[84] Since 2014, the Chinese government has recruited retired officials to participate in the government handling of major petitions, particularly those related to complaints about land acquisition, house demolition and social welfare matters.[85] Retired officials are seen as trustworthy by the petition office, and as skilled and resourceful by petitioners. After retiring from a city-level petition office in 2008, the interviewee started mediating local disputes. In January 2011, a group of more than a dozen local residents submitted a petition to the interviewee, alleging that a government-sanctioned construction project had violently demolished their homes and caused several injuries, and presenting their evidence that consisted of photos of the injured residents and an anonymous testimony of the violent behaviour of the construction team.[86]

The interviewee agreed with the petitioners that he would conduct an on-site investigation and, if the allegations were true, speak with the project manager to request proper redress for the injured residents. The interviewee found that there had been some minor physical conflict (mostly pushing) during the demolition process, but no injuries as claimed by the petitioners were discovered. The interviewee nevertheless contacted the project manager, and asked him to hold an informal dialogue with the petitioning residents during which the manager agreed to investigate the conduct of his team and offer proper compensation to the affected residents if any wrongdoing was found; the residents agreed to suspend their petitioning action during the internal investigation, provided that the investigation was conducted efficiently and honestly. The tripartite process, in which the petition office and a trusted adviser work together to propose an appropriate solution to the petitioners' complaint, was applied in several regions in China in the 2010s.[87]

However, it remains uncertain whether these local practices involving non-governmental advisers can be developed into a nationwide standard procedure. "The relevant government department does not always respond to our request in a

[82] In Jilin Province, for instance, the amount of litigation-related petitions declined from over 7000 in 2010 to 1300 in 2014. People's Daily (2016).

[83] Ibid.

[84] Xiaowei and Chen-wen (2013), p. 129.

[85] Paragraph 7 and 16, in the Advisory Opinions on Innovating Measures for Resolving Major Problems in Petitions.

[86] Author's interviews dated on 20–22 January 2011 in a major municipal government in Central China. The complete information on the interviews are with the author.

[87] Key Tasks of Shenzhen Municipal Government in 2014 (中共深圳市委办公厅 深圳市人民政府办公厅关于印发<2014年全市社会建设工作要点>的通知), issued by the CPC Municipal Committee and the Shenzhen People's Government on 4 April 2014.

timely and meaningful way because they are aware that the cost of not cooperating with us is quite low," said a non-governmental mediator working with the Nanjing Municipal Petition Office in 2016, and "that's a vicious circle. If there is little or no cooperation from the relevant government department, petitioners start to doubt whether we genuinely want to help them or whether we are trying to keep them away from annoying the government."[88] For the lawyer's participation, petitioners prefer to have senior lawyers advise on their cases, while senior lawyers are often too constrained by time or financial reimbursement to accommodate these requests.[89] In short, it is unclear whether the involvement of non-governmental advisers in the petition settlement can achieve the intended goal of reducing forum shopping by petitioners and concluding petition cases before they become confrontational.

3.2.6 Primacy of Legal Accountability of Petition Settlements? Not Yet Instituted

This section has analysed the incorporation of legal accountability rules into the government petition-handling procedure in China, which aims to regulate the power, work procedure and accountability of the petition office. These rules are adopted to make the government petition-handling procedure subsidiary to statutory appeal procedures. After that, the section has identified the main obstacles to the institutionalisation of legal accountability in the receipt and settlement of petitions in general and of collective petitions in particular. The Chinese government has sought to involve non-governmental advisers in order to channel collective petition cases into statutory appeal procedures and to prevent a confrontation between collective petitioners and the government.

In conclusion, Chinese measures for dealing with collective petitions shift from being based on political considerations to being bound by legal accountability. Yet, this shift faces three major challenges: a. the government petition office is not operationally separated from statutory appeal procedures which leads to the continuation of forum shopping by petitioners; b. there is no consensus among petition offices that legal accountability rules are the primary basis for deciding on the petition settlement, and c. there is no social culture in which petitioners trust the statutory appeal procedures and take the legal accountability of the petition office seriously. In this sense, the primacy of accountability law has not been instituted in Chinese measures for addressing petitions, which is particularly evident in the government's handling of collective petitions.

[88] The Nanjing Municipal Bureau for Complaint Letter and Visit (2013).

[89] Yueyang (2018), pp. 87–88.

3.3 The Socialisation of Accountability Law in the News

Since 1995, China has passed and amended national regulations to reorient the government petition-handling procedure as a subsidiary to the statutory appeal procedures, by introducing legal accountability to the petition office and reducing its decisional and remedial powers. To fully understand the juridification of Chinese measures for managing collective petitions, it is necessary to make sense of both the relevant regulatory rules, their amendments and subsequent implementation, and to what extent these legal accountability rules are embedded in social norms.

To this end, I collect a large number of Chinese news reports on collective petitions and their settlements and examine whether the legal accountability rules regulating the petition-handling procedure (in particular, the 1995 National Regulation and its 2005 amendment) are interpreted as normal and important in narrating collective petitions and evaluating their settlements in the news. Specifically, the first part outlines the analytical methods used to compose the news corpus and process it. The second part examines popular vocabulary and recurring narratives in the news coverage of collective petitions and their outcomes. The third part focuses on the news related to senior officials, courts and community advisers who are involved in handling collective petitions and identifies recurring narratives about these actors. The last part summarises the findings of the role of legal accountability in news narratives and framings of collective petitions and their settlements.

3.3.1 Data Collection, Relevance Testing and Processing

The WiseNews is the source for my news data collection, which is the world's largest Chinese news database that captures and stores the full text of Chinese news reports. The search starts on 1 January 1998, the earliest date on which the full text of Chinese news is available, and ends on 1 May 2015, a decade after the 2005 amendment to the National Regulation became effective. To ensure inclusivity of relevant news reports, the search uses fourteen different terms to refer to collective petitions, including both official terms such as collective letter and visit, collective visit, collective letter, and colloquial references and their synonyms, such as collective drop-by, group letter and visit, group visit, group letter, group drop-by, group petition, collective petition, group petition request, collective petition request, receiving group visit, and receiving collective visit.[90]

The collection comprises news reports that match at least one of the fourteen search words in their headline or lead paragraph or at least two search words in the same paragraph of their body text. A total of 2702 news reports are collected, with

[90]The search terms are in simplified Chinese, consisting of: 集体信访, 集体走访, 集体来访, 集体访, 群体访, 群体来访. 群体走访, 群体信访, 集体信访诉求, 群体信访诉求, 集体信访申诉, 群体信访申诉, 集体接访, 群体接访.

newspapers being the primary content producers, accounting for over eighty-five per cent of the collected reports. News agencies account for about nine per cent of the collected reports, and news websites and news journals around four per cent and one per cent, respectively. To analyse how the development of regulatory rules is reflected in the news, the collected reports are divided into three groups, using 1 May 2005 and 1 May 2010 as the dividing point. These two dates mark the enforcement of the amendment to the National Regulation in 2005, and the reinforcement of political intervention in petition settlements with the routinisation of senior officials' reception day in 2010. Accordingly, Group A consists of the collected reports published between 1 January 1998 and 30 April 2005, Group B comprises the reports published between 1 May 2005 and 30 April 2010, and Group C includes the reports published between 1 May 2010 and 1 May 2015, the year that marks the twentieth anniversary of the adoption of the National Regulation and tenth anniversary of its amendment.

Thereafter, a close reading is conducted on randomly selected news reports from each group to test their relevance to collective petitions. Reports are marked as highly relevant if they contain the target term of the collective petition or its synonyms in the headline, or if they mention the target term more than three times in the body text. Reports are marked as moderately relevant if they contain the term at least twice in the body text, but not in the headline. The reports mentioning the term less than twice in the body text are marked as having low or no relevance.

The close reading reveals that approximately eighty per cent of the reports in Group A are either highly or moderately relevant to collective petitions,[91] and about fifty per cent of the reports in Group B[92] and about sixty per cent of the reports in Group C[93] are either highly or moderately relevant. The keywords from the reports with low or no relevance are used to search for similar texts in each group, which are subsequently excluded from further analysis. Following the cleaning process, the

---

[91] Group A contains 819 pages of news reports in the Microsoft Word document. A close reading is conducted on the report listed on every 82nd page. News reports about the following topics are removed from the corpus as they pertain to neither collective petitions nor Chinese measures for resolving them: 'Philip (corporation)', 'Motorola (company)', 'group visits to China', 'Yahoo (company)', 'Sohu (the IT company)', 'TCL (the electronics company)'.

[92] Group B contains 2, 022 pages of news reports in Microsoft Word document. A close reading is conducted on the report listed on every 202nd page. News reports about the following topics are removed from the corpus as they pertain to neither collective petitions nor Chinese measures for resolving them: the teachers' visit to student houses, group visits to China, group visits to USA, Hewlett-Packard, Sildenafil, corporates' collective claim, corporates' collective appeal, patent disputes, group interviews.

[93] Group C contains 1, 973 pages of news reports in the Microsoft Word document. A close reading is conducted on the report listed on every 198th page. News reports about the following topics are removed from the corpus as they pertain to neither collective petitions nor Chinese measures for resolving them: commerce association, entrepreneur, spring festival, European union, Japan, North Korea, South Korea, USA, Taiwan, Russia, BRIC, legislation on keeping dogs as the pet, Hewlett-Packardm Toyota, group visits to China, foreign companies, consumer groups, listed companies, collective leadership.

Table 3.2 The composition of three corpus groups

Corpus Group	Producer of the news				Size of news data (in characters)	
	Newspaper	News journal	News agency	Web news	Before cleaning	After cleaning
A	443	4	27	6	955,121	894,027
B	1073	10	92	9	2,002,869	1,384,017
C	793	16	133	96	2,081,391	1,643,907

size of Group A is over 0.89 million characters, Group B is over 1.38 million and Group C is over 1.64 million (see Table 3.2). The cleaned data are then processed using two software programs: Word Phraser to code the data as computer-readable units and AntConc to analyse the readable data through the chosen qualitative data analysis methods.

The analysis begins with the Word-list method in AntConc, which calculates the frequency of words and phrases in each group.[94] Three types of the results are not analysed. The first type contains meaningless words, such as conjunctions (e.g. '和' that means 'and' or 'with'), modal particles (e.g. '了' that indicates the completion of an action), aspect particles (e.g. '着' that indicates the present state) and structural particles (e.g. '的' that links an adjective to a noun). The second includes the fourteen search words that are naturally frequent throughout the text.[95] Lastly, ambiguous terms that can be interpreted in different ways, such as '保' that can mean 'protect,' 'security' and 'ensure', or '政' that can mean 'politics/political', 'government' and 'policy', are also not analysed further. The analysis continues with the Collocate method to examine the co-occurrence of words or phrases in close proximity to the target term of collective petitions in each group. The popular words that appear on the Word-list result list and those on the Collocate result list are then processed in the Concordance method to uncover typical examples of recurrent narratives in the news, which will be interpreted and analysed in detail.

3.3.2 Popular Words and Recurring Narratives in the News

The word 'problem' and the term 'the mass (*qunzhong*/群众)'[96] are the most frequently used in each of the three groups.[97] They are also the most commonly associated with the term of complaint letters and visits throughout the entire

[94] For further information on the computational methods used in this study, please refer to "4.2. On Analytical Foci and Methods" in Chap. 1.

[95] See: the list of fourteen search word for collecting news data in the WiseNews, supra note 90.

[96] In Chinese political discourse, the term qunzhong is generally used interchangeably with the people.

[97] Please refer to Table 3.5 in the Appendix: the Most Popular Terms in Groups A, B and C.

corpus.[98] In line with this textual feature, this part delves deeper into the news coverage of the problem and the mass to uncover their meanings and implications and explore the role of legal concepts and accountability rules in shaping these meanings.

3.3.2.1 Narratives Concerning the Problem

During the early period of 1998 to 2005, Chinese news reports often depict collective petitions as problematic, with the word 'problem' frequently used in the narratives describing how Chinese State authorities dealt with various problems arising from the occurrence of collective petitions. Accordingly, the measures employed by the authorities to disperse collective petitions and discourage collective petitioners are described as reasonable. There is no mention of legal rules in the news with which the petition office must comply in handling collective petitions, nor is there any reference to the appeal right entitled to petitioners.

The early news narrative is often critical of collective petition(er)s, without explaining the reasons behind collective petitions or whether petition settlements are satisfactory to the petitioners. All randomly selected reports, with the exception of only one news report that questions the extensive use of detention in handling petitions (sample 5), use the officially preferred term 'abnormal' petition to describe collective, jurisdiction-jumping and repetitious petitions.[99] The early news characterises collective petitions as abnormal because they are interruptive to the normal functioning of the petition office (samples 8 and 9). It also portrays the involvement of political bodies (sample 2) and senior officials as contributing positively to the procedural efficiency in concluding the matters petitioned (samples 3, 7 and 10). Almost half of the randomly selected news reports describe the petition office as a body that monitors public opinion on critical issues, leaving its duty to facilitate the exercise of the appeal right not discussed (samples 1, 2, 3 and 6).

In early news, narratives about collective petitions are primarily sourced from government policies and political statements.[100] Out of the ten randomly selected news reports, only one bases its narrative on an academic commentary that questions the legality of the preventive measures for handling collective petitions (sample 9). The remaining news reports build their narratives on official statements, such as periodic reports issued by the petition office (samples 1, 6 and 8) and by the procuratorate (sample 5), political statements issued by the CPC organs (samples 2 and 3), or the local governments' press release (samples 4, 7 and 10). When it comes to the assessment of the handling of collective petitions, the early news

[98] Please refer to Table 3.6 in the Appendix: The Terms Most Frequently Collocated to 'Letters and visits' in Groups A, B and C.

[99] Please refer to List 3 in the Appendix: Original Sources of Ten Randomly Selected Samples Where Petitions and 'Problem' Co-occur in Group A.

[100] Ibid.

focuses on whether the petition office fulfils its duties of keeping the government informed of popular discontent with the government and preventing petitioners from becoming confrontational or resorting to abnormal forms of submitting their claims.

More recent news from 2005 to 2010 shares some similarities with early news in that it narrates 'abnormal' petitions as problematic.[101] Specifically, collective petitions are described as incompatible with the law and government policies, and as undermining the due order of the society (samples 4, 7, 8 and 10). Consistent with this narrative, the more recent news narrates official measures for monitoring and limiting collective petitions as reasonable (samples 1, 2, 3 and 5). It portrays collective petitions negatively, using terms such as 'unreasonable' and 'abnormal', and, or rather therefore, explains the prevention of collective petitions from interrupting social stability as necessary (samples 4, 6, 7, 8 and 10). Additionally, involving senior officials is described as helpful in resolving collective petitions (samples 5 and 9). In short, more recent news often frames collective petitions (as a typical form of 'abnormal' petitions) in a negative light.

Government policies and official statements remain the major source for more recent news on (collective) petitions, as evidenced by randomly selected news samples from Group B. News narratives centre around political statements (samples 1, 8, 9 and 10) and policy briefings issued by local government authorities (samples 2, 5 and 7). It is, however, not to say that more recent news simply republishes official narratives verbatim. They in fact refer to non-governmental sources, such as academic critiques on government measures for concluding abnormal petitions (sample 3), feedback from petitioners (sample 4), and comments from lawyers working with petitioners (sample 6).

The narrative framing of the most recent news from 2010 to 2015 differs from earlier news. It focuses on procedural flaws in petition settlements rather than stressing the problem with 'abnormal' collective petitions.[102] Specifically, it discusses legal requirements for handling major petition cases, such as the inclusion of public hearings (samples 1 and 7), and timely disclosure of decisions by administrative and judicial review bodies (samples 2 and 3). It also highlights the importance of simplifying the petition-receiving procedure (samples 5, 6 and 8), and ensuring procedural legality by petition offices (samples 4, 9 and 10). Furthermore, information sources in the most recent news are more diverse.[103] In addition to citing government reports (samples 1, 6 and 8), the most recent news narratives also reference non-governmental sources such as court opinions (samples 2, 3, 4 and 9), academic analyses (source 3) and opinions from collective petitioners (samples 7 and 10).

---

[101] Please refer to List 4 in the Appendix: Original Sources of Ten Randomly Selected Samples Where Petitions and 'Problem' Co-occur in Group B.

[102] Please refer to List 5 in the Appendix: Original Sources of Ten Randomly Selected Samples Where Petitions and 'Problem' Co-occur in Group C.

[103] Ibid.

To summarise, the news coverage of collective petitions where problem frequently occurs demonstrate an evolving change in the narrative framing. This change is evident in the reports published after 2010, which highlight flaws in the petition-handling procedure and collective petition settlements, as well as legal accountability rules regulating the handling of collective petitions. In contrast, earlier news often depicts collective petitions, along with other 'abnormal' forms of petitions, as hindering the efficiency of the petition-handling process and disrupting orderly public governance, and bases its assessment of petition outcomes on political norms that value social stability and the accordant measures of monitoring and dispersing 'unreasonable' petitions.

3.3.2.2 Narratives Concerning the Mass

In Chinese political discourse, the term 'the mass' carries a more complex connotation beyond simply pluralising the singular form of a person. It implies respect for and conformity to socialist ideologies, such as valuing work ethics and prioritising social interests over individual ones, as is evident in political phrases of "the mass line" and "the relationship between the Party and the mass".[104] Conflicts that are internal to the mass shall be resolved using non-oppressive measures, whereas conflicts between the mass and the antagonistic force may require harsher measures to be settled.[105] The dichotomous implication of the mass has lost much of its relevance in current Chinese measures for managing collective petitions. Nonetheless, petition settlements can still be affected by whether their claims and petitioning methods are considered internal to the mass, which would necessitate a non-confrontational approach to addressing them.[106]

Early news from 1998 to 2005 focuses on whether petition settlements contribute to refining the conduct of Chinese governing authorities.[107] Specifically, early news introduces the petition procedure as a mechanism for monitoring public discontent with government decisions, such as those on government compensation for parties affected by urban development plans or government subsidies for the unemployed (samples 1, 2 and 8), or as an external check on the procedural fairness and decisional enforceability of court procedures (sample 5). It describes regular interaction between government officials and petitioners as strengthening public trust in the government (samples 4, 6, 9 and 10), and interprets the involvement of senior officials as ensuring procedural efficiency in settling petitions (samples 3 and 7).

[104] Lifeng (2018), pp. 146–148.

[105] Goldman and Perry (2002), pp. 292–293.

[106] De-xiong (2002).

[107] Please refer to List 6 in the Appendix: Original Sources of Ten Randomly Selected Samples Where Petitions and 'Mass' Co-occur in Group A.

Overall, the early news narratives are governance-focused, highlighting how petition settlement helps to improve government decision-making and sustain public trust.

The narrative framing of more recent news from 2005 to 2010 differs greatly from earlier news.[108] Instead of focusing on how good petition settlements help improve public trust in the government, more recent news highlights the role of the petition office in assisting petitioners to obtain proper redress for their losses and emphasises the importance of protecting petitioners from threats or repercussions during the petition settlement process (samples 3, 4, 9 and 10). The more recent narratives are built on both official and non-official sources, such as statements from political supervisory bodies (sample 1), inputs from non-governmental advisers (sample 2), the People's Congress (sample 5) and third-party mediators (samples 6 and 8).

This petitioner-focused narrative is also apparent in the most recent news from 2010 to 2015.[109] The tasks of the petition office are narrated as to resolve petitioners' complaints and to monitor and alleviate their discontent (samples 1, 4, 7 and 10). Community engagement is introduced as a desirable approach to dealing with collective petitions in the news, and community workers are narrated as having a better understanding of local situations than those working at higher levels, making them better equipped to handle petitions that reflect local particularities (samples 2, 3, 5, 6, 8 and 9). Overall, the most recent news focuses on whether petitioners receive a timely and appropriate redress for their grievances, demonstrating a petitioner-focused narrative.

3.3.2.3 Summary: A Changing Narrative in the News

This part has examined news narratives related to two terms—the problem and the mass, which are the most commonly used in news coverage of collective petitions. The textual and contextual analyses of the news in three groups reveal that not all political norms underlying Chinese measures for dealing with collective petitions are narrated as reasonable. There is an evolving change in the news narrative in terms of information sources, narrative focus, and evaluative references (see Table 3.3). Noticeably, more recent news highlights the inadequate coordination between judicial and administrative appeal procedures. It also emphasises the increasing importance of legal accountability rules in assessing petition settlements. In contrast, earlier news focuses on whether petition settlements help the government monitor public dissatisfaction with its decisions and maintain public trust in its governance competences.

[108] Please refer to List 7 in the Appendix: Original Sources of Ten Randomly Selected Samples Where Petitions and 'Mass' Co-occur in Group B.

[109] Please refer to List 8 in the Appendix: Original Sources of Ten Randomly Selected Samples Where Petitions and 'Mass' Co-occur in Group C.

Table 3.3 Summary of Chinese news narratives related to the problem and the mass

Corpus group	Information source(s)	Narrative Foci	Assessment of the petition settlement
Group A (January 1998–April 2005)	Official statements such as government reports and political speeches.	Monitoring public discontent; Refining the government decision; Providing an external check on the work of the court.	Based on whether petition offices maintain the petitioning order and monitor public discontent with the government.
Group B (May 2005–April 2010)	Largely official statements; Occasionally non-official inputs from petitioners and mediators.	Monitoring 'abnormal' petitions; Assisting petitioners in identifying a suitable appeal venue.	Based on whether petition offices maintain the petitioning order and sustain public trust in the government.
Group C (May 2010–May 2015)	A combination of court opinions, academic commentaries and official statements.	Weakness in the petition procedure; Improving the effectiveness of petition settlements.	Based on whether the petition settlement resolves the matters petitioned.

3.3.3 Narratives About the Bodies Involved in Petition Settlements

The analysis proceeds with the news reporting of the major bodies involved in handling collective petitions, namely the senior official (or 'the leading cadre' as translated from the Chinese term *lingdao ganbu*), the court and the non-governmental adviser. This section examines recurrent news narratives about these bodies that government petition offices involved in the petition settlement, giving attention to the role of political norms vis-à-vis legal rules in these narratives.

3.3.3.1 Senior Officials in the News

To provide context for understanding political intervention in petition settlements, Chinese central policy mandates that senior officials regularly meet with petitioners who have complaints about the losses caused by governing authorities. Since the late 1990s, the Chinese government has been promoting the rule of morality as a supplement to the rule of law. In July 1999, the then Premier Zhu Rongji, who served as Head of the State Council from 1998 to 2003, urged government officials at all levels to handle complaint letters and visits carefully and oversee the settlement outcome to ensure that petition cases would be properly concluded.[110] In January

[110]Lei (1999), p. 1.

2001, the then General Secretary of the CPC Jiang Zemin announced the aspiration of the central leadership to combine the rule of law with the rule of virtues at the National Convention for Publicity Officials.[111] In September of the same year, the Central Committee of the CPC adopted a resolution that the CPC and government officials should regularly receive petitioners to stay informed of public opinions and popular concerns in the society.[112]

During his visit to the Three Gorges Dam in October 2013, then Premier Wen Jiabao (in office from 2003 to 2013) received a collective petition from migrant workers who complained about the discriminatory labour reimbursement standard set by the local authority; with the support of Premier Wen, the State Council formed a working group to investigate the discriminatory treatment of migrant workers in the region, which later submitted its investigation report to the State Council and triggered the introduction of an amendment to the national labour protection law prohibiting the difference in labour salary made based on one's migrant residence status.[113] In 2019, the Central Committee of the CPC and the State Council jointly issued guiding rules on the "Moral Construction of Civic Morality in a New Era", which includes an essential moral requirement for civil servants to sustain a close relationship with the public.[114] This guidance reaffirms that the proper handling of petitions is both a legal duty and a moral duty of government officials.

The term senior officials is frequently concurrent with complaint letters and visits in all three corpus groups.[115] The early news narratives from 1998 to 2005 generally present a critical view of collective petitions (samples 2, 4, 5, 9 and 10) and justify the regular intervention of government officials in reviewing and settling petition cases (samples 1, 3, 6 and 7); they also describe the adoption of preventive measures to discourage collective petitioners as necessary, and the leaders' reception day as desirable based on that senior officials offer supporting opinions to petitioners.[116]

More recent news from 2005 to 2010 employs a mixed framing when narrating the involvement of senior officials in petition settlements.[117] While it continues to depict political intervention in receiving, reviewing and concluding petitions using positive analogies such as the 'green passage', 'high-way' and 'direct bus' (samples 3, 4, 6 and 8), it also raises doubts about the benefits of political intervention for petitioners' perceptions about the government's public image. A recurring question is whether the intervention of senior officials in the conclusion of collective petitions

---

[111]Zemin (2001).

[112]The CPC Central Committee (2001).

[113]Huo and Gang (2004).

[114]Moral Construction of Civic Morality in a New Era (中共中央 国务院印发新时代公民道德建设实施纲要), jointly issued by the CPC Central Committee and the State Council on 27 October 2019.

[115]Please refer to Table 3.6 in the Appendix.

[116]Please refer to List 9 in the Appendix: Original Sources of Ten Randomly Selected Samples Where Petitions and 'Leader' Co-occur in Group A.

[117]Please refer to List 10 in the Appendix: Original Sources of Ten Randomly Selected Samples Where Petitions and 'Leader' Co-occur in Group B.

positively contributes to the trust of petitioners in the government's overall competence (samples 1, 2, 5 and 9). Meanwhile, more recent news describes the non-governmental bodies, such as the village committee and the lawyers' association, as a positive contributor to mediating petitioners' emotions and selecting a feasible remedy venue (samples 7 and 10).

The mixed framing for narrating political intervention in petition settlements is evident in the most recent news from 2010 to 2015 too.[118] It describes political intervention as a positive factor in the efficient settlement of collective petitions (samples 1 and 2), and in maintaining public trust in the government (samples 6, 7 and 9). On the other hand, while still using the conventional narrative that collective petitions are resolved efficiently with the help of political intervention (samples 3 and 4), it presents negative impacts of political intervention by senior officials which can undermine the procedural regularity of petition settlements and the authority of judicial dispute resolution in the long run (samples 5, 8 and 10).

3.3.3.2 The Court in the News

Early news from 1998 to 2005 is critical of petitions that are presented to the government petition office while being considered before the court or after they have been concluded by the court.[119] It presents litigation-related petitions as a misuse of dispute resolution resources and a potential threat to the already delicate balance between judicial and administrative review powers (samples 1, 2, 3, 5 and 6). Additionally, it explains litigation-related petitions as based on an outdated belief that senior officials are more trustworthy than judges in granting redress for grievances against the government (sample 4). Although the leading narrative problematises litigation-related petitions, early news also draws attention to the procedural weaknesses of the court that political guidance can override its decision, motivating litigants to seek political support, and the urgency to improve the fair and independent functioning of the court (samples 7, 8, 9 and 10).

The narrative in more recent news from 2005 to 2010 is somewhat different. Instead of criticising litigation-related petitions, more recent news focuses on positive actions taken by the court to separate its work from the government petition procedure. It highlights the court's 'soft' measures to reduce the number of litigation-related petitions.[120] For example, it narrates court measures as desirable that the court explains to applicants who have approached the government petition

[118]Please refer to List 11 in the Appendix: Original Sources of Ten Randomly Selected Samples Where Petitions and 'Leader' Co-occur in Group C.

[119]Please refer to List 12 in the Appendix: Original Sources of Ten Randomly Selected Samples Where Petitions and 'Court' Co-occur in Group A.

[120]Please refer to List 13 in the Appendix: Original Sources of Ten Randomly Selected Samples Where Petitions and 'Court' Co-occur in Group B.

office the relevant rules that prohibit government intervention in court work and helps the applicants choose a proper appeal venue (samples 1, 5, 9 and 10).

More recent news positively describes court efforts to address the forum-shopping problem, such as judges being required to work with the petition offices to understand the needs of petitioners and to develop skills to persuade petitioners to discontinue litigation-related petitions (sample 3), and training judges to improve communication with applicants to enhance the court's credibility (samples 2 and 4). It also accredits official measures to improve coordination between different appeal procedures, such as building a data-sharing platform through which the petition office can detect the case under consideration by a statutory appeal body (samples 6, 7 and 8). Comparatively speaking, early news focuses on the problematic nature of litigation-related petitions which are described as wasting public resources while more recent news focuses on positive measures taken by the court to channel such petitions to a proper venue.

The solution-focused narrative is also recurrent in the most recent news from 2010 to 2015.[121] It narrates litigation-related petitions as an obstacle to the proper functioning of the court and explains timely coordination between the court and the government as necessary (samples 1, 6, 8 and 9). Although the most recent news occasionally problematises the expectations of petitioners to receive a favourable court decision by involving the petition office, it stresses the importance of making the subsidiary status of the petition procedure known to petitioners and correcting any belief that the petition office has the power to influence the work of court (samples 2, 3, 4, 5, 7 and 10). In addition, it explains the procedural and enforcement issues with the court as attributing to the petitioners' lack of trust in judicial resolution, which departs from the earlier narrative that blames petitioners.

3.3.4 The Non-Governmental Advisers in the News

Chinese news coverage of collective petitions mentions three types of non-governmental advisers: social organisations (*shehui tuanti*/社会团体), people's associations (*qunzhong zuzhi*/群众组织) and communities (*shequ*/社区). In terms of vocabulary popularity, non-governmental advisers are significantly less discussed than senior officials and courts in the news.[122] Relatively speaking, the term 'community' is more frequently used in the news than social organisations and people's associations, particularly in news reports after 2005.[123]

[121] Please refer to List 14 in the Appendix: Original Sources of Ten Randomly Selected Samples Where Petitions and 'Court' Co-occur in Group C.

[122] Please refer to Table 3.7 in the Appendix: Occurrence of 'Social organisations' in Groups A, B and C.

[123] Please refer to Table 3.8 in the Appendix: The Ten Most Popular Vocabularies Collocated to 'Community'.

More specifically, community advisers are often narrated as a positive supplement to the petition-handling procedure in early news from 1998 to 2005, who play an important role in local consultation and mediation prior to the emergence of collective petitions and during their settlement.[124] They are also described as bridging the legislature and the government to local residents, informing them of the contents of new rules and policies (samples 1, 2 and 8), and as helpful for monitoring local discontents with the government (samples 4, 6, 7, 9 and 10) and maintaining public order at the local level (samples 5 and 7). While early news occasionally mentions the importance of the autonomy of community organisations (e.g. explaining the self-management principle in samples 3 and 9), the dominant narrative is largely government-focused where the involvement of community advisers is described as a supplement to the government's fulfilment of petition-handling and stability-maintaining tasks.

The narrative in more recent news from 2005 to 2010 is identical to the earlier news. It describes community advisers as the facilitators for the government to handle petitions.[125] The narrative focus is on government tasks that community advisers can assist with, such as receiving and hearing complaints from local petitioners (samples 1, 3, 5, 6, 7, 8 and 10), and pacifying 'abnormal' petitioners in collaboration with local authorities (samples 2, 4 and 9). The most recent news from 2010 to 2015 adopts a different narrative where community advisers are depicted as service providers for local petitioners, such as offering advisory and financial support to local residents who intend to petition the government (samples 1, 3, 4 and 9), and mediating between local petitioners and government authorities to reach a mutually acceptable settlement (samples 5, 6, 7 and 10).[126] In short, the news narrative about community advisers is shifting from what the government needs in earlier reports to what can be done for petitioners in more recent ones.

3.3.4.1 Summary: Government-Focused Narratives Dominate the News

This part has analysed the recurring news framings used to narrate the involvement of three bodies in the settlement of collective petitions: senior officials, the court and community advisers. Generally, news reports align with the official stance that collective petitions are problematic and the evaluative reference is often the political consideration to maintain social stability and sustain public trust in the government (see Table 3.4). There is hardly any reference to legal rules in the news that hold petition settlements accountable to regulatory rules, despite occasional criticism of

[124] Please refer to List 17 in the Appendix: Original Sources of Ten Randomly Selected Samples Where Petitions and 'Community' Co-occur in Group A.

[125] Please refer to List 18 in the Appendix: Original Sources of Ten Randomly Selected Samples Where Petitions and 'Community' Co-occur in Group B.

[126] Please refer to List 19 in the Appendix: Original Sources of Ten Randomly Selected Samples Where Petitions and 'Community' Co-occur in Group C.

Table 3.4 Chinese news narratives concerning the bodies engaged in tackling collective petitions

Corpus group	Concerning senior officials	Concerning courts	Concerning community advisors
Group A (Jan. 1998–April 2005)	Focusing on political tasks to demotivate collective petitioners and maintain a non-confrontational interaction between petitioners and the government.	Critical of litigation-related petitions and attributing it to the old-fashioned mindset of petitioners.	Focusing on tasks to facilitate the monitoring and dissolving of collective petitioners.
Group B (May 2005–April 2010)	Focusing on the effectiveness of concluding petition cases and sustaining petitioners' trust in the government.	Focusing on positive actions taken by the court to reduce litigation-related petitions.	Focusing on the supplementary role of the community to the work of government petition offices.
Group C (May 2010–May 2015)	Focusing on the benefits of political intervention for efficiently concluding petition cases while stressing the negative impacts on procedural regularity of the petition settlement.	Critical of litigation-related petitions and attributing it to the weak effectiveness of the court in remedying the losses of complainants	Focusing on the community services to local petitioners and their role in mediating the conflict between petitioners and the government.

the negative effects of political intervention on the procedural regularity of petition settlements. Calls for enhancing the credibility of the court and popularising knowledge of different appeal procedures are also frequently present in the news.

3.3.5 *Accountability Law Important in the News on Collective Petitions? Not Really*

Over the last few decades, the Chinese petition-handling procedure has undergone several reforms. Its decisional and remedial powers have been replaced by statutory appeal procedures, and its political accountability has been merged with legal accountability. As reflected in Chinese news reports on collective petitions and their settlements, official measures that prioritise political considerations to maintain an unrest-free society and the widely trusted government are now being questioned while the measures that focus on protecting the legitimate rights and interests of petitioners are often seen as normal and necessary.

News narratives in which the problem and the mass are discussed reveal an evolving change over time in their information sources, descriptive focuses, and narrative framings. While the recent news highlights procedural flaws in the settlement of petition cases and evaluates these settlements based on whether they promptly resolved the petitioners' grievances, early news portrays collective petitions as undermining the orderly functioning of the petition office and assesses petition settlements based on whether they dispersed collective petitioners and prevented their confrontation with the government. In recent news, there has been a focus on whether the right of petitioners to receive a timely response and a fair redress is safeguarded, whereas early news focuses on political norms to monitor public discontent and sustain public trust in the government. In short, the recent news narratives tend to be petitioner-focused while the earlier ones are governance-focused.

A similar trend is also apparent in the recurring news narratives about the main bodies involved in handling collective petitions: senior officials, the courts and community advisers. The leading narrative in early news centres around political norms that prioritise social stability and popular confidence in the government. Accordingly, it qualifies collective petitions as disruptive and describes political intervention as positive given its role in persuading collective petitioners to avoid contentious actions. The major narrative in recent news, on the other hand, emphasises positive measures taken by the government and the court to reduce the amount of litigation-related petitions and enhance the credibility of the court. In summary, more recent news is solution-focused, discussing the causes for forum-shopping behaviour among petitioners and official efforts to discourage it.

To sum up, Chinese news coverage of collective petitions and their resolutions is often influenced more by political considerations rather than legal rules, with the former being frequently narrated as normal and necessary. However, recent news has shown a shift in the recurrent narrates, prioritising the losses of petitioners caused by the government rather than sustaining public trust in the competence of the government. Although legal rules, particularly legal accountability rules, are not commonly used to describe collective petitions and assess their settlements, their importance is growing in recent news narratives.

3.4 Conclusion: Unsettled Shift from Political Norms to Legal Rules

This chapter presents a case study of Chinese measures for dealing with collective petitions. The chapter first introduces a pressing problem with Chinese practices in effectively settling collective petitions, namely, a mismatch between the intended subsidiary function of the petition procedure and the expectations and choices of petitioners. Therefore, it analyses the legislative development regulating the government petition-handling procedure, and the institutional and social obstacles to its implementation. It also examines the role of legal accountability rules in the Chinese news coverage of the topic.

Petition handlers often seek political guidance when dealing with major petition cases, while complainants may seek political support when seeking redress for the harm or loss caused by the government. This reinforces the traditional political dominance over petition settlements. Since the mid-1990s, the Chinese government has introduced legal accountability rules to regulate the work of petition offices and confirmed the subsidiarity of the petition-handling procedure to statutory appeal procedures. However, despite these jurisdictional and procedural reforms of the petition-handling procedure, the issue of forum shopping by petitioners has not been effectively resolved. The conflict between the political and legal accountabilities of petition offices undermines the institutionalisation of the latter in the government's petition-handling procedure.

This chapter also analyses Chinese news reports on collective petitions and their settlements using a large dataset of over 3.9 million characters. It investigates the narratives and framings used in the news to define collective petitions and assess their settlements. The recurring narratives generally describe collective petitions as problematic and interruptive to the efficiency of the petition-handling procedure. Early news reports from 1998 to 2010 assess the settlement of collective petitions referring to politically important norms and describe official measures for forestalling collective petitions as normal and necessary. In contrast, recent news reports from 2010 to 2015 employ a different framing, highlighting the shared grievances of collective petitioners and explaining their causes. Accordingly, recent news reports focus on the insufficient coordination between China's judicial and administrative review bodies and emphasise legal accountability rules governing petition settlements. Overall, the recurrent news narratives on collective petitions are shifting from governance-focused to petitioner-focused.

In conclusion, this chapter presents a holistic and nuanced account of the juridification of Chinese approaches to managing collective petitions. Existing research has mainly taken a normative approach, emphasising the primacy of law in refining the Chinese petition-handling procedure. However, it is important to understand the changing institutional and social contexts that shape Chinese measures for addressing collective petitions. Neglecting or simplifying their complex dynamics is unlikely to enhance our knowledge of the topic. In this sense, researchers and policy advisers may find the findings presented in this case study useful, which consider legislative, institutional and social aspects of Chinese measures for addressing collective petitions as a whole and explain each aspect in detail.

This chapter also aims to assist those interested in formulating amendment suggestions to tackle the shortcomings of current Chinese measures for settling petitions. A well-functioning procedure for receiving and reviewing petition cases is dependent on an institutional environment in which legal accountability rules are taken seriously, and a social culture in which political support is not considered a must for redressing petitioners' grievances. Merely promoting statutory appeal procedures will not suffice to reduce forum shopping by petitioners or to resolve the mismatch between regulatory rules and agency conduct during petition settlements. It is imperative for petition handlers to take their legal accountability seriously and consistently adhere to legal rules. Besides that, petitioners must have confidence that petition settlements will be held accountable to the law rather than politics.

Appendix

Table 3.5 The most popular terms in Groups A, B and C

Group A		Group B		Group C	
Frequency	Word	Frequency	Word	Frequency	Word
5387	/	4513	/	6939	/
2894	*Problem*	3557	*Masses*	4656	*Problem*
2436	*Masses*	3197	*Problem*	4434	*Masses*
2033	Party	3078	Society	3739	Society
1955	Leaders	2164	Resolve	3077	Resolve
1899	Supervise	1768	Construct	2650	Lawsuit
1829	Construct	1699	Develop	2495	Construct
1796	Develop	1664	Manage	2338	Develop
1769	Strengthen	1487	Contradiction	2317	Government Organs
1632	Cadre	1484	Government Organs	2110	Leaders

Table 3.6 The terms most frequently collocated to 'Letters and visits' in Groups A, B and C

Group A		Group B		Group C	
Frequency	Collocate	Frequency	Collocate	Frequency	Collocate
3508	/	3182	/	5643	/
1641	*Problem*	2299	*Masses*	3250	*Problem*
1464	*Masses*	2207	/	3142	*Masses*
968	Resolve	2009	*Problem*	2931	/
958	/	1804	/	2159	Resolve
951	/	1379	Resolve	2072	/
936	Deal with	1239	/	1986	Government organs
854	Leaders	1213	Leaders	1562	/
729	Government organs	1009	Regulation	1534	Leaders
700	/	967	/	1524	/

List 3: Original Sources of Ten Randomly Selected Samples Where Petitions and 'Problem' Co-occur in Group A

279 KWIC results are produced in Group A with the search term defined as 'problem' and the search window size defined as '100'. Ten samples are selected in accordance with the 'random selection' procedure in Microsoft Excel. The source of each selected news sample is listed below:

1. 《齐抓共管标本兼治——记青岛市劳动保障局信访处》，载于《中国劳动保障报》，2002-03-14，"综合新闻"。
2. 《张惠新在中央纪委、监察部基层信访举报座谈会上强调 狠抓信访问题处理和落实》，载于《人民日报》，2002-06-10。

3. 《以“三个代表”思想为指导全面完成今年各项工作任务为跨世纪的新发展奠定坚实基础——在省委八届十二次全会上的报告闻世》，　载于《辽宁日报》, 2000-08-31。
4. 《实行信访“六联单”落实责任主体》, 载于《光明日报》, 2004-12-21。
5. 《福建省人民检察院工作报告——2002年1月26日在福建省第九届人民代表大会第五次会议上福建省人民检察院检察长鲍绍坤》, 载于《福建日报》, 2002-02-22, 04版。
6. 《实行重点管理改善信访形势》, 载于《江西日报》, 2001-12-26, B02版。
7. 《"信访六联单"联起党群心》, 载于《人民日报》, 2004-12-10,10版。
8. 《预测排查提前介入》, 载于《江西日报》, 2001-12-12。
9. 《信访“变脸”》, 载于《四川日报》, 2004-04-18, 要闻版。
10. 《我省开展重点信访问题集中整治 一批信访疑难问题得以解决》, 载于《河南日报》,2004-12-16, 02版。

List 4: Original Sources of Ten Randomly Selected Samples Where Petitions and ‘Problem’ Co-occur in Group B

630 KWIC results are produced in Group B with the search term defined as ‘problem’ and search window size defined as ‘100’, and ten samples are selected in accordance with the ‘random selection’ procedure in Microsoft Excel. The source of each selected news sample is listed below:

1. 《“信访直通车”焐暖百姓心 淮安信访群众满意率 98.9%》，载于《人民日报》, 2005-08-25, 03版。
2. 《努力把新时期信访工作提高到新的水平——各地各部门贯彻落实中央五号文件精神综述》, 载于《经济日报》, 2007-09-26,02版。
3. 《临淄创新排解机制处纠纷》, 载于《大众日报》, 2009-05-04, 06版。
4. 《信访案件越来越少满意感谢越来越多》，载于《深圳晚报》，2010-01-27, A17版。
5. 《洛宁 贫困乡综合治理实现两年“零上访”》, 载于《河南法制报》, 2007-01-08, 27版。
6. 《“闹访”之痛》, 中国新闻社, 2009-10-10, “国内新闻”。
7. 《灵山:多管齐下抓好信访工作》, 载于《广西日报》, 2009-02-04, 10版。
8. 《陈学亨在全省信访工作会议上强调 全面提高信访工作水平》, 载于《甘肃日报》, 2006-02-24, 01版。
9. 《甘肃信访领导包案解决:省级领导上前线》，载于《中经网》，2005-07-08, 04版。
10. 《在发展中妥善化解人民内部利益矛盾》，载于《中国经济时报》，2008-01-25, 08版。

List 5: Original Sources of Ten Randomly Selected Samples Where Petitions and ‘Problem’ Co-occur in Group C

308 KWIC results are produced in Group C with the search term defined as ‘problem’ and search window size defined as ‘100’, and ten samples are selected in accordance with the ‘random selection’ procedure in Microsoft Excel. The source of each selected news sample is listed below:

1. 《听民声消民怨 解民忧促和谐》, 载于《浙江日报》, 2011-04-26,04版。
2. 《最高法要求集中化解进京重复上访》, 载于《南方都市报(全国版)》, 2011-01-28, A22版。
3. 《省人大常委会会议昨审议《广东省信访条例(草案)》 信访立法应强调群众主体地位》, 载于《南方日报(全国版)》, 2013-11-21, A08版。
4. 《市中院畅通信访渠道 院长接访日倾听民声》, 载于《汕头日报》, 2014-02-23, 11版。
5. 《八步区 打造阳光信访 为民排忧解难》, 载于《广西日报》, 2014-11-13, A04版。
6. 《市政府人民来访接待厅挂牌启用 6职能部门集体接访》, 载于《南方都市报(全国版)》, 2012-09-12, AII03版。
7. 《浙江衢州推行信访公开听证 冀解决集体访、越级访》, 中国新闻社, 2011-04-22, "国内新闻"。
8. 《全国网上信访受理平台将建 市县两级将联合接访》, 中国新闻社, 2013-11-28, "国内新闻"。
9. 《草案强化接访责任, 提出信访首办责任制 接访作风导致矛盾激化 信访首办单位或被问责》, 载于《南方都市报(全国版)》, 2013-11-20, A11版。
10. 《丹心为民——记丰城市信访局局长雷启珍》, 载于《江西日报》, 2010-05-20, A01版。

List 6: Original Sources of Ten Randomly Selected Samples Where Petitions and 'Mass' Co-occur in Group A

183 KWIC results are produced in Group A with the search term defined as 'mass/people' and search window size defined as '100', and ten samples are selected in accordance with the 'random selection' procedure in Microsoft Excel. The source of each selected news sample is listed below:

1. 《上访首破万人次大关》, 载于《南方日报(全国版)》, 2004-01-13, "每日要闻"版。
2. 《新形势下信访工作问题和对策》, 载于《中国社会报》, 2001-07-23, "要闻"版。
3. 《省信访工作领导小组会议提出要求用发展的办法解决信访问题》, 载于《福建日报》, 2002-12-05, 12 版。
4. 《临泉县强化措施抓信访, 张桥镇重视信访促稳定》, 载于《安徽日报》, 2001-12-19, B03版。
5. 《架起一座与人民沟通的桥梁》, 载于《法制日报》, 2004-09-16, 12版。
6. 《五通桥, 流动下访解民忧》, 载于《四川日报》, 2004-10-10, "文娱"版。
7. 《龙陵县抓信访见成效》, 载于《云南日报》, 2003-06-05, 02版。
8. 《信访工作要抓好三个转变》, 载于《经济日报》, 2004-10-24,02版。
9. 《为群众利益就要"管得宽"》, 载于《无锡日报》, 2001-11-20, "今日要闻"版。
10. 《乐为民众解忧愁——记九江市委副秘书长、信访局局长邹沅清》, 载于《江西日报》, 2003-10-04, 01版。

List 7: Original Sources of Ten Randomly Selected Samples Where Petitions and 'Mass' Co-occur in Group B

273 KWIC results are produced in Group B with the search term defined as 'mass/people' and search window size defined as '100', and ten samples are selected in accordance with the 'random selection' procedure in Microsoft Excel. The source of each selected news sample is listed below:

1. 《化解纠纷资金拟入财政预算》, 载于《北京青年报》, 2007-05-14, A01版。
2. 《千名群众代表参与信访处理》, 载于《人民日报》, 2006-04-16, 07版。
3. 《中纪委副书记:依法规范信访举报减少推诿扯皮》, 中国新闻社, 2005-05-19, "国内新闻"。
4. 《中国19省区市100多地级市200多县建立举报网站》, 中国新闻社, 2008-12-03, "国内新闻"
5. 《件件有登记件件有分析件件有落实件件有回音》, 载于《人民日报》, 2005-05-09, 02版。
6. 《信访代理:百姓诉求渠道多了办结快了》, 载于《北京日报》, 2010-03-05, 04版。
7. 《下访听民声主动解民忧》, 载于《浙江日报》, 2006-01-03。
8. 《当前湖北省信访问题的特点、对策与建议》, 中经网通讯社, 2006-07-11.
9. 《专项清理讨回2.75亿欠薪》, 载于《四川日报》, 2005-10-11, "要闻"版。
10. 《合力协调基层化解 安源构建信访调处新机制》, 载于《江西日报》, 2005-11-28, B03版。

List 8: Original Sources of Ten Randomly Selected Samples Where Petitions and 'Mass' Co-occur in Group C

140 KWIC results are produced in Group C with the search term defined as 'mass/people' and search window size defined as '100', and ten samples are selected in accordance with the 'random selection' procedure in Microsoft Excel. The source of each selected news sample is listed below:

1. 《周永康在专题研究部署信访工作时强调实实在在解决好涉及群众切身利益的突出问题》, 载于《光明日报》, 2010-07-17, 03版。
2. 《党报聚焦社会管理难题 : 以人为本才能真正化解矛盾》, 中国新闻社, 2011-02-19, "国内新闻"。
3. 《省人大常委会会议昨审议《广东省信访条例(草案)》 信访立法应强调群众主体地位》, 载于《南方日报(全国版)》, 2013-11-21, A08版。
4. 《全国网上信访受理平台将建 市县两级将联合接访》, 中国新闻社, 2013-11-28, "国内新闻"。
5. 《合江凤鸣镇创建"信访合格村"畅通群众信访》, 载于《四川经济日报》, 2011-10-22, 03版。
6. 《市信访大厅启用 集体信访最多只能有5名代表》, 载于《南方日报(佛山版)》, 2012-09-12,06版。
7. 《把办公地点"搬"到田间地头——检察机关重心下移化解社会矛盾纪实》, 载于《江西日报》, 2010-07-22, B02版。
8. 《桂平创新机制抓信访维稳工作》, 载于《广西日报》, 2014-01-07,03版。
9. 《赞"把接访日当作自己生日一样"》, 载于《江西日报》, 2012-04-04, 02版。

10. 《合江县先市镇:"阳光信访"促和谐》, 载于《四川经济日报》, 2013-11-22, 06版。

List 9: Original Sources of Ten Randomly Selected Samples Where Petitions and 'Leader' Co-occur in Group A

72 KWIC results are hit in Group A with the search term defined as 'leader' and search window size defined as '100', and ten samples are selected in accordance with the 'random selection' procedure in Microsoft Excel. The source of each selected news sample is listed below:

1. 《福建省永定县土地管理信访工作机制有创新变群众上访为领导下访》, 载于《中国矿业报》, 2002-05-23, "矿政观要"版。
2. 《丝丝春雨解民忧》, 载于《湖北日报》, 2009-08-04, 02 版。
3. 《婺城检察院处理集体信访扎实有效 案件全部办结 结案无一复访》, 载于《浙江日报》, 2000-05-17, "政法"版。
4. 《陕西宝鸡市市级领导信访接待日纪实》, 载于《经济日报》, 2000-05-17, 10版。
5. 《坚持例会制接待制包案制下访制 藤县信访调解成功逾9成》, 载于《广西日报》, 2004-12-28, 02版。
6. 《实行信访"六联单"落实责任主体》, 载于《光明日报》, 2004-12-21, 02版。
7. 《做好信访工作是领导干部的重要责任 吕祖善夏宝龙等出席》, 载于《浙江日报》, 2003-12-25, 01版。
8. 《开拓创新路引领春风来 我市纪检监察信访总量连续六年下降》, 载于《无锡日报》, 2003-02-25, "地方新闻"版。
9. 《临泉县强化措施抓信访, 张桥镇重视信访促稳定》, 载于《安徽日报》, 2001-12-19, B03版。
10. 《我省召开电视电话会议要求强化领导开创信访工作新局面钟起煌到会讲话》, 载于《江西日报》, 2001-10-18.

List 10: Original Sources of Ten Randomly Selected Samples Where Petitions and 'Leader' Co-occur in Group B

83 KWIC results are hit in Group B with the search term defined as 'leader' and search window size defined as '100', and ten samples are selected in accordance with the 'random selection' procedure in Microsoft Excel. The source of each selected news sample is listed below:

1. 《尊重群众信访权利保障民意顺畅上达 全国各地畅通信访渠道出实招见成效》, 载于《人民日报》, 2007-03-07,10版。
2. 《丝丝春雨解民忧》, 载于《湖北日报》, 2009-08-04, 02 版。
3. 《信访工作难领导重视就不难九江建立"大信访"察民情解民忧》, 载于《光明日报》, 2005-05-19, 06版。
4. 《焦作:构建"绿色通道"化解社会矛盾》, 载于《河南日报》, 2005-10-02, 02版。
5. 《破解 "四难"为民谋利》, 载于《云南日报》, 2005-06-08,07版。
6. 《"帮你访"缝合信访服务缝隙 龙岗区南湾街道创新信访诉求代理制度破解越级上访难题》, 载于《南方日报(全国版)》, 2010-01-19, 03版。

7. 《江苏省纪检监察信访举报工作巡礼》, 载于《扬子晚报》, 2006-03-20, "江苏新闻"版。
8. 《<太原市领导信访接待日实施方案>出台》, 载于《山西日报》, 2006-06-21, "本省新闻"版。
9. 《聚焦十六大以来浙江发生的巨变》, 中经网, 2007-10-12。
10. 《风雨无阻察民情 ——陇西县领导信访接待日纪实》, 载于《甘肃日报》, 2006-05-30,06版

List 11: Original Sources of Ten Randomly Selected Samples Where Petitions and 'Leader' Co-occur in Group C

74 KWIC results are hit in Group C with the search term defined as 'leader' and search window size defined as '100', and ten samples are selected in accordance with the 'random selection' procedure in Microsoft Excel. The source of each selected news sample is listed below:

1. 《南丹:"四项积极"办理环境信访案件》, 载于《广西日报》, 2011-12-12,10版。
2. 《"领导干部大接访":关注民生 维护稳定》, 载于《青岛日报》, 2009-08-04, 02 版。
3. 《一个"黑老大"的诞生》, 载于《财新周刊》, 2011-10-10, 页80-81。
4. 《苏荣:年轻领导干部要补好"群众路线"这一课》, 载于《信息日报》, 2011-05-05, 02版。
5. 《媒体调查称近九成网络信访者对官方答复不满意》, 中国新闻社, 2012-01-11。
6. 《"春风吹散心上愁——来自省信访局接访一线的报告》, 载于《江西日报》, 2011-07-14, C03版。
7. 《充分发挥新形势下信访工作的重要作用》, 载于《江西日报》, 2012-06-20, B02版。
8. 《信访人"信领导信权力信关系"现象突出》, 载于《南方日报(广州版)》, 2011-12-14, 02版。
9. 《赞"把接访日当作自己生日一样"》, 载于《江西日报》, 2012-04-04, 02版。
10. 《广州大接访 有人通宵排队有人现场跪求》, 载于《南方都市报(全国版)》, 2010-10-19, A12版。

List 12: Original Sources of Ten Randomly Selected Samples Where Petitions and 'Court' Co-occur in Group A

41 KWIC results are produced in Group A with the search term defined as 'court' and search window size defined as '100', and ten samples are selected for close reading. Source of each selected news sample is listed below:

1. 《信访制度面临法治挑战》, 载于《华西都市报》, 2004-07-01, 报章 | 国内(09版)。
2. 《常委会<关于限制开山采石的决定>》, 载于《无锡日报》, 2005-01-28, 报章 | 地方新闻。
3. 《让信访从法律纷争中抽"身"而出》, 载于《解放日报》, | 2004-03-02, 报章 | 05 | 观点。

4. 《信访洪峰"成关注焦点》, 载于《中国剪报》, 2004-11-15, 报章 | 02 | 综合信息 | 新闻热点。
5. 《坚持用"三个代表"重要思想指导党风廉政建设和反腐败工作为全面建设小康社会提供政治保证》, 载于《北京日报》, 2004-02-23, 报章 | 焦点新闻。
6. 《海南省人民检察院工作报告(摘要)》, 载于《海南日报》, 2003-01-28, 报章 | 要闻。
7. 《新形势下信访工作问题和对策》, 载于《中国社会报》, 2001-07-23, 报章 | 要闻 | By 国家信访局局长 周战顺。
8. 《时刻不忘群众利益》, 载于《经济日报》, 2001-07-22, 报章。
9. 《北京市人民检察院工作报告(摘要)》, 载于《北京日报》, 2004-03-22, 报章 | 焦点新闻。
10. 《2003中国遭遇信访洪峰新领导人面临非常考验》, 载于《长江日报》, 2003-12-08, 报章 | 国内新闻。

List 13: Original Sources of Ten Randomly Selected Samples Where Petitions and 'Court' Co-occur in Group B

143 KWIC results are produced in Group B with the search term defined as 'court' and search window size defined as '100', and ten samples are selected for a close reading. Original source of each selected news sample is listed below:

1. 《最高人民法院在第十一届全国人民代表大会第三次会议上的工作报告》, 载于《经济日报》, | 2010-03-19, 报章 | 02 | 要闻。
2. 《解读执行分权制约 与责任追究等制度》, 载于《北京青年报》, 2010-03-12, 报章 | A02 | 全国两会. 解读
3. 《信访:为老百姓提供讲话的地方》, 载于《羊城晚报》, | 2010-02-22, 报章 | A01 | 要闻。
4. 《自治区高院启动"万名法官下访"活动》, 载于《南国早报》, 2010-01-14, 报章 | 12 | 社会新闻。
5. 《建立完善行政效能投诉机制深入推进行政效能监察工作》, 载于《青海日报》, 2009-03-02, 报章 | 5版。
6. 《法治, 才是信访的归途——与省委党校王建华教授谈<信访条例>》, 载于《四川日报》, 2005-06-13, 报章 | 特刊。
7. 《"信访责任倒查"机制的法理评析》, 载于《法制日报》, | 2007-08-26, 报章 | 13 | 法学院。
8. 《肖扬与贾春旺分别作高法、高检工作报告(要点)》, 中国新闻社, 2007-03-13, 通讯社 | 国内新闻。
9. 《三河法院 集体接访形成制度》, 载于《法制日报》, 2005-05-15, 报章 | 02 | 综合新闻。
10. 《北京法院对执法不公造成重复上访将追查责任人》, 中国新闻社, 2005-08-10, 通讯社 | 社会新闻。

List 14: Original Sources of Ten Randomly Selected Samples Where Petitions and 'Court' Co-occur in Group C

147 KWIC results are produced in Group C with the search term defined as 'court' and search window size defined as '100', and ten samples are selected for close reading. Source of each selected news sample is listed below:

1. 《夫债妻还 离婚女不能承受之重》, 中国新闻网, 2015-03-20, 网站| 生活。
2. 《网上申诉仍有门槛》, 载于《南方都市报(全国版)》, 2015-03-14, 报章 | A06 | 重点。
3. 《本月起涉诉信访实施新规 家门口可进行 市内任何法院信访登记》, 载于《南方日报(惠州版)(数字报) 》| 2014-11-21, 网站| HC01 | 惠州观察。
4. 《提高信访工作科学化水平 ——解读4月1日起正式施行的新的<上海市信访条例>》, 载于《解放日报》, 2013-04-02, 报章 | 02 | 要闻。
5. 《湖北省高级人民法院工作报告》, 载于《湖北日报》, 2013-02-07, 报章 | 04 | 时政要闻。
6. 《中国社会转型多领域矛盾凸显 调解促社会更和谐》, 中国通讯社, 2012-09-26, 通讯社。
7. 《法律的归法律 信访的归信访 民诉法修改为信访困局"破题"》, 载于《新京报》, 2012-09-08, 报章 | B03 | 评论周刊·观察。
8. 《一位信访工作者— 老百姓的事比天大》, 载于《经济日报》, 2012-08-20, 报章 | 07 | 科学发展。
9. 《济阳法院全省首创信访保证金制度》, 载于《济南日报》, 2011-03-07, 报章 | 07 | 法治。
10. 《清远市人民检察院窗口部门推"四个一"承诺 》, 载于《南方日报(清远版)》| 2014-03-25, 报章 | PC05 | 清远观察。

Table 3.7 Occurrence of 'Social Organisations' in the collocational format

Group A		Group B		Group C	
Frequency	Collocate	Frequency	Collocate	Frequency	Collocate
5	Strengthen	5	Grassroots	24	Mediate
4	/	4	/	24	Grassroots
4	/	3	/	20	Elder
4	Disputes	2	/	13	Party
3	Resolve	2	/	12	Self
3	Self-management	2	/	12	/
3	Village	2	/	12	/
3	Legality	2	Law	12	/
2	/	2	/	12	Society
2	/	2	/	12	/

Table 3.8 The ten most popular vocabularies collocated to 'Community'

Group A		Group B		Group C	
Frequency	Collocate	Frequency	Collocate	Frequency	Collocate
83	Construction	219	Grassroots	559	Service
75	Organisation	164	People	407	Management
53	Party	154	Contradiction	399	Residents
38	Management	125	Construction	276	Society
37	Employment	112	Residents	261	Streets
36	Urban	106	Society	256	Grassroots
33	Reform	104	Disputes	212	People
32	Streets	101	Resolution	197	Disputes
31	People	88	Rural	185	The senior
26	Residents	87	Agents	161	Internet

List 17: Original Sources of Ten Randomly Selected Samples Where Petitions and 'Community' Co-occur in Group A

46 KWIC results are produced in Group A with the search term defined as 'community' and search window size defined as '100', and ten samples are selected for close reading. The original source of each selected news sample is listed below:

1. 《福田区纪委三结合抓好纪检监察信访举报》, 载于《深圳特区报》, 2005-04-25, 报章 I 今版·关注。
2. 《维护群众合法权益着力构建和谐社会 我省探索建立信访工作长效机制》, 载于《甘肃日报》, 2005-03-08, 报章 I 06 I 法制经纬
3. 《打浦桥街道社区信访工作"三会一代理"纪实》, 载于《解放日报》, 2005-04-25, 报章 I 03 I 要闻·国际新闻。
4. 《创新信访机制转变工作作风 省信访局深入一线办信访见成效》, 载于《江西日报》, 2005-01-25, 报章 I B03 I 读者之声。
5. 《实行信访"六联单"落实责任主体》, 载于《光明日报》, 2004-12-21, 报章 I TMP02。
6. 《创新信访机制江汉区集体上访案逐年减少》, 载于《长江日报》, 2004-12-13, 报章 I 武汉新闻。
7. 《"大信访"助建"平安历下"》, 载于《大众日报》, 2004-10-14, 报章 I TMP08。
8. 《依法信访维护稳定 副市长张桂华就我市开展依法信访工作答记者问》, 载于《哈尔滨日报》, 2004-08-13, 报章 I TMP01。
9. 《探索统筹兼顾、标本兼治的大信访工作格局》, 中经网, 2004-08-04, 通讯社 I TMP01。
10. 《做好社区服务这篇大文章——平顶山新华区构建老城区服务型社区的几点启示》, 载于《河南日报》, 2003-11-25, 报章 I 06 I 理论与实践。

List 18: Original Sources of Ten Randomly Selected Samples Where Petitions and 'Community' Co-occur in Group B

247 KWIC results are produced in Group B with the search term defined as 'community' and search window size defined as '100', and ten samples are selected for close reading. The source of each selected news sample is listed below:

1. 《信访代理:百姓诉求渠道多了办结快了》, 载于《北京日报》, 2010-03-05, 报章 | 04 | 时政新闻。
2. 《第一时间在基层解决问题》, 载于《深圳晚报》, 2010-02-03, 报章 | A24 | 特别报道。
3. 《"帮你访"缝合信访服务缝隙　龙岗区南湾街道创新信访诉求代理制度破解越级上访难题》, 载于《南方日报(全国版)》, 2010-01-19, 报章 | AII03 | 深圳观察·时政。
4. 《件件有回音 事事有着落》, 载于《深圳晚报》, 2010-01-13, 报章 | A24 | 特别报道。
5. 《百姓动嘴 政府跑腿》, 载于《青岛日报》, 2010-01-05, 报章 | 01 | 首页。
6. 《罗湖打造"信访终点站"》, 载于《深圳晚报》, 2009-12-25, 报章 | A25 | 今日城事。
7. 《和谐春风暖人心》, 载于《江西日报》, 2009-12-25, 报章 | A02 | 要闻。
8. 《直面新形势构建信访维稳新模式》, 载于《深圳特区报》, 2009-09-04, 报章 | A05 | 综合要闻。
9. 《科学发展观是解决当前突出信访问题的金钥匙》, 载于《四川法制报》, 2009-04-15, 报章。
10. 《透明带来信任公开重在惠民》, 载于《人民日报》, 2007-12-27, 报章 | 12 | 综合。

List 19: Original Sources of Ten Randomly Selected Samples Where Petitions and 'Community' Co-occur in Group C

86 KWIC results are produced in Group C with the search term defined as 'community' and search window size defined as '100', and ten samples are selected for a close reading. Original source of each selected news sample is listed below:

1. 《免费法律顾问化解矛盾纠纷奉新县创新社会管理取得实效》, 载于《青岛日报》, 2014-03-29, 报章 | 05 | 理论周刊。
2. 《细微处入手　全方位发力——钦州市创新社会综治观察》, 载于《广西日报》, 2014-01-29, 报章 | 11 | 法 治。
3. 《合江县先市镇:"阳光信访"促和谐》, 载于《四川经济日报》, 2013-11-22, 报章 | 06 | 财经新闻。
4. 《民政局引进专业社工服务复退军人》, 载于《南方日报(中山版)》, 2013-11-21, 报章 | AC02 | 中山观察。
5. 《省人大常委会昨日就<广东省信访条例(草案)>向社会各界公开征求意见　<广东省信访条例>有望明年上半年出台》, 载于《南方日报(全国版)》, 2013-11-20, 报章 | A06 | 时局·南粤。
6. 《重心下移, 让社区管理事半功倍——龙城"综治信访维稳"特色之路》, 载于《南方日报(全国版)》, 2010-06-23, 报章 | AIII04 | 龙岗视窗·时政。

7. 《给干部念"紧箍咒"南溪区创新"停职停薪"制度》, 载于《华西都市报》, 2012-11-29, 报章 | 072 | 城市读本/宜宾。
8. 《恭城:打造廉政文化大县》, 载于《广西日报》, 2013-03-22, 报章 | 02 | 要闻。
9. 《为群众服务不分份内份外》, 载于《青岛日报》, 2011-03-18, 报章 | 01 | 首页。
10. 《从服务群众入手创新基层社会管理服务》, 载于《北京日报》, 2011-04-23, 报章 | 01 | 头版。

References

Article 11, in the Rules on Disclosing the Petition-handling Records (国家信访局政府信息公开管理办法), issued by the National Bureau for Complaint Letters and Visits on 2 August 2019. Available at: www.gjxfj.gov.cn/gjxfj/zfxxgk/zfxxgkzd/xxgkfgzd/webinfo/2019/08/1590610201924747.htm

Article 41, in the Constitution of the People's Republic of China (2018 Amendment). Available at: http://www.npc.gov.cn/npc/c505/201803/e87e5cd7c1ce46ef866f4ec8e2d709ea.shtml:

Article 5 in the Interim Regulation on Sanctioning the Non-compliance of Complaint Letter and Visit Working Disciplines, adopted by the Ministry of Supervision (replaced by the National Supervisory Commission in 2018), the Ministry of Human Recourses and Social Security, and the National Public Complaint Commission in June 2008. Available at: www.gjxfj.gov.cn/gjxfj/xxgk/fgwj/flfg/webinfo/2008/07/1541706492397919.htm

Articles 1, 2 and 5, in the Rules on the Petitioning Work, adopted by the Central Committee of the CPC on 24 January 2022 and promulgated by the Central Committee of the CPC and the State Council on 25 February 2022. Available at: http://www.gov.cn/zhengce/2022-04/07/content_5683923.htm

Articles 1, 8, 9, 14, 18, 21, and 22, in the 1995 National Regulation on Complaint Letters and Visits, Order of the State Council of the People's Republic of China (No. 431), adopted on 28 October 1995. Available at: www.gjxfj.gov.cn/gjxfj/xxgk/fgwj/xftl/webinfo/2016/03/1460416222479578.htm

Articles 16, 20, 21, 32, 40, and 47, in the 2005 National Regulation on Complaint Letters and Visits, adopted by the State Council of the People's Republic of China on 1 January 2005 (Order of the State Council No. 431), its full text available at: https://www.gjxfj.gov.cn/gjxfj/xxgk/fgwj/xftl/webinfo/2016/03/1460416222479578.htm

Articles 2, 3, 7 and 8, in the Working Rules on Handling Petitions in Accordance with Law, adopted by the National Bureau for Complaint Letters and Visits and effective on 12 July 2017. Available at: https://www.gjxfj.gov.cn/gjxfj/xxgk/fgwj/zdwj/webinfo/2018/08/1534706062636624.htm

Articles 5 and 6, in the Interim Provisions on the Violation of Disciplinary Measures in Handling Complaint Letters and Visits (关于违反信访工作纪律处分暂行规定), issued by the Ministry of Supervision, Ministry of Human Resources and Social Security, and the National Bureau for Complaint Letters and Visits on 30 June 2008. www.gjxfj.gov.cn/gjxfj/xxgk/fgwj/flfg/webinfo/2008/07/1541706492397919.htm. Accessed 3 April 2017

Benney J (2016) Weiwen at the Grassroots: China's stability maintenance apparatus as a means of conflict resolution. J Contemp China 25(99):389–392

Bing-yi W (2010) The origin of the Xinfang procedure: Mao Zedong and Xinfang between 1949 and 1976 (信访制度的奠基:毛泽东与信访制度1949-1976). Rev Polit Law 1:154

Chao W (2018) The historical evolution of the petition mechanism in China (中国信访制度的历史变迁). J Soc Dev 2:164–167, 171–172

Chinese Public Administration Research Team (ed) (2009) Causes and solutions on mass spontaneous incidents in China (中国群体性突发事件成因及对策). 1st edn. The Chinese Academy of Governance Press, pp 34–36, 93–94

De-xiong Z (2002) What does the political concept of the 'People' mean? (作为中国政治概念的"人民"是什么?). Mod China Stud (4). Available at: www.modernchinastudies.org/cn/issues/past-issues/79-mcs-2002-issue-4/1258-2012-01-06-08-38-50.html

Dong-yu P (2013) Administrative Reconsideration: Lessening the Tension between the Officials and the People. People's Congr China J 348(24):28. Available at: www.npc.gov.cn/zgrdw/npc/zgrdzz/site1/20131227/0a1111111111427687e03.pdf

Goldman M, Perry EJ (eds) (2002) Changing meanings of citizenship in modern China. Harvard University Press, pp 292–293

Guiding Opinion on the Admissibility of Protests Against the Decision of the Letter-and-visit Bureau Before the Court (最高人民法院关于不服县级以上人民政府信访行政管理部门、负责受理信访事项的行政管理机关以及镇(乡)人民政府作出的处理意见或者不再受理决定而提起的行政诉讼人民法院是否受理的批复), issued by the Supreme People's Court on 12 December 2005. Available at: www.pkulaw.cn/fulltext_form.aspx?Db=chl&Gid=1a8b0df0f2ff856abdfb&keyword=&EncodingName=&Search_Mode=accurate&Search_IsTitle=0. Accessed 19 Oct 2016

Guiding Opinions on Establishing the System for Lawyers to Participate in Resolving and Representing Petitioned Cases (关于建立律师参与化解和代理涉法涉诉信访案件制度的意见(试行)), issued by the CPC Central Committee of Political and Legal Affairs on 9 November 2015. Available at: www.xinhuanet.com/politics/2015-11/09/c_1117086504.htm. Accessed 14 Aug 2016

Heurlin C et al. (2017) Responsive authoritarianism in China: land, protests, and policy making. Cambridge University Press, p 90

Hou R (2020) Maintaining social stability without solving problems: emotional repression in the Chinese petition system. China Q 243:638

Huihua L (2014) Resolving the problem with challenging petitions to litigations (破解入口不顺程序空转出口不畅难题 推动诉访分离依法治访). People's Court Daily, 12 September 2014. Available at: https://www.chinacourt.org/article/detail/2014/09/id/1437213.shtml

Huo H, Gang L (2004) Premier concerned about the salary of migrant workers (讨薪农妇熊德明的心愿: 总理继续关心保护农民). Xinhua News, 15 March 2004. Available at: https://news.sina.com.cn/c/2004-03-16/10162062249s.shtml. Accessed 10 Aug 2016

Interim Rules on the Handling of Petitions by the CPC and Government Organs [Draft] (党政机关信访工作暂行条例(草案)), issued by the Central Committee of the CPC and the State Council on 8 April 1982. Available at: https://baike.baidu.com/item/%E5%85%9A%E6%94%BF%E6%9C%BA%E5%85%B3%E4%BF%A1%E8%AE%BF%E5%B7%A5%E4%BD%9C%E6%9A%82%E8%A1%8C%E6%9D%A1%E4%BE%8B%28%E8%8D%89%E6%A1%88%29

Key Tasks of Shenzhen Municipal Government in 2014 (中共深圳市委办公厅 深圳市人民政府办公厅关于印发<2014年全市社会建设工作要点>的通知), issued by the CPC Municipal Committee and the Shenzhen People's Government on 4 April 2014. Available at: https://www.sz.gov.cn/zfgb/2014/gb886/content/post_4964944.html. Accessed 8 Sept 2017

Lei M (1999) Premier Zhu Rongji Speaking about Statutory Governance and Administration at the National Administrative Conference (朱镕基在全国依法行政工作会议上强调认真贯彻依法治国方略, 切实全面推进依法行政), published 7 July 1999 at People's Daily: 1

Lifeng L (2018) Ambiguous subject: the "Masses" (qunzhong) discourse in modern China. Int J Philosophy Cult Axiol 15(2):146–148

Lin LI et al. (ed) (2008) The China legal development yearbook Vol. 1 (On the Development of Rule of Law in China). Brill, p 290

Liu LJ, Stern RE (2020) State-adjacent professionals: how Chinese lawyers participate in political life. China Q 10

Min'an J (2005) Improving administrative remedial mechanisms and its role in building a fair society (完善行政救济机制与构建和谐社会). Legal Stud 5:22

Minzner CF (2006) Xinfang: an alternative to formal Chinese legal institutions. Stanford J Int Law 42:105. Available at: https://ir.lawnet.fordham.edu/cgi/viewcontent.cgi?referer=&httpsredir=1&article=1005&context=faculty_scholarship

Moral Construction of Civic Morality in a New Era (中共中央 国务院印发新时代公民道德建设实施纲要), jointly issued by the CPC Central Committee and the State Council on 27 October 2019. Available at: http://www.gov.cn/gongbao/content/2019/content_5449646.htm. Accessed 2 Dec 2020

Paragraph 2, Subsection 4 in Section 5 "Strengthen the Rule-of-law Concept amongst the People, and Deepen the Building of the Rule-of-law Society", in the CPC Central Committee's Decision on Major Issues for Comprehensively Building the Rule-of-law Country (中共中央关于全面推进依法治国若干重大问题的决定), adopted by the Fourth Plenary Meeting of the 18th Central Committee of the CPC on 23 October 2014. Available at: www.npc.gov.cn/zgrdw/npc/zt/qt/sbjszqh/2014-10/29/content_1883449_5.htm

Paragraph 3, in the explanatory notes on the Working Rules on the Handling of Complaint Letters and Visits, issued by the National Bureau for Complaint Letters and Visits on 2 August 2017. Available at: http://www.gov.cn/zhengce/2017-08/02/content_5215574.htm

Paragraph 3, in the No. 29 Guiding Opinion of the National Public Complaints and Proposals Administration on the Cross-departmental and Separated Procedures for Handling Complaint Letters and Visits (国家信访局协调"三跨三分离"信访事项工作规范(国信办发〔2013〕29号), published in 2013. Available at: http://www.jx-xinfang.gov.cn/zcfg/flfg/201502/t20150209_360184.html. Accessed 4 May 2020

Paragraph 6 in the "Advisory Opinions on Innovating Measures for Resolving Major Problems in Petitions", jointly issued by the General Office of the CPC Central Committee and the General Office of the State Council in December 2013, full text accessed 29 July 2019 via: http://www.gov.cn/jrzg/2014-02/25/content_2621605.htm

Paragraph 7, in the Advisory Opinions on Improving the Handling of Complaint Letters and Visits in the New Era, jointly issued by the Central Committee of the CPC and the State Council on 10 March 2007. Available at: http://pkulaw.cn/fulltext_form.aspx?Gid=245551&Db=chl

Paragraphs 5, 6, 7 and 16, in the Advisory Opinions on Innovating Measures for Resolving Major Problems in Petitions, jointly issued by the General Office of the CPC Central Committee and the General Office of the State Council in December 2013, full text accessed 29 July 2019 via: http://www.gov.cn/jrzg/2014-02/25/content_2621605.htm

Paragraphs 7 and 16, in the Advisory Opinions on Innovating Measures for Resolving Major Problems in Petitions

People's Daily (2016) Lawyers Involved in Handling Litigation-relation Petitions: A Helpful Third Party (律师参与化解涉法涉诉信访 做好信访第三方), published on 8 November 2016. Available at: https://www.gjxfj.gov.cn/gjxfj/news/gzdt/dfdt/webinfo/2016/05/1479456772811586.htm

Qinghua W (2018) Social governance through judiciary: conclusion of petitions and the crime of picking quarrels and provoking troubles (通过司法的社会治理: 信访终结与寻衅滋事). Zhejiang Soc Sci 1. http://www.cicjc.com.cn/zh/node/9063

Qing-hua W (2018) Concluding petitions and the crime of picking quarrels and provoking trouble. Zhejiang Soc Sci 1:51–52

Section "The confirmation of receiving the complaint visitor by senior officials", in the summary of the petition-handling work at the Sixth National Conference on Handling Complaint Letters and Visits (第六次全国信访工作会议以来信访工作成就综述), published by the National Bureau for Complaint Letters and Visits 13 July 2012. Available at: https://www.gjxfj.gov.cn/gjxfj/zw/webinfo/2012/07/1540671423989512.htm

Sina News (2004) The central authority will set up joint-meeting mechanisms to reduce petitions (中央将建立处理信访联席会议制度减少上访人数), published 3 December 2004.

Available at: http://news.sina.com.cn/o/2004-12-03/07184418785s.shtml. Accessed 7 May 2020

Suli J (2006) The role of public hearing in resolving petitions in China (我国信访听证制度研究). CASS J Polit Sci 4:45–46

Tables of "Statistics of Complaint, Appeal and Letter-and-visit Handled by Courts" and "Cases of Reporting, Accusation and Petition Handled by People's Procuratorate", in the Law Yearbook of China 1995-2000

The Centre for Education and Study of Human Rights of the South West University of Political Science and Law (2008) Survey on Grassroots Petition in China: An Example on Petition Situation of Lintong District of Xi'an. the Investigation Reports Series: 37 (Table 21)

The CPC Central Committee (2001) Resolution on Integrity-building among the CPC Members (中共中央关于加强和改进党的作风建设的决定), issued on 26 September 2001, in the Selected Important Documents since the 15th Plenary Conference of the Communist Party of China. Available at: http://www.gov.cn/test/2008-07/11/content_1042443.htm)

The Decision of the State Council on the Work of Handling People's Letters and Visits (政务院关于处理人民来信和接见人民工作的决定), promulgated by Premier Zhou Enlai on 7 June 1951. Available at: www.china.com.cn/guoqing/2012-09/04/content_26746268.htm

The Guiding Opinions for Handling Litigation-related Petitions in Accordance with Law (关于依法处理涉法涉诉信访问题的意见), issued by the General Office of the CPC and the General Office of the State Council on 19 March 2014. Available at: www.humanrights.cn/html/special/2015/0515/160.html

The Nanjing Municipal Bureau for Complaint Letter and Visit: "The Report on the Implementation of Joint-meeting for Dealing with Difficult Petitions and Mass Group Incidents", published 12 November 2013. Available at: http://xfj.nanjing.gov.cn/xwzxn/201810/t20181016_1855230.html. Accessed 3 Aug 2016

The National Bureau for Complaint Letters and Visits (2006) regarding the implementing measures for the Guiding Opinion of the Central Committee of the CPC and the State Council on Improving the Petition Work (中共中央、国务院关于进一步加强新时期信访工作的意见), published 25 June 2006. Available at: www.gjxfj.gov.cn/gjxfj/xxgk/fgwj/zcjd/webinfo/2016/03/1460416222582372.htm

The National Bureau for Complaint Letters and Visits (2015a) Completing the Legislative Draft on Petition Law Soon (国家信访局:将尽快起草信访法草案). Xinhua News on 13 May 2015. Available at: http://politics.people.com.cn/n/2015/0513/c70731-26994295.html

The National Bureau for Complaint Letters and Visits (2015b) The amount of petitioners to Beijing has dropped by 36 per cent following the abolition of the performance ranking (取消信访排名后进京上访人次降36%). Available at: http://politics.people.com.cn/n/2015/0131/c70731-26483177.html

The Regulation on the Function, Structure and Personnel of the State Bureau for Complaint Letters and Visits, jointly issued by the General Office of the CPC and the General Office of the State Council on 13 February 2000

The State Bureau for Complaint Letters and Visit (2006) Petitioners' Actions Getting Rational and Lawful (国家信访局负责人: 群众上访行为更趋于理性合法). People's Daily (29 April): 5

The State Council listed an item of 'drafting a petition law' in its work plan in 2016, which has not been shown on the list of its new work plans since 2017. See http://www.gov.cn/zhengce/content/2016-04/13/content_5063670.htm

Working Rules on the Handling of People's Petitions (中国人民政治协商会议全国委员会暨省、市协商委员会关于处理人民意见的试行办法), adopted by the National Committee of the National Political Consultative Conference on 19 July 1951. Available at: www.cppcc.gov.cn/2011/09/06/ARTI1315304517625189.shtml

Xiaowei Z, Chen-wen K (eds) (2013) Elites and petitions in rural China. Routledge, p 129

Xiao-yong H (2011) The right choice for the reform of the petition system: comments on the disputes over petition reform. China Public Adm Rev 10:125–127

Xing Y (2004) On petition remedy, a special administrative remedial procedure (作为特殊行政救济的信访救济). Chinese J Law 3:58–61

Xinhua News (2014) Petitioners' Tendency to Resort to Judicial Venues for Litigation-related Complaints (涉法涉诉信访"两升一降" 呈现"弃访转法"良好势头). www.gov.cn/xinwen/2014-09/11/content_2749303.htm. Accessed 9 July 2017

Xiucheng Z (2007) A Study of China's Petition System after 1978: A Case on Weihai in Shandong Province (1978年以来中国信访工作研究——以山东威海为个案). Central Party School Thesis Database: 150. Available at: www.cnki.net/kcms/detail/detail.aspx?FileName=2007083301.nh&DbName=CDFD2007&DbCode=CDFD. Accessed 2 July 2016

Xi-xin W (2003) Rules, appropriation and governance: a study on probability and applicability of alternative dispute resolution in administrative matters (规则、合意与治理——行政过程中ADR使用的可能性与妥当性研究). Stud Law Bus 5(97):71

Yi C (2013) Risk, accountability and institutions: a study of government reactions to mass group incidents (风险、责任与机制: 责任政府化解群体性事件的机制研究). Central Compilation & Translation Press, pp 238–239

Yongtao W, Peng C (2015) On typology and governance of litigation-involved letters and visits (涉诉信访的基本类及其治理研究). Sociol Rev China 3(2):18–19

Yueyang L (2018) A reflection on the effectiveness of engaging lawyers in handling litigation-related petitions. Chinese Lawyer 5:87–88

Zemin J (2001) Vigorously promote the spirit of unremitting efforts (大力弘扬不懈奋斗的精神). In: The selected works of Jiang Zemin (Vol. 3). Available at: www.reformdata.org/2001/0110/5867.shtml)

Zhe L (2009) Function, status and reforming trend of the letter-and-visit system (信访制度的功能、属性及其发展趋势). J Party School Central Committee CPC 1:89

Chapter 4
Chinese Measures for Handling Labour Actions: The Rise of Labour Protection Rules and Its Challenges

4.1 Rights Protection and Stability Maintaining: Balanced or Conflicting Ends?

Labour relations have become a dispute-intensive area in contemporary China. Labour actions, which involve a group of workers collectively complaining against the violation of their labour rights or interests,[1] have revealed several challenges to Chinese labour dispute resolution procedures in effectively addressing the losses suffered by workers.[2] Between 2000 and 2013, for example, approximately one-third of mass actions involving more than one hundred complainants were due to unresolved labour grievances.[3] The English-language and Chinese-language research literature on Chinese measures for handling labour actions is either State-centric that focuses on legislative developments related to the legal protection of labour rights and their subsequent implementation by administrative and judicial bodies,[4] or protester-centric that focuses on the claims and strategies made by labour complainants, the consequential confrontation with the employer and the government and their outcomes.

These analyses often isolate labour action settlements in China from the institutional and social contexts that shape the rules and practices for managing them. The attribution of the causes for labour action settlements to the authoritarian nature of

[1] The definition of labour action is not unified under existing Chinese labour law and regulations. A labour complaint brought by ten or more workers is typically classified as a collective labour complaint, according to Article 7 of the Law of the People's Republic of China on Mediation and Arbitration of Labour Dispute. In some cases, local governments may register a labour complaint involving 100 or more complainants as a collective labour complaint. See: the National Bureau of Statistics of China's annual report on 'Labour Disputes Accepted and Settled' from 2012 to 2014.

[2] In this chapter, the terms 'labour action', 'collective labour complaint', and 'collective labour dispute' are used interchangeably.

[3] Lin and He (2014), pp. 270–288.

[4] Kai (2013), p. 93.

C.-r. Qiao, *Chinese Rules and Procedures for Addressing Mass Actions*,
https://doi.org/10.1007/978-3-031-62201-4_4

the Chinese State is an oversimplification. As discussed in Chap. 1, it is crucial to make sense of Chinese approaches to dealing with labour actions in the light of their institutional and social cultures as well as their changes, in a holistic and nuanced manner. To this end, the chapter examines the institutional reform of Chinese labour management starting in the 1980s, focusing on the shift from State-dependent labour management that supported the centrally commanded economy, to employment-contract-based labour management in accordance with statutory rules.

Specifically, this section first analyses the formation and dismantling of State-dependent employment relations between the 1950s and the 1980s, outlining their benefits and costs (Sect. 4.1.1). It then details the introduction of labour dispute resolution rules to Chinese labour management and their subsequent implementation (Sect. 4.1.2). It proceeds by identifying the problems with Chinese labour dispute resolution measures in handling labour actions (Sect. 4.1.3). The section concludes by summarising the importance of labour protection rules in Chinese approaches to addressing labour complaints in general and labour actions in particular (Sect. 4.1.4).

4.1.1 Chinese Workers Enjoying Iron Rice Bowl and Its Outcomes

At the start of the twentieth century, hundreds of thousands of Chinese peasants shifted from agricultural work to industrial jobs in urban areas. In 1916, the estimated amount of factory workers was 560,000, which is thought to be a conservative estimate compared to the actual size of the factory labour force at the time.[5] In 1920, the weaving and dyeing sector employed 301,544 workers, the machinery and mechanical manufacturing sector employed 17,951 workers, the chemical industry such as the production of porcelain, lacquerware and paper, employed 42,002 workers, the food manufacturing sector employed 36,762 workers, and the railway construction sector employed 50,000 workers.[6] As the number of Chinese workers increased, organisations emerged in major cities to protect workers' employment interests from exploitative practices by employers.

A study conducted in Beijing from 1917 to 1930 revealed that despite heavy workloads, the average income of eighty-two factory workers remained so low that they could barely make ends meet.[7] Consequently, labour associations that aimed to represent workers rapidly developed in labour-intensive sectors, which propagated the socialist idea that the root cause of the unfair treatment workers suffered was a structural inequality between capitalists who owned the means of production and workers whose only valuable commodity was their labour force.[8] Organising

[5]Russel (1922), Chapter XIV "Industrialism in China".

[6]Da (1929), pp. 7–19.

[7]Menghe (2011), pp. 26–27, 37–46 and 69.

[8]Yuan (2016), pp. 287–288.

themselves was the only way for workers to strengthen their bargaining power against capitalists in seeking fair labour relations. During the 1920s and 1930s, labour strikes erupted against employers in several cities.[9] Following the establishment of the People's Republic of China in 1949, its interim constitution confirmed that the Chinese State would be led by the working class, with the means of production owned by workers and land owned by peasants.[10]

The 1954 Chinese Constitution reaffirmed the political leadership of Chinese workers and peasants. It established the State's duty to safeguard the labour rights of Chinese citizens, including the right to work, to decent working conditions, to fair wages and labour benefits, to rest and leisure, and to material assistance in the event of old age, illness and disability, and to overseeing the socialist transformation of the national economy.[11] The Chinese government's first Five-Year Plan for Developing the National Economy, which was adopted in 1953, prioritised the development of socialist economic sectors that were collectively owned by the people, over capitalist ones that were privately owned. The principle that the Chinese economy was centrally commanded and aimed to improve the material and cultural well-being of the people was also incorporated into the Chinese Constitution in 1954.[12]

The Chinese command economy has two operational features. Firstly, State-owned enterprises (hereafter referred to as the "SOE") made their production and sales plans based on government commands rather than market prices and demands; secondly, labour resources were allocated by the government to sectors that the government deemed critical to the strategic development of China, such as heavy industry and defence equipment manufacturing due to Cold War tensions between China and Occidental States.[13] Chinese workers were not given the right to choose their work or employers. Instead, they were assigned to a workplace based on their educational qualifications and experiences, to maximise their contribution to the national development plans. By the end of 1957, the contribution of the SOEs to China's Gross National Product had increased from 19.1 per cent in 1952 to 32.2 per cent, the contribution of collectively owned enterprises (namely, owned by the working class) increased from 1.5 per cent in 1952 to 53.4 per cent, and cooperatively owned enterprises (namely jointly owned by the State and private bodies) increased from 0.7 per cent in 1952 to 7.3 per cent, whereas privately owned enterprises decreased from 71.8 per cent in 1952 to 7.1 per cent in 1957.[14]

After the nationwide extension of the command economy in 1957, a State-dependent labour system was gradually set up, resulting in almost all Chinese

[9] Perry (1993), pp. 65–66.

[10] Articles 1, 3 and 28, in the Common Program of The Chinese People's Political Consultative Conference, adopted on 29 September 1949.

[11] Articles 1, 10, 91, 92 and 93, in the Constitution of the People's Republic of China, adopted on 20 September 1954.

[12] Article 15, in the Constitution of the People's Republic of China of 1954.

[13] Naughton (1996a), pp. 26–30.

[14] The Research Institute of the History and Archives of the CPC (2017).

workers becoming State employees in some capacity. In 1978, the Chinese urban labour force numbered 95.1 million, with the vast majority, 99.8 per cent, employed by the SOEs (74.5 million),[15] and collectively owned enterprises (20.5 million).[16] In accordance, labour relations in China were managed through a permanent State employment mechanism known as the work unit (*danwei*/单位), which was metaphorically referred to as the iron rice bowl. The work unit mechanism was designed to maintain the functioning of the command economy across China.

When an employee entered an employment relationship, whether it was in a factory, retail shop, hotel, restaurant or other types of service and production sectors, the employee became a member of the work unit to which their employer belonged. The work unit was responsible for managing not only the professional lives of workers, such as career promotions and job transfers, but also certain aspects of their private lives, such as issuing approval letters with which they could travel by public transport and stay at hotels, and verification letters with which they could register their marriages with the government civil affairs department.[17] The work unit members received a variety of labour and social benefits,[18] including a comprehensive welfare scheme that subsidised the costs of healthcare, housing, vocational training and recreational leisure, and also the costs of education and healthcare for their children.[19]

The Chinese government controlled not only the production and employment plans of enterprises but also the founding and functioning of workers' representative bodies of labour unions. In Shanghai, for example, the municipal government supported local enterprises in establishing more than 980 labour unions between 1949 and 1950, which enrolled around 667,900 workers as their union members.[20] The labour unions, in turn, supported the implementation of government decisions. During government-sanctioned political movements, labour union officials mobilised workers to report misconduct by managerial members of the SOEs, which resulted in a large number of revelations being submitted to the government.

The mass whistleblowing had unintended consequences on the productivity of the SOEs. In 1952, the municipal government of Shanghai received over 300,000 letters of revelation from workers, exposing the wrongful conduct of managerial personnel.[21] In 1956 and 1957, more than 10,000 workers went on strike to complain about the widespread shortage of daily necessities. The Chinese government attributed the

[15] China's State Bureau for Statistics (2019).

[16] China's State Bureau for Statistics (2009).

[17] Perry and Xiaobo (1997), pp. 10–11 and 51–52.

[18] Perry and Xiaobo (1997), p. 4.

[19] Articles 4, 12, 15, 16 and 20, in the Labour Insurance Regulations of the People's Republic of China, adopted on 23 February 1951.

[20] Perry and Xiaobo (1997), p. 8.

[21] Qizhu (2005), p. 62.

suffering of workers to corrupt management at the SOEs and launched political movements to identify those responsible and re-educate them.[22] Around 85 per cent of factories in the Eighth Textile District in Beijing agreed to sell their equipment to increase wages for workers, due to the managerial boards' concerns about political repercussions.[23]

In general, labour disputes and labour conflicts were infrequent under work-unit labour management. The work unit served as both an employment management tool and a social governance tool.[24] Labour recruitment in the SOEs was based on government economic planning, and labour dismissals were rare due to political reasons.[25] Workers who reached retirement age or experienced a serious work-related injury could request that their work unit transfer their job positions to their children. Between 1978 and 1983, more than nine million new workers were hired through internal job transfers from parents to their qualified children.[26] In addition to meeting the production goals set by the government, the SOEs also fulfilled non-production duties, such as providing healthcare and educational services to their employees.[27]

In 1990, there were 316,875 work units in China; and by 1994, approximately 113.7 million work unit members had free or otherwise low-cost access to work unit facilities such as clinics, nurseries, cafeterias, bathhouses, entertainment centres, and nursing care for their children, the costs of which were largely financed by the responsible employers.[28] However, the social governance functioning of the work units had several negative economic consequences on the national economy in China. By the mid-1990s, more than one-third of the SOEs experienced consecutive periods of negative growth.[29]

In 1993, then Premier Zhu Rongji identified the provision of social welfare to workers and internal job transfers as key factors contributing to the malfunctioning of the SOEs and the slow growth of China's economy, evidenced by financial and overstaffing burdens of the SOEs.[30] As a result, the Chinese government decided to dismantle the work unit mechanism at the SOEs in 1995. Between 1995 and 1999, the SOEs laid off around fifteen million workers who had only a nominal affiliation to their original work units and received little or no access to labour and social benefits.[31] This large-scale unemployment provoked a rocketing number of labour

[22] The Guiding Opinion of the Central Committee of the Communist Party of China on Handling Labour Strikes and Student Strikes, issued on 25 March 1957.

[23] China's State Archives Bureaus (1994), p. 88.

[24] Meng et al. (2003), pp. 145–146.

[25] Jian (2007), pp. 30–31.

[26] Aiyun (2011).

[27] Xinchun (2001), pp. 36–37.

[28] Perry and Xiaobo (1997), p. 9.

[29] Lee (2000), p. 91.

[30] Rongji (2009).

[31] Qiang et al. (2001), p. 66.

complaints across the country. In 1995, the number of labour actions was officially estimated to be around 1.1 million and in 1998, the number of labour protesters was officially estimated to be no fewer than 3.6 million.[32]

Despite widespread worker discontent, the Chinese government was determined to implement market-oriented labour reforms. The government argued that the current hardships being endured by workers were an unavoidable cost of reviving the national economy in the long term, which would ultimately benefit the public.[33] The 1993 amendment to the Chinese Constitution confirmed the legitimacy of the market economy in China and stipulated that the Chinese State should improve its economic legislation and its regulatory role to further marketise the Chinese economy.[34] In July 1994, the National People's Congress passed the first Chinese Labour Law after more than 500 closed-door meetings with labour relations and management experts.[35] Subsequently, labour management in China was recognised as market-oriented, establishing legal principles of equal employment opportunities, freedom to choose one's occupation and employer, and fair settlement of labour disputes.[36] The era of China's work unit labour management, where workers were provided with the iron rice bowl, entered its final days in the late 1990s. Individual and collective complaints from Chinese workers about the loss of job security grew in both quantity and intensity.

4.1.2 The Expansion of Labour Complaints and Official Responses

In 1986, the Chinese government implemented market-oriented labour reforms that granted increased autonomy to the SOEs in managing employer-employee relations and deciding on employment plans. As a result, there was a surge in labour complaints about new labour management practices in the SOEs, such as recruiting workers, confirming and modifying employment contracts, and deciding on labour dismissals, all on the basis of the enterprise's production and growth needs.[37] In 1989, the SOEs replaced internal job inheritance with an open and merit-based recruitment procedure.[38] These reform measures led to the lay-off of 42,300

[32] Feng (2000), p. 41.

[33] Hurst (2008), pp. 75 and 80.

[34] Article 7 of the amendment to Article 15 of the Chinese Constitution.

[35] Yan-sui (2004), p. 128.

[36] Articles 1 and 3, in the Labour Law of the People's Republic of China, adopted on 5 July 1994.

[37] Four Regulations on Labour Reforms (No. 77), adopted in 1986.

[38] Article 5, in the Interim Regulations on Recruiting Workers at the State-Owned Enterprises, adopted on 12 July 1986.

permanent and temporary workers, which accounted for 0.5 per cent of the entire urban workforce at the time.[39] Although this percentage was modest, it was unprecedented for the SOEs.

Chinese workers were worried about the growing risk of unemployment and frustrated by the reduction in labour and social benefits. Previously, the Chinese government directly heard and handled labour complaints related to employment conditions, confirmation and termination of employment relations, and internal promotion or sanction; if a labour complaint was revolved through the enterprise's internal procedure, the settlement records and outcome had to be registered with the government.[40] Under the work unit mechanism, workers seldom filed complaints against their employers through government mediation or arbitration procedures,[41] due to the considerable control that employers had over both their professional and private lives.[42] However, China's shift from a command economy to a market economy gradually dissolved workers' dependence on their work units, making it feasible for workers to confront employers in internal and external dispute resolution forums.[43]

In 1987, the Chinese government mandated the SOEs to set up the Labour Dispute Mediation Committee as part of their corporate governance to deal with the surging number of labour complaints regarding employment conditions and benefits. The labour dispute mediation committee consisted of representatives from the workers' assembly, the labour union and the company's managerial board.[44] The workers' assembly, which was originally assigned to oversee management decisions and promote harmonious labour relations within the company,[45] assisted the labour dispute mediation committee in addressing labour grievances and mediating labour complaints.[46] By the end of 1992, more than sixty percent of the SOEs had set up internal mediation committees (their number totalling 108,460); and in 1993, the labour dispute mediation committees recorded around ninety percent of labour complaints as resolved through internal mediation.[47] In 1993, the internal mediation procedure was also extended to privately owned enterprises, to

[39] Naughton (1996b), p. 212.

[40] Articles 4–6, in the Regulation on the Labour Dispute Resolution Procedure, adopted on 16 November 1950.

[41] Qingjun and Yu (2013), p. 83.

[42] Jian (2007), pp. 30–31.

[43] Jian (2007), pp. 30–32.

[44] Articles 2 and 7, in the Interim Regulation on Resolving Labour Disputes within the State-Owned Enterprises, adopted on 31 July 1987.

[45] Articles 2 and 3, in the Interim Regulation on Worker's Assembly at the State-Owned Enterprises, adopted on 15 June 1981.

[46] Article 7, in the Interim Regulation on Resolving Labour Disputes within the State-Owned Enterprises.

[47] Wenjia (2013), p. 150.

which an employee could complain about dismissal decisions, labour benefit provisions, or other employment-related matters.[48]

Despite the government requirement, many small enterprises could not afford the operational and personnel costs of internal mediation.[49] Even medium and large enterprises struggled to handle the increasing number of labour complaints that overwhelmed their mediation committees.[50] Efficiently addressing labour complaints and redressing the loss of workers was, and still is, a concern for the Chinese government, as a socialist State is supposed to safeguard the interests and welfare of the working class.[51] In 1993, the Chinese government started subsidising the Labour Dispute Arbitration Committee as an external mechanism to handle labour complaints that could not be resolved through internal mediation. Labour dispute arbitrators were representatives from the labour union, the government's labour management and economic management departments.[52] By 1994, over 2800 arbitration committees at the municipal and provincial levels had begun to accept and hear labour complaints.[53]

Since the enforcement of the Chinese Labour Law on 1 January 1995, Chinese courts have been able to hear labour complaint cases if the complainants object to the decision of labour dispute arbitration.[54] However, the court's adjudication was not a popular choice for labour complainants due to the actual or perceived unfairness of court procedures and decisions.[55] Procedurally, labour dispute litigation was the last resort for resolving labour complaints, and it should always be preceded by labour dispute mediation and arbitration. By 1995, internal labour dispute mediation, government-led labour dispute arbitration and labour dispute litigation had formed the contemporary Chinese labour dispute resolution mechanism known as "one mediation, one arbitration and two trials (*yitiao yicai ershen*/一调一裁二审)".

In the 2000s, China's labour dispute resolution mechanism faced widespread criticism for its inefficiency. In Guangdong Province, for example, a labour complaint could take up to thirty months before the labour dispute arbitrator(s) began hearing it in 2006.[56] The judicial resolution of labour disputes was also overwhelmed. In 2008, Chinese local courts received around 280,000 labour dispute cases, almost double the number of cases from the preceding year, while the number of judges remained almost unchanged.[57] The frequent delays in resolving labour disputes were blamed for intensifying labour complaints rather than concluding

---

[48] Article 2, in the Regulation on Resolving Labour Disputes at the Companies, adopted on 11 June 1993.

[49] Kun (2014), p. 25.

[50] Feng and Mengxiao (2013), p. 573.

[51] Chen (2011), pp. 110–112.

[52] Article 13, in the Regulation on Resolving Labour Disputes at the Companies of 1993.

[53] Jingwen (2007), p. 475.

[54] Article 79, in the Chinese Labour Law of 1995.

[55] Wenjia and Feng (2015), p. 381.

[56] Wenjia (2013), p. 155.

[57] Wanhua et al. (2009), pp. 27–28.

them.[58] In 2002, the Supreme People's Court and the Ministry of Justice in China made a joint decision to redirect labour complaints from arbitration and litigation venues to labour dispute mediation and to strengthen the role of the people's mediation committees, which numbered over 900,000 with more than eight million mediators, to deal with the sheer volume of labour disputes awaiting settlements.[59]

The Chinese Labour Dispute Mediation and Arbitration Law, which was passed in 2007, legally confirms the importance of mediation in resolving labour disputes in China. The law provides for three types of mediation to deal with labour complaints based on voluntary participation and equal negotiation:[60] informal mediation by the people's mediator, government-led mediation and in-court mediation. Prior to the formal recognition of the extended use of mediation in settling labour complaints, similar practices were experimented with at the local level. Between 2004 and 2007, local courts in Shanghai, Hubei, and Sichuan Provinces invited labour union representatives and labour dispute arbitrators to court hearings on labour complaint cases and had them propose mediation agreements to be considered by the disputing parties.[61] In 2009, the Chinese Supreme People's Court recognised the local inclusion of mediation settlements in the court handling of labour complaints as a good practice, which has been promoted nationwide to achieve speedy settlements of labour disputes since then.[62]

Labour disputes regarding employment confirmation, fulfilment of the employment contract, work-related injury compensation, and dismissal decisions are typically first handled by labour dispute mediators before being presented to the labour dispute arbitration committee or the court.[63] The process of settling a labour dispute usually starts with an internal consultation where the complainant presents their complaint and claim to the employer and seeks a settlement with the employer, with or without the participation of a labour union representative; if the consultation does not result in an agreement, or is not complied with by either party, the complainant may proceed to the internal labour dispute mediator, or the local mediation committee (overseen by the local government or court), or the grassroots association that conducts dispute mediation; if either party fails to reach or comply with the mediation agreement, the labour dispute arbitration may commence, which is a mandatory procedure before litigation; lastly, if either party objects to or refuses to comply with the arbitral settlement, the case may be brought to the court for adjudication whose decision can be appealed once.[64] During the arbitration process, the

[58] China's Youth Daily (22 April 2008).

[59] Paragraph 2, in the Advisory Opinion on Strengthening the Work of People's Mediation. Issued on 26 February 2002.

[60] Article 2, in the Labour Dispute Mediation and Arbitration Law of the People's Republic of China, adopted on 29 December 2007.

[61] Jinglun and Wenjia (2014), pp. 72–73.

[62] Paragraph 4, in the Advisory Opinion of the Supreme People's Court on Doing a Good Job in the Trial of Labour Dispute Cases. Issued on 6 July 2009.

[63] Article 2, in the Chinese Labour Dispute Mediation and Arbitration Law.

[64] Articles 5, 15 and 29, in the Chinese Labour Dispute Mediation and Arbitration Law.

arbitration committee must propose a mediation agreement to the disputing parties before formulating its arbitral decision.[65]

To be eligible as a labour dispute arbitrator, a candidate must have experience working as a judge or have completed legal research and education with a professional certificate, or have worked in a human resources office or for a labour union for at least five years, or have practiced labour law or a related field for at least three years.[66] As of the end of 2012, there were over 36,900 qualified labour dispute arbitrators in China, with thirty-four per cent holding a university degree in law.[67] The role of labour dispute mediators is to remain impartial and connected with the public, and they must have a good understanding of Chinese laws, government policies and customary traditions.[68] In 2016, there were 784,000 registered mediation committees across China, including 7027 specialised in handling labour dispute cases.[69] These committees resolved more than 300,000 labour complaint cases in 2016.[70]

Before 2008, complainants in labour disputes were responsible for paying some or all of the costs associated with the arbitration process. The registration fee for arbitration ranged from 20 to 50 Yuan (approximately three to seven Euro) and must be paid by the complainant(s) within five days of registration; the settlement fee for arbitration was charged based on the estimated costs of the arbitration process, including evidence identification, travel and accommodation of arbitrators and witnesses, which should be paid by both the complainant and the employer within five days of registration.[71] The government now covers the costs of both materials and personnel for the labour dispute arbitration procedure.[72] In 2014, the labour dispute mediation, arbitration and litigation procedures settled 715,613 labour complaint cases.[73] Of these, around forty-five per cent were handled through labour dispute mediation, and forty-four per cent through labour dispute arbitration in 2014, which is six times the amount of labour dispute arbitration settlements in 2000.[74]

The Chinese government has favoured labour dispute mediation over other procedures because it is subject to fewer procedural regulations, allowing relevant authorities to exert some directional power and expedite the conclusion of labour disputes.[75] Government labour management departments, in particular, have

---

[65] Article 42, in the Chinese Labour Dispute Mediation and Arbitration Law.

[66] Article 20, in the Chinese Labour Dispute Mediation and Arbitration Law.

[67] Xian (2013), p. 666.

[68] Article 11, in the Chinese Labour Dispute Mediation and Arbitration Law.

[69] Legal Daily (29 June 2017).

[70] ibid.

[71] Regulatory Rules on Charging the Labour Contract Identification Cost and Labour Dispute Arbitration Costs. Adopted on 10 June 1992.

[72] Article 53, in the Chinese Labour Dispute Mediation and Arbitration Law.

[73] National Bureau of Statistics of China (2015).

[74] Hongwen (2015), p. 347.

[75] Wenjia and Feng (2015), pp. 389–390.

reportedly compelled employers to agree to some of the requests of the complaining workers, and the workers to accept the mediation settlement and dissolve their labour actions.[76] By the end of 2010, nearly a quarter of labour complaints were resolved through government-led mediation; of these, seventeen per cent were resolved before the town-level mediation committees and five per cent before the county-level and district-level mediation committees.[77]

Labour complainants, on the other hand, have varying reactions to mediation settlements. While some appreciate the efficiency of the mediation procedure compared to labour dispute arbitration and litigation, others remain sceptical. According to a 2012 survey conducted in Guangzhou, eighty-seven per cent of labour complainants preferred the government to play an active role in labour dispute mediation to pressure employers to satisfy workers' requests and comply with the settlement.[78] Enterprises cannot afford to disagree with or embarrass the government, as this could jeopardise their long-term business operations and development.[79] Labour complainants respond that the engagement of the local government helped to ensure both procedural efficiency and enforceability of the dispute settlement.[80]

However, the extensive and rapid use of mediation settlements undermines the principle of voluntariness. It has become increasingly challenging for labour complainants to avoid labour dispute mediation, even though it is not a mandatory procedure under the law. In some regions, local courts are under political pressure to apply mediation to conclude labour disputes. In Hunan Province, for instance, judges at the municipal and town-level courts were required to impel or deceive disputing parties into mediation between 2004 and 2014, and the rate of 'successful dispute mediation' carried significant weight in their performance assessment.[81] In addition, cases accepted by the labour dispute arbitration committee are sometimes referred to the mediation procedure, with or without the consent of the labour complainants; if the first mediation fails to reach an agreement, a second mediation will be conducted with the presence of an arbitrator.[82] Labour complainants have reported feeling somewhat coerced into accepting the mediation result and not feeling free to object to the mediation process.[83]

In summary, the development of the Chinese labour dispute resolution mechanism has undergone significant changes in line with the transition from a command economy, where Chinese workers' labour rights and benefits were policy-mandated, to a market economy, where workers' labour rights and interests are legally protected. China's market-oriented labour reforms have left tens of millions of

[76] Wenjia and Feng (2015), p. 393.

[77] Wenjia (2013), pp. 156–157.

[78] Wenjia and Feng (2015), p. 398.

[79] Wenjia and Feng (2015), p. 396.

[80] Wenjia and Jinglun (2014), p. 148.

[81] People's Daily (22 January 2014).

[82] Jinglun and Wenjia (2014), pp. 72–73.

[83] Wenjia and Feng (2015), pp. 389–390.

workers dissatisfied with their dismissal and frustrated with their income crisis. Labour dispute mediation, arbitration and litigation procedures were established to provide a proper settlement of labour complaints. The widespread use of mediation settlements helps to tackle the frequent delays in labour dispute arbitration and litigation whereas it also poses a critical challenge to the legal principles of voluntary participation and equal consultation.

4.1.3 Legal Rules and Political Norms in Handling Labour Actions

Labour actions have been observed in both the SOEs that have laid off numerous workers and privately owned manufacturing factories that have failed to comply with working conditions and labour reimbursement requirements.[84] Historically, collective labour complaints about unfair treatment or mistreatment of workers are not unique to the economic transition in China.[85] Yet, Chinese rules and procedures are in several aspects characteristic in terms of how they balance the protection of labour rights with the maintenance of economic and social stabilities when resolving labour actions. The following are some key factors that shape Chinese approaches to dealing with labour actions.

Firstly, there is no constitutional or legal basis for Chinese workers to initiate labour action as a means of having their work-related complaints heard and their requests considered. Neither the Chinese Constitution nor the Chinese Labour Law recognises the right to strike.[86] The leading reason why the right to strike is not protected in China is doctrinal. Labour strikes are seen as a disruptive threat to the self-interest of capitalists whereas in the Chinese socialist economy, the means of production are owned by the people, the production planning and profits are for the people, and any suspension or interruption of production can lead to damage to the interests of the people.[87] Labour actions are legally restricted due to the absence of legal protection of labour strikes and the presence of doctrinal denial of their necessity in China.

Chinese labour dispute resolution venues are often unwilling to handle cases with multiple complainants due to legal restrictions. In the mid-1980s, the State Council mandated that when the number of labour complainants exceeded ten, they should

---

[84] Chang and Cooke (2015), p. 445.

[85] Kai and Brown (2013), p. 105.

[86] The right to strike is internationally recognised as "an essential corollary of the right to organise", protected by Convention 87 of the International Labour Organisation. However, the right to strike is not a necessary part of labour legislation, which exists in some countries where the right to strike is recognised and protected, but not in others where workers can still go on strike. See: The right to strike, updated by the International Labour Organisation on 10 December 2001.

[87] Youyu (2003), p. 14.

assign one or no more than three representatives to present their joint complaint to the labour dispute mediation or arbitration venue.[88] In 1993, the national regulation imposed further a limitation that a labour complaint involving three or more workers should be presented by a single representative before the labour dispute arbitration committee or the court.[89] In 2007, the Labour Dispute Mediation and Arbitration Law also limited the number of labour complainants who could approach dispute resolution venues. When ten or more workers file a labour complaint together, they shall choose a representative to act on behalf of the group during mediation, arbitration or litigation procedures.[90]

Secondly, collective labour complaints in China are not limited to employer-employee relations but also extend to government policies. The Chinese government used to attribute the suffering of workers to the malfeasance of managerial personnel, downplaying a general issue to individual misconduct. During the 1950s, when there were several large-scale labour actions, the government attributed workers' discontent to a fraction of corrupt managers at the SOEs; mass whistleblowing was therefore encouraged to help the government identify and sanction the wrongdoers.[91] During the market-oriented labour management reform of the 1990s, there was no external or mass oversight to ensure the fairness of government decisions, which could have blocked or highlighted policy elements that were disproportionately harmful to workers.

The SOEs adhered to government economic and labour policies when making decisions on dismissals and welfare deductions, which caused large-scale dissatisfaction among workers. From 1995 to 2002, the restructuring policy mandated the merger or closure of thousands of unprofitable enterprises within a decade, leading to the dismissal of over sixty million workers.[92] In 1996 alone, 5335 SOEs were merged or went bankrupt, leading to the short-noticed layoff of around 4.3 million employees and causing widespread shock and frustration among the affected workers and their families.[93] In 1998, the Chinese government passed guidance that required the SOEs to provide a dismissal allowance to laid-off workers, which was intended to cover basic living costs during the initial months following the dismissal.[94]

However, the dismissal allowance policy was poorly implemented due to the financial inability of the SOEs and weak government oversight. According to a survey conducted in ten cities in 1998 and 1999, thirty-one per cent of laid-off

[88] Article 4, in the Interim Regulation on Resolving Labour Disputes within the State-owned Enterprises.

[89] Articles 5 and 6, in the Regulation on Resolving Labour Disputes at the Companies of 1993.

[90] Article 7, in the Chinese Labour Dispute Mediation and Arbitration Law.

[91] A Guiding Opinion on Handling Labour Strikes and Student Strikes. Issued on 25 March 1957.

[92] Jiemian News (19 August 2021).

[93] Yifu and Zhiyun (2003), p. 10.

[94] The Notice on Handling Problems Rising from the Laid-off Workers at the SOE and Their Re-employment. Issued on 9 June 1998.

workers received no allowance at all, while sixty-seven per cent had to rely on loans.[95] In February 2000, approximately 10,000 workers who were dismissed organised a petition to the mining management department of the local municipal government, accusing their employer the Chinese Non-ferrous Metal Industrial Corporation (then owned by the State Council) of implementing an irresponsible re-organisational plan that contained unfair labour dismissal decisions.[96] In short, labour actions crying about the working and living adversities of numerous workers are often the result of a combination of flawed government decisions and problematic implementation by employers.

Similarly, the Chinese residence management policy exposes rural residents who seek jobs in urban areas to discriminatory treatment. The combination of inappropriate government policy and unlawful decisions of employers leads to recurrent complaints from migrant workers. In the context of the Chinese labour market, migrant workers refer to citizens who hold rural residences but work and live in the city, or who are usually called "rural workers (*nongmin gong*/农民工)". Their household registration is categorised as 'peasant/farmer'. As of 2018, there were more than 288 million rural workers, with around sixty percent having migrated from their hometown or home province for non-agricultural employment in urban areas.[97]

To understand the discriminatory impact of Chinese labour management policies on rural residents and rural workers, it is essential to consider a range of historical, economic and social factors. However, these factors are intricate and require a separate study. What is relevant here is the government's requirement for employers to conclude an employment contract with rural workers is weak, leaving these workers in a legal conundrum when seeking remedies for the violation of their labour rights without an employment contract. The Chinese government has implemented several policy amendments to protect the labour rights of rural workers. Since 2008, employers who fail to conclude employment contracts with rural workers on time are subject to financial sanctions.[98] Employers who intentionally and severely infringe on the labour rights of rural workers may face criminal charges.[99] However, the implementation of these protection rules is weak. In 2014, as many as sixty-two per cent of the 274 million rural workers did not sign

[95] Feng (2000), p. 47.

[96] Xiucheng (2007), p. 73.

[97] Section One in the Monitor Report on Rural Workers in 2018.

[98] Article 82, in the Chinese Labour Contract Law, adopted on 29 June 2007.

[99] For example, the Standing Committee of the National People's Congress amended the Criminal Law of China in 2011 to include an article stating that "anyone who evades the payment of a relatively large amount of labour remuneration by transferring property or by fleeing and hiding, or who refuses to pay a relatively large amount of labour remuneration even though he is able to do so and still refuses to pay after being ordered to do so by the relevant government department" is liable to criminal prosecution. Article 276, in Criminal Law of the People's Republic of China.

employment contracts with their employers, leaving their labour rights and interests outside government oversight and legal protection.[100]

Thirdly, Chinese labour unions were initially established as a mass organisation to defend workers' rights.[101] However, during the command economy, labour unions lacked the power to influence employment terms and their major function was to organise educational and recreational activities in the workplace.[102] In 1992, labour unions were granted the power to amend employment terms related to worker-employer relations and to mitigate worker-employer conflicts. Specifically, labour unions could provide input on employers' decisions to dismiss or penalise employees, review employers' reasons for terminating employment contracts,[103] and participate in internal labour dispute mediation.[104] They are also responsible for inspecting the implementation of decisions of workers' assemblies[105] and assisting the labour dispute mediation committee in accepting and hearing labour complaints.[106]

Labour unions, which are supposed to collaborate closely with the labour dispute mediation and arbitration committees in labour dispute resolution processes, are not well trusted by labour complainants.[107] In cases of labour actions, such as collective work stoppage or delays, the labour union is responsible for promptly normalising the interrupted production by consulting with the government and mediating conflicts between workers and employers.[108] Employees at privately owned and foreign-owned enterprises often lacked access to labour unions as their employers were not legally required to implement workers' right to form and participate in the labour union; in cases where labour complainants are members of the union, they may not trust the union during labour conflict settlements.[109]

Fourthly, although the right to strike is not recognised or protected by law in China, workers are entitled to certain procedural and substantive rights related to the defence of labour interests, such as the right to fair labour dispute resolution, to equal employment, to fair labour reimbursement,[110] and to collective labour bargaining as a mechanism for protecting the interests of employees with collective labour

[100] Lee (2016), p. 320.

[101] Article 2, in the Chinese Labour Union Law of the People's Republic of China, adopted on 3 April 1992.

[102] Siming and Feng (2008), p. 35.

[103] Article 19, in the Chinese Labour Union Law.

[104] Article 20, in the Chinese Labour Union Law.

[105] Article 30, in the Chinese Labour Union Law.

[106] Article 4, in the Interim Regulation for Implementing Labour union's Role of Assisting with Resolving Labour Disputes, adopted in 1995.

[107] Chang and Cooke (2015), pp. 447–448.

[108] Article 25, in the Chinese Labour Union Law.

[109] Chang and Cooke (2015), pp. 447–448.

[110] Article 3, in the Labour Law of the People's Republic of China, adopted on 5 July 1994.

contracts.[111] Before the conclusion of a collective labour contract, it is legally required to engage in collective labour bargaining between employees and employers; and during the bargaining process, the labour union is obliged to represent the legitimate rights and interests of workers.[112] The implementation of workers' employment rights, particularly collective labour bargaining and collective labour contracts, is intended to prevent potential labour conflicts.

In the early 1990s, it was already required to submit the draft of collective labour contracts to the workers' assembly for review and discussion before finalising them.[113] In 2007, the Chinese Labour Contract Law reaffirmed the principle of equal negotiation that workers or their representative body and employers should negotiate equally on the employment and labour benefit terms, and the collective labour contract agreed upon through collective labour bargaining should be submitted to the workers' assembly for the final adoption.[114] Collective labour bargaining is a process where workers and employers agree on the contents of an employment contract and subsequently, comply with it. This is a preventive measure aimed at reducing labour actions from the start of an employment relationship; and in the event of a collective labour dispute, the collective labour contract serves as the basis for resolving the dispute. In 2015, labour dispute resolution venues concluded 10,466 collective labour complaints (brought by 341,588 workers), which is nearly three times the amount in 1996 (that is 3150 cases brought by 92,203 workers).[115]

The impact of collective labour bargaining on reducing the number of labour conflicts is not yet clear, despite increased government promotion of this mechanism.[116] In 2014, more than eighty per cent of enterprises in industrially prosperous regions claimed to have included collective labour bargaining in the employment contract confirmation process; however, in the following years, there was an increase in labour complaints presented to labour dispute resolution venues in the same regions.[117] The government labour management department has reportedly focused on formal records of whether collective labour bargaining took place during the conclusion of employment contracts, rather than whether it resulted in substantive amendments to employment terms as requested by workers.[118] This raises questions about the effectiveness of collective labour bargaining in preventing the occurrence of labour actions.

Lastly, Chinese labour dispute resolution venues have the dual duty of protecting workers' labour rights and interests on the one hand, and promoting harmonious

[111] Kai (2013), pp. 98–99.

[112] Articles 6 and 51, in the Chinese Labour Contract Law.

[113] Article 18, in the Chinese Labour Union Law.

[114] Articles 6 and 51, in the Chinese Labour Contract Law.

[115] China's National Bureau of Statistics (2016) Labour Statistical Yearbook of 2016 and Labour Statistical Yearbook of 2005.

[116] Chinese Premier's Report on the Work of the Government to the Second Session of the Twelfth National People's Congress on 5 March 2014.

[117] Workers' Daily (17 February 2016).

[118] Qingjun (2012), pp. 81–83.

labour relations and sustaining social harmony on the other, which are not always compatible with each other. Procedural efficiency is a guiding principle that labour dispute settlements must adhere to.[119] In the aftermath of the 2008 global financial crisis, the Chinese government has been promoting integrated development goals to secure economic growth, improve people's livelihoods, and maintain social stability, which is encapsulated in the phrase '*bao zengzhang, bao minsheng, bao wending* (保增长、保民生、保稳定)'. Officially, mass group incidents, including labour actions, are explained as challenges to social stability.[120]

Local governments in China are responsible for monitoring and preventing labour actions from escalating into mass group incidents, which are considered to undermine social stability."[121] To maintain social stability, local governments often prefer to have collective labour complaints concluded through flexible and efficient mediation procedures, rather than the more time-consuming procedures such as labour dispute arbitration and litigation.[122] Enterprises often prefer to resolve labour disputes through mediation rather than arbitration or litigation, to quickly resolve the issue.[123] However, this preference can leave labour complainants in a passive and vulnerable position.[124] It is unclear whether equal negotiation can be guaranteed during the mediation process. In brief, prompt mediation settlements of labour actions can help achieve the policy goal of maintaining economic stability, while it may not fully satisfy the legal objective of fairly addressing workers' grievances or fairly compensating workers for their losses.

4.1.4 The Compromised Protection of Labour Rights in Resolving Labour Actions

The preceding parts have analysed Chinese rules and procedures for managing labour complaints in general and collective labour complaints in specific. The impact of the national market-oriented labour reform on the labour management system has been analysed in detail. The system has shifted from a State-dependent regime where the government planned labour relations and handled labour complaints mainly through government-sanctioned movements, towards a legally regulated system. In the new labour management system, labour relations at both the SOEs and private enterprises are confirmed by the legally valid employment contract, and labour

[119] Articles 1 and 3, in the Chinese Labour Dispute Mediation and Arbitration Law.

[120] Xinhua News (24 July 2009a).

[121] Article 7 and Article 34, in the Provisions on the Negotiation and Mediation of Enterprise Labour Disputes. Issued on 30 November 2011.

[122] Wenjia and Feng (2015), p. 382.

[123] Wenjia and Jinglun (2014), p. 151.

[124] Xin and Ying (2013), pp. 94–95.

Table 4.1 Characteristics of Chinese labour dispute resolution rules and procedures

	Pre-reform	Present
Qualifying labour conflicts	Caused by corrupt conduct of managerial personnel	Caused by a failure to comply with the lawfully concluded employment contract
Grounds for labour dispute resolution	Government policies and political decisions	Chinese Labour Law (effective in 1995) Chinese Labour Contract Law (effective in 2008) Chinese Labour Dispute Mediation and Arbitration Law (effective in 2008)
Measures for handling labour complaints	Political movements; Government-led mediation and arbitration	Internal consultation and negotiation; Labour dispute mediation and arbitration; Court adjudication
Dispute resolution venues	The government labour management department	Workers' assembly and labour union; The government labour management department; Labour dispute mediation and arbitration committees; The court

complaints are dealt with through statutory procedures that are subject to legal regulation (see Table 4.1).

The rise of labour actions is not unique to the development of the Chinese market economy. However, how the Chinese government deals with labour actions is characteristic of its institutional culture. In situations where there is a conflict between politics and law, policy priorities often take precedence over the power of law. Chinese workers do not have constitutional or legal grounds to organise labour strikes. There is also a lack of public oversight or external review of government labour policies. Therefore, inappropriate elements of government decisions relating to labour rights and interests may not be timely detected. Furthermore, labour unions are not primarily responsible to workers and have not functioned as a trusted intermediary between labour complainants and employers. It remains uncertain whether collective labour bargaining effectively safeguards labour rights and reduces labour actions.

In summary, Chinese workers now enjoy legal recognition and protection of their right to fair labour dispute resolution. Procedurally, labour complainants can resort to a tripartite labour dispute resolution mechanism. This section has examined in detail three venues for labour action settlement: first, labour dispute mediation, which was first set up internally within enterprises in 1987 and has since been extended to internal and external mediations since 2008; second, labour dispute arbitration that has been expanded nationwide since 1993; and third, court adjudication that was introduced in 1995. Labour dispute resolution venues must comply with labour protection laws and relevant legal rules, and also fulfil government policies aimed at harmonising labour relations and sustaining economic and social stabilities. It is important to note that the handling of labour actions in China is not solely for the protection of the rights and interests of labour complainants, but rather is influenced by the venues' adherence to policy goals.

4.2 Is the Handling of Labour Actions a Legal Story in the News?

The preceding section has analysed the legislative and institutional developments of the Chinese labour management system and its impact on the rules and practices for dealing with labour actions. This section further examines how the Chinese news coverage introduces and narrates labour actions and their settlements, with a focus on the role of labour protection legal rules in the recurring news narratives and framings. A large collection of Chinese news reports on labour actions and their settlements, published between 1998 and 2015 by official and non-official news media, has been gathered for further analysis in the following parts.

Specifically, the first part introduces the methods used to collect relevant Chinese news reports, conduct the relevance test of the collected reports, and process the cleaned data. The second part identifies the recurrent news narratives about labour actions and labour complainants. The third part investigates the recurrent news narratives concerning the major procedures for handling labour actions, examining the importance of legal rules in those narratives. The fourth part examines news narratives about collective labour relations and labour conflicts arising from them. The final part summarises the findings and their implications.

4.2.1 Data Collection, Relevance Test and Data Processing

The WiseNews database, the largest Chinese news database in the world which captures and stores the full text of a wide range of Chinese news, is the source of Chinese news reports on labour actions and their settlements in this case study. Three sets of data are collected to reveal the relevance of labour protection rules in the recurring news narratives about labour actions, labour action settlements, and collective labour relations. To compose the first dataset, two sets of search terms are defined.

The first dataset consists of sixteen terms that describe various forms of labour action, such as labour group incident, labour group resistance, labour group protests, labour group processions, labour group rights defence, labour group work stoppages, and labour group petitions, as well as their synonyms. The results of this search are included in corpus Group 1.1.[125] The second set comprises fifteen terms that

[125] Sixteen search terms for Group 1.1 are: labour group incident, labour mass group incident, labour group resistance, labour group protest, labour group procession, labour group rights defences, labour group work stoppage, labour group petition, worker group incident, worker mass group incident, worker group resistance, worker group protest, worker group procession, worker group rights defence, worker group work stoppage and worker group petition (in Chinese: 劳动群体事件or劳动群体性事件or劳动群体抗争or劳动群体抗议or劳动群体游行or劳动群体维权or劳动群体游行or劳动停工or劳动群体信访or职工群体事件or职工群体性事件or职工群体抗争or职工群体抗议or职工群体游行or职工群体信访or职工群体维权).

formally refer to labour actions and their synonyms, such as collective labour dispute, collective labour conflict, collective labour litigation, collective labour case and collective labour lawsuit. The results of this search are included in corpus Group 1.2.[126]

The second dataset concerns labour action settlements. Three sets of search terms are defined, namely, the combination of forty-two formal and colloquial references to labour actions with mediation (Group 2.1),[127] with the arbitration

[126]Fifteen search terms for Group 1.2 are: collective labour dispute, collective labour conflict, collective labour litigation, collective labour case, collective labour lawsuit, group labour dispute, group labour conflict, group labour litigation, group labour case, group labour lawsuit, mass labour dispute, mass labour conflict, mass labour litigation, mass labour lawsuit, and mass labour case (in Chinese: 集体劳动争议 or 集体劳动纠纷 or 集体劳动诉讼 or 集体劳动官司 or 集体劳动起诉 or 群体劳动争议 or 群体劳动纠纷 or 群体劳动诉讼 or 群体劳动官司 or 群体劳动起诉 or 群体性劳动争议 or 群体性劳动纠纷 or 群体性劳动诉讼or 群体性劳动官司 or 群体性劳动起诉).

[127]Forty two search terms for Group 2.1 are: (collective labour dispute and mediation) or (collective labour conflict and mediation) or (collective labour relation and mediation) or (collective labour incident and mediation) or (collective labour work and mediation) or (collective worker conflict and mediation) or (collective worker relation and mediation) or (collective worker incident and mediation) or (mass labour dispute and mediation) or (mass labour conflict and mediation) or (mass labour relation and mediation) or (mass labour incident and mediation) or (mass group labour dispute and mediation) or (mass group labour conflict and mediation) or (mass group labour relation and mediation) or (mass group labour incident and mediation) or (mass group labour dispute and mediation) or (mass group labour conflict and mediation) or (labour group incident and mediation) or (labour group protest and mediation) or (labour group resistance and mediation) or (labour group procession and mediation) or (labour group rights defence and mediation) or (labour group work stoppage and mediation) or (labour group strike and mediation) or (labour group work slowdown and mediation) or (labour group petition and mediation) or (labour group letter and mediation) or (labour group visit and mediation) or (labour group procession and mediation) or (labour group case and mediation) or (labour group protest and mediation) or (worker group incident and mediation) or (worker group protest and mediation) or (worker group resistance and mediation) or (worker group procession and mediation) or (worker group rights defence and mediation) or (worker group work stoppage and mediation) or (worker group strike and mediation) or (worker group work slowdown and mediation) or (worker group petition and mediation) or (worker group letter and mediation) or (worker group visit and mediation) or (worker group procession and mediation) or (worker group case and mediation) or (worker group protest and mediation). In Chinese, they are: (集体劳动争议 and 调解) or (集体劳动纠纷 and 调解) or (集体劳动关系 and 调解) or (集体劳动事件 and 调解) or (集体职工争议 and 调解) or (集体职工纠纷 and 调解) or (集体职工关系 and 调解) or (集体职工事件 and 调解) or (群体劳动争议 and 调解) or (群体劳动纠纷 and 调解) or (群体劳动关系 and 调解) or (群体劳动事件 and 调解) or (群体性劳动争议 and 调解) or (群体性劳动纠纷 and 调解) or (群体性劳动关系 and 调解) or (群体性劳动事件 and 调解) or (劳动群体事件 and 调解) or (劳动群体抗议 and 调解) or (劳动群体抗争 and 调解) or (劳动群体游行 and 调解) or (劳动群体维权 and 调解) or (劳动群体停工 and 调解) or (劳动群体罢工 and 调解) or (劳动群体怠工 and 调解) or (劳动群体信访 and 调解) or (劳动群上访 and 调解) or (劳动群体走访 and 调解) or (劳动群体游行 and 调解) or (劳动群体案件 and 调解) or (职工群体事件 and 调解) or (职工群体抗议 and 调解) or (职工群体抗争 and 调解) or (职工群体游行 and 调解) or (职工群体维权 and 调解) or (职工群体停工 and 调解) or (职工群体罢工 and 调解) or (职工群体怠工 and 调解) or (职工群体信访 and 调解) or (职工群上访 and 调解) or (职工群体走访 and 调解) or (职工群体游行 and 调解) or (职工群体案件 and 调解).

(Group 2.2),[128] and with litigation (Group 2.3).[129] The last dataset concerns typical areas of labour actions where workers hold collective labour contracts and defend their labour rights collectively. Sixteen search terms are defined, including laid-off worker, rural worker, collective worker and their colloquial variants (Group 3).[130]

The search results include news reports that meet three criteria: they are published in the region of Mainland China, between 1 January 1998 and 31 December 2015, and contain at least one search term in the news headline or at least two search terms within the same paragraph in the news body text. A total of 3300 news reports are collected, containing nearly 9.5 million characters. Subsequently, a close reading is conducted on ten randomly selected news reports from each corpus group. News reports are evaluated based on their content relevance to labour actions and the number of times they mention labour actions in the text. News body text that is directly relevant is marked as highly relevant. If there are more than three mentions of labour actions in the news body text, it is marked as moderately relevant. If a news report mentions labour actions fewer than three times, it is marked as having low relevance. News reports that are irrelevant to labour actions are marked as having no relevance.

Based on the relevance test of randomly selected news reports, around ninety per cent of the news reports in Group 1.1 are highly or moderately relevant to labour actions,[131] and around sixty per cent of Group 1.2 are highly relevant to labour actions while the remaining forty per cent have moderate relevance.[132] For Group 2 on labour action settlements, about seventy per cent of the news reports are highly relevant to labour action, around twenty per cent are moderately relevant, while

[128] Search terms for Group 2.2 are the combinations of arbitration with the 42 references to labour actions that are the same as those in Group 2.1.

[129] Search terms for Group 2.3 are the combinations of litigation with the 42 references to labour actions that are the same as those in Group 2.1.

[130] Sixteen search terms for Group 3 are: (laid-off and collective dispute), or (rural worker and collective dispute), or(labour work and collective dispute), or(laid-off and collective complaint), or (rural worker and collective complaint), or(labour work and collective complaint), or(workers group and dispute), or(employees group and dispute), or(workers group and complaint), or (employees group and complaint), or(state-owned enterprise and labour dispute), or(collectively-owned enterprise and labour dispute), or (public enterprise and labour dispute), or (state-owned enterprise and labour complaint), or (collectively-owned enterprise and labour complaint), or (public enterprise and labour complaint). In Chinese, they are: (下岗+集体争议) or (农民工+集体争议) or (劳工+集体争议) or (下岗+集体纠纷) or (农民工+集体纠纷) or (劳工+集体纠纷) or (工人集体+争议) or (职工集体+争议) or (工人集体+纠纷) or (职工集体+纠纷) or (国有企业+劳动争议) or (集体企业+劳动争议) or (事业单位+劳动争议) or (国有企业+劳动纠纷) or (集体企业+劳动纠纷) or (事业单位+劳动纠纷).

[131] Group 1.1 contains 322 pages of news reports in the Microsoft-word document. The news report that appears on every 32nd page is chosen for a close reading to check its relevance to labour actions.

[132] Group 1.2 contains 1693 pages of news reports in the Microsoft-word document. The news report that appears on every 169th page is chosen for a close reading to check its relevance to labour actions.

Table 4.2 The composition of the cleaned corpus groups

Corpus group	Producer of the news				Size of news data (in characters)
	Newspaper	News journal	News agency	Web news	
1.1	319	1	23	3	537,741
1.2	520	5	55	7	1,121,157
2.1	251	1	22	5	545,133
2.2	344	1	31	6	514,033
2.3	55	0	4	2	94,685
3	450	0	4	2	5,241,017

around ten per cent are of little or no relevance.[133] For Group 3 on collective labour relations, around eighty per cent of the news reports are highly or moderately relevant to labour actions.[134] The keywords in the reports that are marked as having little or no relevance are used to search for similar texts in the entire news data. These texts are then removed from the corpus and excluded from further analysis. The cleaned data consists of 2111 news reports, totalling approximately 8.05 million characters (see Table 4.2).

The cleaned data are then processed using two software programs: Word Phraser to code the data as computer-readable units and AntConc to analyse the readable data through the chosen methods.[135] Four methods in the AntConc are used to process the coded data. Firstly, the Word-list method shows the most frequent words or terms in the chosen corpus. Secondly, the Collocate method calculates the words or terms frequently concurrent with labour actions in the chosen corpus. Thirdly, to understand typical news texts where the target term is shown, the data are processed using the Concordance method. When analysing the difference between a target corpus and a reference corpus, the data are processed using the Keyword-list method.

Two types of the AntConc results are not analysed. First, the results of meaningless structural particles will not be reported, such as: and (和), de (的), in/on/at (在), be (是), with (有/与), le (了), for (为), will/would/must/should (要), yi (以), ge (个), as for (对), amidst (中), above (上) and negativity (不). Second, the results of incomplete words that can be read differently, such as cai (裁), zhang (障), and fu (服), and ambiguous words that do not present a clear meaning, such as ren (人), work (工作), our country (我国) and per cent (百分点), will not be reported and marked with "/" in the result list.

[133] Group 2 contains 1245 pages of news reports in the Microsoft-word document. The news report that appears on every 124th page is chosen for a close reading to check its relevance to labour actions.

[134] Group 3 contains 4815 pages of news reports in the Microsoft-word document. The news report that appears on every 481st page is chosen for a close reading to check its relevance to labour actions.

[135] For more detail of the computational methods employed in this study, please refer to "1.4.2. On Analytical Methods" in Chap. 1.

4.2.2 Chinese News on Labour Actions: Favouring a Victim Narrative

As discussed in the first section, the increase and spread of labour actions in China are a result of the structural reform of the Chinese labour management system. The dismantling of the 'iron rice bowl' labour management mechanism resulted in tens of millions of Chinese workers becoming unemployed. The Chinese government promoted the idea of a market-oriented mentality, which framed workers who complained about losing their permanent jobs as being dependent on government planning and unwilling to value their competence in the job market.[136] The narrative that blames labour complainants for holding outdated employment expectations has been controversial. Even the official news agency Xinhua advised against using the phrase 'deluded or misled workers' when reporting on labour actions, which is inappropriate in suggesting that workers are ignorant and empty-headed.[137]

In light of different narratives about labour actions in Chinese news, this part examines whether the leading framing underlying these news narratives is critical of labour complainants, or critical of employers and the government. To start with popular vocabulary, the news mostly uses neutral vocabulary, including 'society', 'development', 'company', 'labour union' and 'work unit'.[138] This result does not imply a negative or critical association with labour actions or those who file labour complaints. To further explore the news, the analysis defines 'collective' and 'mass/group' as the target terms, assuming that the collective form of labour complaints would have an impact on the news framing.

The assumption that news narratives that contain the terms of collective or mass/group are more likely to be critical of labour actions is not supported by the results generated in AntConc. The most concurrent words with collective and mass/group, such as 'company', 'negotiation', 'salary', 'labour union', 'regulation', 'arbitration', and 'society' are neutral and do not indicate any particular judgement or sentiment.[139] On the other hand, it is worth noting that the terms 'problem' and 'contradiction/conflict' also appear frequently, albeit with a lower ranking, in the result lists.[140] At this point, it is unclear in which context the news reports use the terms 'problem' and 'conflict' in narrating labour actions.

With that question, the analysis then proceeds to the Concordance method and closely examines the results where the target term 'collective' and its synonyms are

---

[136] Lee (1998), p. 17.

[137] Xinhua News (28 July 2009b).

[138] Please refer to Table 4.4 in the Appendix: Top Twenty Popular Vocabularies in Groups 1, 1.1 and 1.2.

[139] Please refer to Table 4.5 in the Appendix: Top Twenty Popular Vocabularies Collocated to 'Collective/Mass'" in Groups 1.1 and 1.2.

[140] Ibid.

shown.[141] In general, a victim narrative stands out. The terms 'adverse', 'vulnerable', 'misfortune' and 'poor' are frequently used in the news reports, and workers who make collective claims or take part in labour actions are often described as economically vulnerable and socially disadvantaged (samples 1, 3, 4, 5, 7, 8, 9 and 10). For instance, in sample 10, delayed or denied payment is narrated as a shameless violation of workers' labour rights, and a trigger for workers' collective dissatisfaction.

When explaining the expansion of labour actions, the news reports often portray labour complainants as being unfairly treated and describe the infringement of their labour rights and interests (samples 1, 2, 7, 9 and 10) as the cause for them to take collective action. In sample 2, for example, workers are narrated as key players in reviving the Chinese market economy, yet they have restricted access to dividends of the country's economic achievement. In contrast, the narrative that blames labour actions for interrupting social stability and describes the government's preventive measures as necessary is only occasionally present (sample 6).

In summary, Chinese news coverage of labour actions typically uses neutral terms in its descriptions and often presents a victim narrative that is sympathetic to labour complainants when explaining the expansion of labour actions. The recurring victim narrative portrays labour complainants as being unfairly treated by their employers and as being restricted from enjoying the economic and social achievements that correspond to their contribution to the Chinese economy and society.

4.2.3 Chinese News on Settling Labour Actions: Little Relevance to Legal Rules

The extensive use of mediation to resolve labour disputes has raised concerns about the observance of procedural voluntariness and equality principles. This part looks into the recurring news narratives and framings of various labour action settlements, with a focus on the role of legal principles of voluntariness and equality in these narratives and framings. To start with, the news on labour dispute mediation and arbitration is substantially more frequent than that on labour dispute litigation: the size of each of the former two corpus groups is over five times larger than the latter.[142] This suggests that mediation and arbitration settlements are more prevalent than litigation in Chinese news reports.

The analysis then examines the contents of news reports on mediation and arbitration settlements. On the whole, these reports tend to emphasise procedural efficiency and minimal impact on social stability when describing and evaluating

[141] Please refer to List 1 in the Appendix: Original Sources of the Ten Randomly Selected Samples Where 'Collective/Group/Mass' Occurs in the Context of Group 1.

[142] Please refer to Table 4.2 "Composition of the Cleaned Corpus Groups" in Sect. 4.2.1 above.

labour action settlements.[143] The news narrative regarding labour dispute mediation settlements (samples 1, 4, 6, 7, 9 and 10) focuses on the quick resolution of collective labour disputes and the alleviation of collective labour discontent. The news describes the speediness and flexibility of mediation as helpful to the work of labour dispute arbitration committees and courts in concluding labour actions (samples 3, 4, 6, 7, and 10), in accordance with this efficiency-focused narrative.

Chinese news often presents government-directed mediation as a reasonable and effective method for resolving labour disputes and ensuring compliance by both workers and employers parties (samples 3 and 5). On the other hand, news reports sometimes expose the vulnerability of labour complainants who feel pressured to accept settlements proposed by their employers due to their desperate need for money (sample 2).[144] In brief, the coverage of mediation settlements usually focuses on procedural efficiency and occasionally highlights the compromised voluntariness of labour complainants during the mediation settlement process.

The Chinese news on arbitration settlements focuses on procedural efficiency as well, and their impact on lessening collective confrontation of labour complainants. Specifically, the news narrative describes whether labour dispute arbitrators, using their legal knowledge and mediation skills, help to alleviate workers' discontent (samples 4, 8 and 9) and dissolve labour actions (samples 1, 2 and 3). The news narrates the arbitration settlement as successful when it meets policy objectives, such as preventing labour complainants from becoming contentious and maintaining their trust in labour dispute resolution venues (samples 6 and 10). To a lesser degree, the news highlights the weak enforcement of arbitration settlements, with employers failing to comply with arbitral decisions (sample 5), and the high arbitration costs that labour complainants find too burdensome (sample 7).[145] There is no mention of the protection of labour rights for labour complainants or the observance of legal rules during the arbitration settlement process.

As to the distinction between the news on mediation settlements and the news on arbitration settlements, relevant news reports are processed using the Keyword-list method. The results show that Chinese news on arbitration settlements more frequently mentions the terms 'fee', 'rural workers' and 'legal aid' than the news on mediation. The news often portrays labour dispute arbitration as a costly procedure, as evidenced by the frequent use of terms such as 'arbitration fee', 'registration fee' and 'investigation fee' (which was an officially recognised issue with labour dispute arbitration settlement prior to 2008).[146]

---

[143] Please refer to List 2 in the Appendix: Original Sources of Ten Randomly Selected Samples Where 'Mediation' Occurs in the Context of Group 2.1.

[144] Please refer to List 2 in the Appendix: Original Sources of Ten Randomly Selected Samples Where 'Mediation' Occurs in the Context of Group 2.1.

[145] Please refer to List 3 in the Appendix: Original Sources of Ten Randomly Selected Samples Where 'Arbitration' Occurs in the Context of Group 2.2.

[146] Please refer to Table 4.6 in the Appendix: The Unusually Popular Vocabularies in Groups 2.1 and 2.2 by Comparison.

Lastly, Chinese news coverage tends to be critical of court settlements of labour actions, as evidenced by the randomly selected news reports.[147] The narrative focus is on the court's strict admissibility and limited hearing capacity, as well as the relatively high cost of initiating a labour lawsuit (samples 1, 3 and 8). The news narrative frequently highlights two problems with labour litigation procedures. The first issue is caused by unscrupulous labour lawyers who exploit court procedures, leading to lengthy labour action settlements (samples 4, 7 and 9). The second issue concerns the inadequate enforcement of court decisions that support the claims of labour complainants (sample 10). The news on court settlements does not mention the contents of applicable law or the court's reasoning and decision. The only news narrative relevant to the labour protection law describes the legal service department at the court that explains the contents of labour dispute resolution rules to labour complainants and directs them to mediation or arbitration venues (samples 5 and 6).

In summary, Chinese news coverage of labour dispute resolution procedures primarily focuses on procedural efficiency in concluding labour actions, followed by their contribution to restoring harmonious relations between workers and employers. Mediation and arbitration settlements are portrayed more positively in the news compared to court settlements, which are generally criticised. Labour protection legal rules are not commonly mentioned in the recurring news narratives about any of the settlement procedures.

4.2.4 *Chinese News on Collective Labour Relations: A Rising Equality Narrative*

During China's labour management reform, labour actions have occurred to complain about the misconduct of employers and weak supervision of the government. The Chinese government has strengthened its regulation of collective labour relations in the hope of reducing factors that could provoke collective labour unrest. The Chinese Labour Contract Law, in particular, which came into force on 1 January 2008, establishes the collective labour contract instrument and stipulates that the wage standard, vacation days and holiday pay, and social benefits concluded in individual labour contracts cannot be lower than those concluded in the collective labour contract.[148]

In this light, this part examines whether legislative developments have an impact on changing social norms by processing Chinese news reports on collective labour relations using the Keyword-list method. A comparison is made between news reports produced before and after 1 January 2008.[149] The more recent news mentions

[147] Please refer to List 4 in the Appendix: Original Sources of Ten Randomly Selected Samples Where 'Litigation' Occurs in the Context of Group 2.3.

[148] Articles 51–54, in the Chinese Labour Contract Law.

[149] Please refer to Table 4.7 in the Appendix: Composition of the Divided News Data in Group 3.

'new generation' and 'equality' more frequently than the earlier news.[150] In the context of labour relations in China, the term 'new generation' refers to young workers born in the 1980s and 1990s, who are better educated and more familiar with online communication tools than the older generation. In 2018, the majority of China's workforce was composed of the new generation of workers, who accounted for 51.5 per cent of all rural workers.[151] Young workers are less likely to tolerate unfair treatment in the workplace and are more assertive in defending their labour rights and interests than older workers.[152] Recent news narratives often highlight young workers' awareness of the legal protection of labour rights and their willingness to seek it when necessary.

Besides the increased attention to legal awareness and activeness, the more recent news narrative of labour actions is also more focused on labour equality than the earlier news.[153] Specifically, the recurring narrative advocates for equal treatment of rural workers, ensuring they have access to the benefits of China's economic growth, social advancement and legal development (samples 1, 3, 6 and 7). Additionally, the narrative calls for equal treatment in the labour market and dispute resolution forums for handling labour complaints (samples 4, 5, 8 and 10). In line with the focus on labour equality, recent news reports portray it as the legal duty of employers to treat rural workers equally when concluding employment contracts, with legal sanctions for failing to do so (samples 2 and 9). In short, Chinese news coverage of collective labour relations is increasingly focused on legal awareness and equal treatment of workers, particularly rural workers.

Chinese news about employment contracts increasingly emphasises their legal significance in defending workers' rights in the event of labour disputes.[154] Specifically, the recurrent news narrative introduces employment contracts as a necessary foundation for legally safeguarding workers' labour rights and interests (samples 3, 4 and 9). The recurrent news narrative explains the delay or refusal to pay workers their wages as a typical violation of the employment contract, and when it happens, labour complainants need to be able to present the employment contract in seeking redress (samples 1, 5, 7 and 9). The news often frames labour actions as a result of the dispute over the fulfilment of the employment contract (samples 1, 2, 5, 6 and 10). The blame narrative targets the employers who fail to sign or comply with the employment contract, describing them as responsible for labour unrest (samples 7 and 8). Employers who fail to pay workers on time are also criticized in the news as

---

[150] Please refer to Table 4.8 in the Appendix: The Unusually Popular Terms in Group 3.1 and 3.2 by Comparison.

[151] Monitor Report on Rural Workers in 2018.

[152] Peilin and Feng (2011), pp. 20–22.

[153] Please refer to List 7 in the Appendix: Original Sources of Ten Randomly Selected Samples Where 'Equal' Occurs in the Context of Group 3.2.

[154] Please refer to List 5 in the Appendix: Original Sources of Ten Randomly Selected Samples Where 'Employment Contract' Occurs in the Context of Group 3.

'malicious',[155] 'outrageous',[156] and 'unreasonable'.[157] In summary, recurrent news narratives tend to be critical of the employers who do not fulfil their duties as concluded in the employment contract and focus on the legal role of the employment contract in narrating the cause for labour actions.

Lastly, Chinese news coverage of labour unions generally focuses on how they assist the government in mitigating collective labour conflicts.[158] In particular, the recurring news narrative highlights the monitoring role that labour unions play in identifying the causes of labour discontent and advising both the enterprise and the government on how to effectively detect collective labour complaints (samples 1, 3, 4, and 7). The news portrays the unions' close communication with the government as normal and necessary to facilitate the government's economic development and labour management policies (samples 2, 5 and 6). Less frequently, the news describes the services labour unions provide in non-confrontational situations, such as training and preparing the unemployed for job search (sample 10) and advising workers in collective labour bargaining with the employer (samples 8 and 9). Overall, the Chinese news coverage of labour unions focuses more on their work in implementing government policies than on protecting the labour rights of complainants, which differs from the recurrent news narratives about collective labour relations and employment contracts that are largely sympathetic to labour complainants.

4.2.5 A Legal Account of Labour Actions in the News? Not Quite

This section has examined in detail Chinese news narratives and framings regarding labour actions and their resolutions, and the significance of labour protection legal rules in the news. A substantial dataset of 2111 news reports, comprising over eight million characters, has been meticulously processed and analysed. The analytical focus is first on recurring news narratives about labour actions and their synonyms, then labour dispute mediation, arbitration and court settlements, and lastly, collective labour relations, employment contracts and trade unions.

Chinese news coverage of labour disputes tends to emphasise the efficiency of settlement processes and the restoration of harmonious labour relations, rather than whether such settlements comply with labour protection laws or satisfy complainants. Nonetheless, news reports often portray labour complainants sympathetically,

---

[155] Southern Weekly (13 November 2003); Legal Daily (7 December 2003).

[156] South China Morning Post (4 October 2004); Caixin News Weekly (4 July 2011).

[157] Shenzhen Economic Daily (21 October 2008); Daily Sunshine (19 June 2012); Southern Daily (20 December 2013).

[158] Please refer to List 6 in the Appendix: Original Sources of Ten Randomly Selected Samples Where 'Labour union' Occurs in the Context of Group 3.

Table 4.3 The summary of Chinese news on labour actions and their settlements

Corpus group	Narrative foci	Recurrent narratives
On labour actions	Sufferings and claims of labour complainants; Various misconducts of employers.	Labour complainants are vulnerable and understandable, and complained employers are blameable.
On labour action settlements	Mediation and arbitration settlements; Efficiency of labour action settlement; Harmonious labour relations.	Whether the labour action settlement is efficient and contributes to normalising the harmony of labour relations.
On collective labour relations	Equal treatment of rural workers; Legal significance of the employment contracts; Economic growth and uninterrupted production.	Rural workers are not equally treated; The employment contract is necessary for seeking legal protection; Labour unions monitor the workplace factors that can lead to collective discontent and mitigate labour unrest.

depicting them as victims of unfair treatment by employers and as the root cause of labour unrest. In recent years, news coverage has increasingly highlighted the growing legal awareness of workers and the importance of equal treatment of workers in its narratives (see Table 4.3).

The findings presented above may come as a surprise to those who browse the existing research literature on labour actions in China. With diverse portrayals of labour complainants and labour action settlements in Chinese news coverage, there is a recurring sympathetic narrative that emphasises legal protection and equal treatment as key factors in understanding labour actions and assessing their outcomes. However, it is important to note that the leading news framing is not based on legal rules for labour protection, but rather on policy considerations for economic and social stabilities. As a result, Chinese news has not developed a legally relevant framing that qualifies labour actions as a means to redress the violation of workers' rights, nor evaluates settlements of labour actions based on applicable legal protection rules.

4.3 Conclusion: Rising Importance of Labour Protection Law and Limitations

This chapter has offered a comprehensive and nuanced analysis of the legislative, institutional and social aspects surrounding Chinese practices for managing labour disputes, with a specific focus on collective labour disputes. The discussion begins by exploring the institutional context of China's labour management reforms in the 1980s and 1990s, during which the country adopted labour protection legal rules and shifted labour relations from being based on government commands to being based on legally concluded employment contracts. Subsequently, it delves into the question of whether labour protection law is commonly understood as a fundamental and essential component of managing labour relations and resolving labour disputes.

China has implemented a tripartite mechanism to address the growing number of labour complaints, consisting of mediation, arbitration, and litigation procedures. This mechanism seeks to provide workers with appropriate remedies to address violations of their labour rights and interests. While labour dispute mediation plays a significant role in reducing delays in arbitration and litigation procedures and promoting harmonious labour relations, concerns have been raised about compliance with legally mandated principles of voluntary participation and equal consultation during the mediation settlement process. Furthermore, labour dispute resolution venues must strike a balance between promoting economic growth and maintaining social stability while upholding the legal obligation to hear allegations of labour rights violations and formulate settlements. Unfortunately, when these violations result from flawed government decisions, there is often a lack of external review procedures in place for affected workers to seek compensation for the harm caused by inappropriate policies. As a result, the focus of labour dispute resolution venues may not always be on protecting labour rights, which ultimately impedes the institutionalisation of Chinese labour protection rules in settlements of labour actions.

After conducting careful legal and institutional analyses, this chapter delves into a vast dataset of more than eight million Chinese characters of news reports related to labour actions and their settlements. The findings reveal a lack of legally grounded framing in Chinese news when it comes to narrating labour actions and evaluating their outcomes. Although news stories tend to show sympathy towards labour complainants and advocate for more legal protection and fair treatment of workers, they often prioritise the procedural efficiency of labour action settlements and their role in promoting workplace harmony for economic growth. Additionally, news coverage of labour unions and collective labour bargaining tends to be government-centric, with a focus on their role in facilitating government policies rather than assisting labour complainants in seeking proper redress for violations of their labour rights. In conclusion, labour protection laws and relevant legal regulations have not become a basic ground for assessing the normalcy of labour actions and their resolutions.

In summary, this chapter provides a detailed examination of Chinese rules and measures for addressing labour actions, including their contexts and characteristics, outcomes and limitations. By employing automated content analysis techniques to process extensive sets of news data, it presents a deeper comprehension of how labour protection laws are communicated from the Chinese legislature to the public. These findings have significant policy implications, such as the necessity to ensure that labour complainants can participate voluntarily and equally in the labour dispute mediation settlement process and that the public may react unfavourably to harsh government responses to labour actions. There is also potential for future research to investigate whether common narratives that sympathise with labour complainants are positively associated with changes in the number and form of labour actions and whether narratives that promote equal treatment and legal protection are positively associated with changes in the expectations of labour complainants regarding preferred settlements. Overall, this case study underscores the increasing importance of labour protection law in Chinese measures to resolve labour disputes in general and labour actions in particular, while acknowledging the conflicting impact of political norms on the institutionalisation and socialisation of these labour protection rules.

Appendix

Table 4.4 Top twenty popular vocabularies in Groups 1, 1.1 and 1.2

Group 1		Group 1.1		Group 1.2	
Frequency	Word	Frequency	Word	Frequency	Word
11,722	Company	3057	Employee	9559	Company
10,248	/	2163	Company	8992	/
8326	Employee	1885	Labour union	6267	/
7284	/	1256	/	6264	/
7162	/	1017	/	6041	Labour disputes
6265	Labour disputes	1010	/	5269	Employee
5543	Labour union	951	*Society*	4006	/
4847	/	898	/	3927	Arbitration
4797	*Society*	783	Relation	3846	*Society*
4422	Relation	739	/	3837	/
4101	*Development*	708	/	3808	Case
4100	/	649	/	3658	Labour union
4044	/	642	*Development*	3639	/
4003	Arbitration	636	Salary	3465	*Development*
3902	Work unit	608	/	3336	/
3884	Case	603	Work unit	3299	Work unit
3805	/	585	Employment	3258	/
3566	/	585	/	3099	Mediation
3278	Workers	556	Economy	3090	Workers
3244	Mediation	547	/	3055	/

Table 4.5 Top twenty popular vocabularies collocated to ‘Collective/Mass’ in Groups 1.1 and 1.2

Collective (*jiti*/集体)		Mass/group (*qunti xing*/群体)	
Frequency	Collocate	Frequency	Collocate
1964	Labour disputes	761	Labour disputes
1791	Company	584	Incident
1730	Negotiation	476	Labour
1570	Salary	439	Employee
1330	/	411	Case
1124	Labour	335	Dissension
1002	/	334	/
917	Case	313	Company
848	Employee	304	/
584	Labour union	259	/
569	Regulation	233	/
496	Arbitration	208	/
495	/	205	Relation
486	/	174	/
475	Relation	166	/
468	/	160	Society
456	/	158	Problem
431	/	158	Mediation
391	/	145	Collective
383	/	145	Contradiction

List 1: Original Sources of Ten Randomly Selected Samples Where ‘Collective/Group/Mass’ Occurs in the Context of Group 1

384 KWIC results are produced in Group 1 with the search term defined as ‘collective or group or mass’ and search window size defined as ‘100’. Ten samples are selected in accordance with the ‘random selection’ procedure in Microsoft Excel. The original source of each selected news sample is listed below:

1. 《尉健行与政协社会福利界和工会界委员座谈并强调建立健全调整劳动关系有效机制努力为职工群众困难群体办实事》, 《人民日报》, 2002年3月5日, 02版。
2. 《劳资矛盾忧患:忽略农民工的权益保护》, 《中国新闻社》, 2002 年7月20日, 13-16版。
3. 《国家基本公共服务体系 “十二五” 规划》, 《经济日报》, 2012年12月13日, 08版。
4. 《三大诱因成群体诉讼“导火索” 法官审案遇四难题》, 《中国新闻社》, 2009年5月6日, 国内新闻。
5. 《为职工免费配备“私人律师”值得推广》, 《西部商报》, 2015年1月12日, A03版。
6. 《雁塔建立劳动关系预警机制》, 《西安日报》, 2003年11月16日, 02版。
7. 《企建立健全有效机制 努力为职工办实事时间》, 《浙江日报》, 2002年3月5日, 国内新闻版。

8. 《2010:成果骄2011:民生为本》,《深圳特区报》, 2011年1月22日, A07版。
9. 《清障把关收尾唱好解除终止劳动合同"三步曲"》, 《中国劳动保障报》, 2002年3月12日, 法律服务版。
10. 《全总将重点监测 企业破产和裁员》, 《北京青年报》, 2010年9月3日, A09版。

List 2: Original Sources of Ten Randomly Selected Samples Where 'Mediation' Occurs in the Context of Group 2.1

2199 KWIC results are produced in Group 2.1 with the search term defined as 'mediation' and the search window size defined as '100'. Ten samples are selected in accordance with the 'random selection' procedure in Microsoft Excel. The source of each selected news sample is listed below.

1. 《劳动争议仲裁有时效劝君莫错过时机》,《西安晚报》, 2001-03-15, 报章
2. 《劳动争议案近5年高发维权成本令劳动者难以承受》, 《法制晚报》, 2013-01-10, 报章 | A51
3. 《南京工会特邀调解员明年上岗》,《浙江日报》, 2005-12-06, 报章
4. 《构建和谐的劳动关系》,《河南日报》, 2004-11-19, 报章 | 05 | 理论
5. 《职工维权亟须 "补课" 》,《四川日报》, 2002-08-30, 报章 | 视点新闻
6. 《前三季劳动争议逾7成调解解决》,《新闻晨报》, 2004-10-27, 报章 | 19 | 上海·民生
7. 《组建调解委员会, 规定调解和审案期限劳动纠纷有望不再打 "持久战" 》于《春城晚报》, 2008-10-10, 报章 | B03 | 滇中四城·社会
8. 《劳动争议仲裁五一提速》,《深圳商报》, 2008-04-28, 报章 | B01 | 都市新闻
9. 《加强仲裁机构队伍建设优先受理群体争议》, 《中国劳动保障报》, 2001-11-27, 报章 | 要闻
10. 《"大调解"促进社会大和谐》,《深圳特区报》, 2009-03-09, 报章 | A07 | 综合要闻

List 3: Original Sources of Ten Randomly Selected Samples Where 'Arbitration' Occurs in the Context of Group 2.2

2683 KWIC results are produced in Group 2.2 with the search term defined as 'arbitration' and the search window size defined as '100'. Ten samples are selected in accordance with the 'random selection' procedure in Microsoft Excel. The source of each selected news sample is listed below:

1. 《劳动争议案件结案率达到97% 南京劳动争议仲裁作用日益加强》, 江南时报 | 2007-01-04报章 | 15 | 江苏·各地 |
2. 《江西省劳动争议处理实施办法》(征求意见稿), 江西日报 | 2004-07-19报章 | B02 | 文件 |
3. 《构建多级调解网络快速有效化解争议纠纷》, 深圳特区报 | 2009-05-08报章 | A10 | 特别报道 |
4. 《服务和谐社会建设完善劳动争议仲裁体系》, 中国劳动保障报 | 2007-02-06报章 |
5. 《是诈骗还是劳动纠纷》, 中国商报 | 2002-01-29报章 | 商报商务/商事 | By 袁贵远

Table 4.6 The unusually popular vocabularies in Groups 2.1 and 2.2 by comparison

News on arbitration as target		News on mediation as target	
Keyness	Keyword	Keyness	Keyword
534.622	Arbitrate	191.764	Mediate
516.832	/	137.124	/
127.369	/	107.791	*Judge*
124.425	Chu jianxing	106.205	Airlines
121.631	*Fee*	96.451	*Judicial*
71.509	*Rural worker*	96.141	*Court*
70.732	/	94.131	Water supply
70.106	Accept	93.771	Labour union
64.209	/	73.444	Privately owned
58.695	*Legal aid*	69.395	Japan

6. 《员工边讨欠薪边说老板不容易理性妥协之后181万元欠薪案提前78天结案》, 广州日报 | 2008-03-19报章 | A22 | 拍案惊奇 | By 蒋悦飞
7. 《"天价仲裁费用"折射劳动者维权困境》, 江南时报 | 2008-01-23报章 | 04 | 时报观点 | By 杨涛
8. 《3328宗劳动争议案无一错案》, 南方日报(全国版) | 2007-04-03报章 | C10 | 龙岗视窗·专题 | 蛤2006年数字解读
9. 《昨起正式启动 企业减员周报制》, 南方日报(全国版) | 2008-11-20报章 | C01| 佛山观察| By 刘三琴
10. 《罗湖首创"两横一纵"联动调解模式》, 深圳特区报 | 2010-06-30报章 | A09 | 深圳新闻

List 4: Original Sources of Ten Randomly Selected Samples Where 'Litigation' Occurs in the Context of Group 2.3

288 KWIC results are produced in Group 2.3 with the search term defined as 'litigation' and the search window size defined as '100'. Ten samples are selected in accordance with the 'random selection' procedure in Microsoft Excel. The source of each selected news sample is listed below:

1. 《新法出台, 劳动争议案件激增 劳动关系协调员出现人才荒》, 《南方日报(全国版)》, 2008-03-05, 报章 | B08 | 人才周刊
2. 《新型劳动纠纷考验执法智慧》, 《楚天金报》, 2010-01-13, 报章 | 32 | 冰点焦点
3. 《公民代理人深陷争议:维权斗士还是"讼棍"》, 中国新闻社, 2012-03-14, 通讯社
4. 《"维权斗士"还是"诉讼掮客"?》, 《南方日报(中山版) 》, 2012-01-17, 报章 | AC03 | 中山观察
5. 《法院开启民工维权"阳光通道》, 《无锡日报》, 2007-12-15, 报章 | 综合新闻
6. 《打官司, 法官叫我们推代表有依据吗?》, 《四川工人日报(网络版) 》, 2009-05-04, 报章 | 03 | 专题·维权
7. 《让仲裁成为劳动者的制度福利》, 《新京报》, 2007-08-28, 报章 | A02 | 社论·来信

8. 《有效化解劳动争议 构建和谐劳动关系》,《青岛日报》, 2009-12-12, 报章 I 05 I 理论周刊
9. 《群体诉讼逐年递减恶意诉讼日趋严重》,《广州日报》, 2014-06-11, 报章 I A16 I 身边纸·关注
10. 《法院支持政府撑腰海珠仲裁执行不难》,《中国劳动保障报》, 2003-09-16, 报章 I 01 I 要闻 I 综合信息/社会

List 5: Original Sources of Ten Randomly Selected Samples Where 'Employment Contract' Occurs in the Context of Group 3

3683 KWIC results are produced in Group 3 with the search term defined as 'employment contract' and search window size defined as '100'. Ten samples are selected in accordance with the 'random selection' procedure in Microsoft Excel. The source of each selected news sample is listed below:

1. 《劳动争议案五大现象令人关注》, 钱江晚报 I 2005-07-05报章 I
2. 《关注大学生就业 为领文凭 "突击就业" 调查 就业协议 "换回" 学位证》, 北京娱乐信报 I 2006-08-14报章
3. 《新劳动法实施后新型案件激增双倍工资索赔居首》, 中国新闻社 I 2008-04-04通讯社 I 社会新闻 I
4. 《预计新类型劳动争议将猛增》, 晶报 I 2011-12-21报章 I A15 I 深圳市情I By 吴欣
5. 《全市劳动争议案明显增加用人单位败多胜少》, 兰州日报 I 2001-07-22报章 I
6. 《企业构建和谐劳动关系的实践与思考》, 中国商贸 I 2013-08-01杂志 I 32-35 I 管理研究 I By 杨诗华
7. 《保护劳动者权益共建共享和谐社会———实施《劳动合同法》《就业促进法》述评》, 广西日报 I 2008-01-26报章 I 01 I 要闻 I By 廖庆凌 陈仕平
8. 《华为 "辞职门" 引热议新法考验企业智慧》, 中国工业报 I 2007-11-14报章 I A03 I 企业. 管理 I
9. 《企业明知会败诉仍拖延劳动者拒签合同还索赔》, 羊城晚报(全国版) I 2014-06-11报章 I A03 I 焦点 I
10. 《提升政务能力 服务改善民生 促进区域发展》, 北京日报 I 2014-01-07报章 I 04 I 专版

List 6: Original Sources of Ten Randomly Selected Samples Where 'Labour Union' Occurs in the Context of Group 3

4263 KWIC results are produced in Group 3 with the search term defined as 'labour union' and search window size defined as '100'. Ten samples are selected in accordance with the 'random selection' procedure in Microsoft Excel. The source of each selected news sample is listed below:

1. 《全总"攻关"下的外企困惑》, 中国经营报, 2006年10月23日, 要闻版.
2. 《维权:新的目标、新的境界》, 四川工人日报(网络版) I 2009-08-27报章 I 01 I 要闻 I.
3. 《广东省总工会积极贯彻落实十八大精神 全面推进"四个一万"工程》, 南方日报(全国版) I 2013-01-08报章 I A05 I 专题I By 黄应来 姚文军.

4. 《从机制上确保劳动关系和谐稳定全市劳动合同签订率近九成》, 汕头日报|2006-10-19报章|01 |.
5. 《工会系统以维护农民工合法权益为切入点, 参与流动人口管理, 落实平安建设》, 法制日报 | 2008-04-14报章 | 03.
6. 《关注劳动报酬与资本收益的失衡》, 中国经济时报 | 2005-12-22报章 | 05 | 新视点 | 大势观察 | By 宋晓梧.
7. 《全总就进一步加强工会劳动争议处理工作出台意见》, 中国新闻社|2008-07-15通讯社|国内新闻|.
8. 《工会开热线温暖万人心》, 辽宁日报 | 2002-11-26报章 | 星期二焦点新闻
9. 《广州立法规范劳动三方协商系国内首次, 相关规定将于明年颁布实施》, 南方都市报(全国版) | 2011-10-29报章 | A11 | 城事 | By 吴渤 刘文慧 史功汇
10. 《三年解决一百五十万》, 三秦都市报 | 2002-11-12报章 | TMP7

List 7: Original Sources of Ten Randomly Selected Samples Where 'Equal' Occurs in the Context of Group 3.2

166 KWIC results are produced in Group 3.2 with the search term defined as 'equal' and the search window size defined as '100'. Ten samples are selected in accordance with the 'random selection' procedure in Microsoft Excel. The source of each selected news sample is listed below:

1. 《政府工作报告》, 中国经济导报, 2008年3月20日, B01-03版.
2. 《确保春节前农民工工资无拖欠》, 羊城晚报(全国版) | 2011-12-31报章 | A04 | 政闻 |.

Table 4.7 Composition of the divided news data in Group 3

Corpus group	Producer of the news				Size (in characters)
	Newspaper	Magazine	News agency	Web news	
3.1	186	0	0	2	2,608,589
3.2	264	0	4	0	2,632,428

Table 4.8 The unusually popular terms in Groups 3.1 and 3.2 by comparison

Early news (1998–2007) as target		Recent news (2008–2015) as target	
Keyness	Word	Keyness	Word
2044.024	Labour	3238.258	Capital
1424.653	/	3124.957	/
1367.004	Labour union	2807.002	/
1128.604	/	1908.533	/
996.830	Company	1903.760	/
991.404	Society	1875.194	Equality
903.076	/	1641.607	New generation
849.633	Labour contracts	1641.458	Company
703.561	/	1598.907	/
662.347	Case	1520.638	/

3. 《劳资关系转型 关乎中国崛起》, 民营经济报 | 2011-04-29报章 | T12 | 阳光五月 |.
4. 《<湖北省企业工会条例>12月1日正式施行》, 湖北日报 | 2010-11-30报章 | 10 | 专版 |.
5. 《劳务派遣能否真正同工同酬》, 深圳商报 | 2013-08-22报章 | A06 | 要闻·综合 |.
6. 《劳动关系不稳定诱发争议》, 今晚报 | 2014-04-29 报章 | 12 | 警法新闻 |.
7. 《降低公务员热还要思考其他职业之冷南方日报(全国版) | 2009-10-28报章 | 封二 | 评论| By 陈聪.
8. 《工资集体协商之争》, 《中国经营报 | 2010-12-27报章 | 18 | 新闻 |.
9. 《深圳普遍实行"信访代诉制" 90%问题解决在基层》, 中国新闻社 | 2010-11-30通讯社|国内新闻|.
10. 《劳动仲裁当事人可查阅案卷》, 信息日报 | 2009-01-16报章 | 11 | 权威发布| By 王欢.

References

Aiyun W (2011) Job transfer to children in the history of the People's Republic of China (试析中华人民共和国历史上的子女顶替就业制度). CPC Hist Stud 12. Available at: https://www.aisixiang.com/data/122186.html

Article 276, in Criminal Law of the People's Republic of China, amended 25 February 2011. Available at: http://www.mohrss.gov.cn/SYrlzyhshbzb/rdzt/gznmgqxwt/zcfg/201906/t20190601_318995.html

Article 3, in the Labour Law of the People's Republic of China, adopted at the Eighth National People's Congress on 5 July 1994 and effective as of 1 January 1995, amended at the 7th session of the 13th National People's Congress on 29 December 2018. Available at: http://www.npc.gov.cn/zgrdw/npc/xinwen/2019-01/07/content_2070261.htm

Article 4, in the Interim Regulation for Implementing Labour Union's Role of Assisting with Resolving Labour Disputes, adopted in 1995 by the All-China Federation of Labour Unions. Available at: http://law.lawtime.cn/d628856633950.html

Article 5, in the Interim Regulations on Recruiting Workers at the State-Owned Enterprises, adopted by the State Council on 12 July 1986. https://www.gov.cn/gongbao/shuju/1986/gwyb198625.pdf. Accessed 3 May 2017

Article 7 and Article 34, in the Provisions on the Negotiation and Mediation of Enterprise Labour Disputes. Issued by the Chinese Ministry of Human Resources and Social Security on 30 November 2011. Available at: http://www.gov.cn/flfg/2011-12/05/content_2010833.htm

Article 7, in the Interim Regulation on Resolving Labour Disputes within the State-Owned Enterprises

Article 7 of the amendment to Article 15 of the Chinese Constitution, states that "The State shall adopt a planned economy based on socialist public ownership. It shall ensure the proportional and coordinated growth of the national economy through the overall balance of economic planning and the complementary regulatory role of the market", adopted at the First Session of the Seventh National People's Congress on 29 March 1993. Available at: www.gov.mo/en/content/laws/constitutional-documents/constitution-of-prc-amendment-1993/

Articles 1, 10, 15, 91, 92 and 93, in the Constitution of the People's Republic of China, adopted at the First Session of the First National People's Congress on 20 September 1954. Available at: web.archive.org/web/20160628133639/http://e-chaupak.net/database/chicon/1954/1954bilingual.htm

Articles 1, 3 and 28, in the Common Program of The Chinese People's Political Consultative Conference, adopted by the Chinese People's Political Consultative Conference on 29 September 1949. Available at: http://www.cppcc.gov.cn/2011/12/16/ARTI1513309181327976.shtml

Articles 1, 3 and 79, in the Labour Law of the People's Republic of China, adopted at the Eighth National People's Congress on 5 July 1994 and effective on 1 January 1995. Available at: http://www.asianlii.org/cn/legis/cen/laws/llotproc353/

Articles 1-5, 7. 11, 15, 20, 29, 42 and 53, in the Labour Dispute Mediation and Arbitration Law of the People's Republic of China, adopted on 29 December 2007 and enforced on 1 May 2008. http://www.lawinfochina.com/display.aspx?lib=law&id=6584. Accessed 18 Oct 2016

Articles 2, 18-20, 25 and 30, in the Chinese Labour Union Law of the People's Republic of China, adopted at the 5th Session of the 7th National People's Congress and effective on 3 April 1992. Available at: https://law.pkulaw.com/chinalaw/d122aaf1594f5eaabdfb.html

Articles 2, 4-7, in the Interim Regulation on Resolving Labour Disputes within the State-Owned Enterprises, adopted by the State Council on 31 July 1987 and effective on 15 August 1987, invalidated by the passage of the Regulation on Resolving Labour Disputes at the Enterprises on 11 June 1993. Available at: https://law.pkulaw.com/chinalaw/151670.html

Articles 2 and 13, in the Regulation on Resolving Labour Disputes at the Companies, adopted by the State Council on 11 June 1993 and released by the State Council on 6 July 1993. Available at: http://www.gov.cn/ziliao/flfg/2005-08/06/content_20937.htm

Articles 2 and 3, in the Interim Regulation on Worker's Assembly at the State-Owned Enterprises, released by the State Council on 15 June 1981. Available at: www.reformdata.org/1981/0713/5627.shtml

Articles 4, 12, 15, 16 and 20, in the Labour Insurance Regulations of the People's Republic of China, adopted by the Central Government on 23 February 1951 and revised in 1953

Articles 4–6, in the Regulation on the Labour Dispute Resolution Procedure (劳动部关于劳动争议解决程序的规定), adopted by the Chinese Ministry of Labour Affairs on 16 November 1950. Available at: http://www.hljcourt.gov.cn/lawdb/show.php?fid=25&key=%D0%D0%D5%FE

Articles 6, 51-54, and 82, in the Chinese Labour Contract Law, adopted at the Tenth National People's Congress of the People's Republic of China on 29 June 2007 and effective on 1 January 2008. Available at: http://www.lawinfochina.com/display.aspx?id=6133&lib=law

Chang K, Cooke FL (2015) Legislating the right to strike in China: historical development and prospects. J Ind Relat 57(3):445–448

CHAPTER V: Substantive provisions of labour legislation: The right to strike, updated by the International Labour Organisation on 10 December 2001. Available at: https://www.ilo.org/legacy/english/dialogue/ifpdial/llg/noframes/ch5.htm

Chen X (2011) Social protest and contentious authoritarianism in China. Cambridge University Press, pp 110–112

China's State Archives Bureaus (eds) (1994) Workers' salaries and employment-related benefits in China's economic archives between 1949 and 1952 (1949年-1952年中华人民共和国经济档案资料选编(劳动工资和职工福利卷)). China Social Sciences Press, p 88

China's State Bureau for Statistics (2009) The communique on the outcomes of the national economic development plan of 1978 (关于一九七八年国民经济计划执行结果的公报) (Section Seven). Published on 27 June 1979. Available at: https://www.cnstats.org/tjgb/200912/zgzg-1978-zag.html

China's State Bureau for Statistics (2019) National records on the economic and social developments since the founding of new China (新中国成立70周年经济社会发展成就系列报告之十九) (Paragraph 2 in Section One). Published on 20 August 2019. Available at: https://www.gov.cn/xinwen/2019-08/20/content_5422616.htm

China's Youth Daily (2008) A Report on Labour Dispute Cases before the Court. Published by the on 22 April 2008 http://zqb.cyol.com/content/2010-01/19/content_3045611.htm. Accessed 10 Nov 2016

Chinese Premier's Report on the Work of the Government to the Second Session of the Twelfth National People's Congress, delivered on 5 March 2014. http://www.china.org.cn/chinese/2014-03/17/content_31806665_3.htm. Accessed 14 Nov 2016
Da C (1929) The Chinese labour problem (中国劳工问题). Commercial Press, pp 7–19
Feng C (2000) Subsistence crises, managerial corruption and labour protests in China. China J 44: 41–47
Feng C, Mengxiao T (2013) Labour conflicts in China: typologies and their implication. Asian Survey 53(3):573
Four Regulations on Labour Reforms (No. 77) (国务院关于发布改革劳动制度四个规定的通知), adopted by the State Council in 1986. http://www.gov.cn/zhengce/content/2012-09/21/content_7444.htm. Accessed 25 Nov 2016
Hongwen Y (ed) (2015) China labour statistical yearbook (中国劳动统计年鉴(2015)). China National Bureau of Statistics Press, p 347
Hurst W (2008) Mass frames and worker protest. In: O'Brien KJ (ed) Popular protest in China. Harvard University Press, pp 75 and 80
Jian Q (2007) Transition in China's labour relations and its characteristics. J China Univ Labour Relat 2:30–31
Jiemian News (2021) A generation of falling and confused workers: after losing the iron rice bowl (铁饭碗"砸碎后，一代工人的沉浮与迷茫). Published on 19 August 2021. https://m.jiemian.com/article/6485827.html
Jinglun Y, Wenjia Z (2014) On effectiveness and innovation of the grand mediation framework for resolving labour disputes in China: a perspective of state mediation capacity (国家调解能力建设:中国劳动争议"大调解"体系的有效性与创新性). Monthly J Manag World 8:72–73
Jingwen Z (ed) (2007) Report on China law development (中国法律发展报告数据库和指标体系). The Remin University Press, p 475
Kai C (2013) The transition towards collective labour relations and its implications on labour policies (劳动关系的集体化转型与政府劳工政策的完善). Soc Sci China 6:93–99
Kai C, Brown W (2013) The transition from individual to collective labour relations in China. Ind Relat J 44(2):105
Kun H (2014) Progress and outlook: refectory remarks on the 20th anniversary of the adoption of the labour law (<劳动法>颁布二十年来中国劳动立法的成就与展望). China Law 5:25
Lee CK (1998) The labour politics of market socialism: collective inaction and class experiences among state workers in Guangzhou. Mod China 24(1):17
Lee HY (2000) Xiagang, the Chinese style of laying off workers. Asian Survey 40(6):91
Lee CK (2016) Precarisation or empowerment? Reflections on recent labour unrest in China. J Asian Stud 75(02):320
Legal Daily (2017) Cases Settled by the People's Mediation Committees since the 18th CPC National Congress (十八大以来全国人民调解组织化解矛盾纠纷4600万余件，筑牢维护社会和谐稳定第一道防线). Published 29 June 2017. Available at: http://news.china.com.cn/2017-06/26/content_41098242.htm?f=pad&a=true
Lin L, He T (eds) (2014) China's legal development yearbook (No. 12, 2014) (中国法治发展报告 No.12). Social Sciences Academic Press, pp 270–288
Meng L, Fengzhou Z et al (2003) Danwei: internal mechanisms of the institutionalised system. In: Institute of Sociology of the Chinese Academy of Social Sciences (eds) Sociology of China, vol 2. Shanghai Renmin Press, pp 145–146
Menghe T (2011) The study of living costs in Peking (北平生活费之分析). Commercial Press, pp 26–27, 37–46 and 69
National Bureau of Statistics of China (2015) China Labour Statistical Yearbook of 2015 (Table 8-2: "Labour Disputes Accepted and Settled by Regions 2014). http://www.mohrss.gov.cn/SYrlzyhshbzb/zwgk/szrs/tjsj/201803/t20180302_289123.html. Accessed 8 Nov 2019
Naughton B (1996a) Growing out of the plan: Chinese economic reform, 1978-1993. Cambridge University Press, pp 26–30

Naughton B (1996b) Growing out of the plan: Chinese economic reform, 1978-1993. Cambridge University Press, p 212

Paragraph 2, in the Advisory Opinion on Strengthening the Work of People's Mediation (最高人民法院、司法部关于进一步加强新时期人民调解工作的意见). Issued by the Central Committee of the CPC and the State Council on 26 February 2002. Available at: http://www.12348.gov.cn/pub/12348/ztj/flfg/201803/t20180322_393.html

Paragraph 4, in the Advisory Opinion of the Supreme People's Court on Doing a Good Job in the Trial of Labour Dispute Cases. Issued by the Supreme Court on 6 July 2009. Available at: http://law.51labour.com/lawshow-87550.htm

Peilin L, Feng T (2011) The new generation of migrant workers: social attitudes and behavioural choices. Chin J Sociol 31(3):20–22

People's Daily (2014) A critical comment on over- emphasised goal for case withdrawals (切莫片面追求调解率撤诉率). Published on 22 January 2014. http://opinion.people.com.cn/n/2014/0122/c1003-24190158.html. Accessed 10 Nov 2016

Perry EJ (1993) Shanghai on strike: the politics of Chinese labour. Stanford University Press, pp 65–66

Perry EJ, Xiaobo L (eds) (1997) The Danwei: changing Chinese workplace in historical and comparative perspectives (in Chapter 2 "From Native Place to Workplace: Labour Origins and Outcomes of China's Danwei System"). M.E. Sharpe, Armonk, N.Y., pp 4–11 and 51–52

Qiang L et al (2001) A comparative study of laid-off and unemployed worker (失业下岗问题比较研究)s, 1st edn. Tsinghua University Press, p 66

Qingjun W (2012) On collective negotiations and government coordination in managing labour relations (集体协商与国家主导下的劳动关系治理). Sociol Stud 3:81–83

Qingjun W, Yu L (2013) Marketisation of labour relations and protection of labour rights: labour relation policies in China (劳动关系市场化与劳工权益保护——中国劳动关系政策的发展路径与策略). J Renmin Univ China 1:83

Qizhu H (2005) A study of the five-anti political campaign in 1952: an interaction among workers, capitalists and the CPC (工人、资本家与共产党——1952年"五反"运动研究). Twenty-First Century J 92:62

Rongji Z (2009) A response to the German Press on 6 May 1993 (朱镕基1993年5月6日接受德国《商报》记者柴德立兹采访). In: The Zhu Rongji Meets the Press, 1st edn. People's Publishing House

Russel B (1922) The problem of China (in its chapter XIV "Industrialism in China"). The electronic version was released on 3 November 2004. Available at: http://www.gutenberg.org/files/13940/13940-h/13940-h.htm#FNanchor_108_108. Accessed 19 Jan 2017

Section 2 Labour Dispute Arbitration Costs, in the Regulatory Rules on Charging the Labour Contract Identification Cost and Labour Dispute Arbitration Cost (劳动合同鉴证和劳动争议仲裁收费管理办法 价费字268号). Adopted by the Ministry of Finance on 10 June 1992 and effective on 1 July 1992, repealed by the passage of the Labour Dispute Mediation and Arbitration Law on 29 December 2007. Available at: http://www.nc.gov.cn/ncszf/rsjr/199210/292c804503a44f0da3e5f0b90a9044c5.shtml

Section One in the Monitor Report on Rural Workers in 2018 (2018年农民工监测调查报告)", published by the State Bureau for Statistics on 29 April 2019. Available at: http://www.stats.gov.cn/tjsj/zxfb/201904/t20190429_1662268.html

Shenzhen Economic Daily (21 October 2008) Bosses Postponed Salary Pay, Legal Aids Intervened (老板欠工薪 法律援助讨回). Daily Sunshine (19 June 2012) Equal work, but Half Pay (干同样活, 收入不到正式工一半). Southern Daily (20 December 2013) Cracking Down Wage Arrears (狠治欠薪要将 "年终关怀" 变为 "终年关怀")

Siming L, Feng C (2008) Continuity and changes: political, economic and social developments in contemporary China (持续与变迁:当代中国的政经、社会与空间发展). Hong Kong Educational Publishing Company, p 35

South China Morning Post (4 October 2004) Hidden Traps in Labour Contracts (设置合同陷阱"死伤概不负责"). Caixin News Weekly (4 July 2011) Legal Reform on Occupational Disease: Empowerment Better Than Supervision (职业病防治修法:监管不如赋权)

Southern Weekly (13 November 2003) Legal clinic empowering the powerless (法律诊所让无力者有力). Legal Daily (7 December 2003) Resorting to Law to Get Hard-earned Money Back (法律助劳动者讨回血汗钱)

Table 8-2: "Labour Disputes Accepted and Settled by Regions (2015)". In: China's National Bureau of Statistics (2016) Labour Statistical Yearbook of 2016. http://www.mohrss.gov.cn/SYrlzyhshbzb/zwgk/szrs/tjsj/201803/t20180302_289122.html

Table 9-1: "Labour Disputes Accepted and Settled between 1996 and 2004". In: China's Labour Statistical Yearbook of 2005. http://www.mohrss.gov.cn/ImportedImageFile/27110316153762520791.pdf. Accessed 8 Nov 2016

The Guiding Opinion of the Central Committee of the Communist Party of China on Handling Labour Strikes and Student Strikes (中共中央关于处理罢工、罢课问题的指示), issued on 25 March 1957, in the Selection of Important Policies and Decisions After the Establishment of People's Republic of China (vol 10). Available at: http://www.ce.cn/xwzx/gnsz/szyw/200706/04/t20070604_11595959.shtml. Accessed 22 Oct 2016

The National Bureau of Statistics of China's annual report on 'Labour Disputes Accepted and Settled' from 2012 to 2014

The Notice on Handling Problems Rising from the Laid-off Workers at the SOE and Their Re-employment (关于妥善处理国有企业下岗职工出中心再就业有关问题的通知). Issued by the Central Committee of the CPC and the State Council on 9 June 1998. Available at: www.reformdata.org/1998/0629/19396.shtml

The Research Institute of the History and Archives of the CPC (2017) The grant victory of the basic completion of socialist transformation (基本完成社会主义改造的伟大胜利). The History of the CPC Website. Available at: www.dswxyjy.org.cn/n1/2017/1215/c244520-29710356.html

Wanhua D et al (2009) Interpretation and application of the advisory opinions of the Supreme People's Court on doing a good job in the trial of labour dispute cases (关于当前形势下做好劳动争议纠纷案件审判工作的指导意见》的理解与适用). People's Judicature 15:27–28

Wenjia Z (2013) Is the mediation-first principle effectively implemented? An empirical inquiry based on provincial panel statistics between 1999 and 2011 (调解优先"能缓解集体性劳动争议吗?基于1999-2011年省际面板数据的实证检验). Sociol Stud 5:150–155

Wenjia Z, Feng C (2015) Mediate first: the revival of mediation in labour dispute resolution in China. China Q 222:381–398

Wenjia Z, Jinglun Y (2014) From court to street: how the grand mediation discouraged workers from seeking institutional remedies (从法庭走向街头:"大调解"何以将工人维权行动挤出制度化渠道). J Sun Yatsen Univ (Soc Sci Ed) 54(247):148–151

Workers' Daily (2016) A Report at the 16th Meeting of the All-China Federation of Labour Unions (李玉赋在全总十六届四次执委会议上的工作报告). Published on 17 February 2016. http://acftu.people.com.cn/n1/2016/0217/c67560-28130008.html. Accessed 17 June 2017

Xian H (ed) (2013) China human resources and social security yearbook (中国人力资源和社会保障年鉴2013年). China Human Resources Publishing Group, p 666

Xin Y, Ying J (2013) An institutional analysis of the current settlement of major labour disputes in China (我国重大集体劳动争议现状及处理机制分析). J Beijing Adm Coll 4:94–95

Xinchun L (2001) Economic features of Danwei. Econ Stud 7:36–37

Xinhua News (2009a) Commentary on Safeguarding Growth, Safeguarding People's Livelihood and Safeguarding Stability (再论 "保增长、保民生、保稳定"). Published on 24 July 2009. Available at: http://www.gov.cn/jrzg/2009-07/24/content_1374390.htm

Xinhua News (2009b) Refrain from naming participants in mass group incidents 'Deluded' (群体性事件中少用 "不明真相"). Published on 28 July 2009. Available at: http://news.cctv.com/china/20090729/105213_1.shtml

Xiucheng Z (2007) A study of China's petition system after 1978: a case on Weihai in Shandong Province (1978年以来中国信访工作研究——以山东威海为个案). Central Party School

Thesis Database: 73. Available at: www.cnki.net/kcms/detail/detail.aspx?FileName=2007083301.nh&DbName=CDFD2007&DbCode=CDFD. Accessed 2 July 2016

Yan-sui Y (2004) A new outline of Chinese labour law (新劳动法概论). Tsinghua University Press, p 128

Yifu L, Zhiyun L (2003) Reform of the state-owned enterprises and financial system in China. In: China Centre for Economic Research Working Paper Series, No. C2003027, p 10. Available at: https://www.nsd.pku.edu.cn/attachments/e98d2092574b48159f291a094e72346b.pdf

Youyu Z (2003) Several problems about constitutional amendments (关于修改宪法的几个问题). In: The selected treatises on constitutional studies. The Social Sciences Academic Press, p 14

Yuan G (2016) The emergence of the three central political themes in the legitimacy-building of Chinese revolutionary politics, 1921–1923. Mod China 42(3):287–288

Chapter 5
Sending Law to the Countryside: Local Acceptance and Resistance

5.1 Unravelling Legal Dimensions of Farmers' Protests in China

In recent decades, China has witnessed a significant number of complaining actions from farmers, ranging from small-scale rallies to massive protests with thousands of participants. The complaining farmers are demanding transparency and accountability from governing powers in rural areas. It is worth noting that in 2012, almost half of the documented mass actions in China were related to farmers' complaints about the decision-making of rural governing powers.[1] Although farmers' protests are prevalent and dynamic, research on the topic has been limited to a few analytical perspectives and conclusions. In particular, assuming that the Chinese government has a homogeneous coercive stance towards farmers' complaining actions has hindered a nuanced understanding of the context and content of farmers' protests and their outcomes in contemporary China (that is, from the 1970s to the present in this chapter).

The existing body of research literature has utilised three primary theories to account for the phenomenon of farmers' protests in China. The first is social movement theory which focuses on farmers' collective actions for challenging the status quo of rural governance and identifies their tactics for organising protesters and negotiating with government authorities.[2] The second theory is the principal-agent analysis, which centres around the underlying incentives and choices of rural governing powers and examines local agencies' behaviours that antagonise local farmers.[3] The third approach concerns legislative gaps that impede the enjoyment of economic, social and political rights by Chinese farmers, as well as flaws in the

[1] Public Opinion Monitoring Centre (2012) Annual Report on Mass Group Incidents.

[2] O'Brien and Lianjiang (2012), pp. 51–59.

[3] Chen (2014), pp. 189–196.

C.-r. Qiao, *Chinese Rules and Procedures for Addressing Mass Actions*,
https://doi.org/10.1007/978-3-031-62201-4_5

appeal procedures that further frustrate rural complainants.[4] These theories have yielded useful insights into the factors that contribute to the emergence and intensification of farmers' protests. However, they have not adequately combined the legislative, institutional and social dimensions to examine these protests and their eventual settlements.

To fill gaps in the research literature, this chapter develops a holistic and nuanced account that contextualises Chinese measures for addressing rural disputes with a particular focus on farmers' protests. It collects and analyses a wide range of data on Chinese rural governance policies, rural dispute resolution rules and practices, as well as Chinese news coverage of farmers' protests published by both official and non-official media. The chapter first examines the rural-urban governance divide, a long-standing characteristic of Chinese State governance tradition. This is a critical starting point for understanding the relationship between Chinese farmers, their local governing body and the Central Government. Following that, it identifies the historical and structural factors that contribute to the injustice experienced by Chinese farmers, as well as contemporary legislation that confirms the legal entitlements of rural residents who have shifted their identity from duty bearers to rights holders (Sect. 5.2).

The next section investigates Chinese news reports on the Wukan protests and their aftermath, which have received more extensive media coverage than other farmers' protests in recent years and garnered widespread attention to the tension between rural residents and rural governing powers.[5] Drawing on a vast dataset of news reports published between January 2010 and December 2013, the section examines recurrent news narratives for depicting farmers' protests and assessing government responses and uncovers the relevance of legal rules protecting the political and economic rights of rural residents to these narratives (Sect. 5.3).

The chapter concludes by summarising its findings and suggesting future research directions (Sect. 5.4). This chapter makes two contributions to understanding the complexities of farmers' protests and their settlements in China. Firstly, it contextualises the changing status and identity of Chinese rural residents and its impacts on their demands from rural governing powers. Secondly, it opens up new opportunities to analyse the dynamics of farmers' protests in China and their resolutions and has the potential to improve the current rules and practices for managing rural disputes in general and farmers' protests in particular.

[4] He (2014a), pp. 852–853.

[5] Caixin News (13 March 2013).

5.2 The Shifting Status of Chinese Farmers from Duty Bearers to Rights Holders

To comprehend the emergence and growth of farmers' protests in China, it is necessary to examine the country's rural governance tradition and its contemporary reforms. These reforms have transformed Chinese farmers from duty bearers who were reliant on rural governing powers towards rights holders who are entitled to making their own political and economic choices. To start with, the Chinese term of farmers, referred to as *nongye renkou* (农业人口) in Chinese, is determined not only by one's occupation but also by their household registration type.[6] The household registration, known as *hukou* (户口) in Chinese, is used to identify a person's place of origin and determine their eligibility for social welfare, educational access and other public services provided by the Chinese government.[7]

Chinese rural governance has, until recently, restricted the individual agency of rural residents. Notably, the economic activities of Chinese farmers used to be decided by the rural cooperative, a grassroots governing power accountable to the government. Besides that, Chinese farmers were underrepresented in the decision-making process. Before 2010, rural representatives were only assigned one-fourth of the seats assigned to urban representatives in China's legislative body, the People's Congress.[8] As China transitioned from a centrally commanded to a market-oriented economy, rural residents gradually became autonomous rights holders and decision-makers, both formally and practically. In 2015, Chinese farmers participated in over 170,000 mass actions, with the most common issue being the infringement of farmers' land and political rights, for which rural governing powers were allegedly responsible.[9]

In light of institutional and social changes in China's rural governance, this section outlines the legislative developments that are changing the status of Chinese rural residents and their relationship and interactions with rural governing powers. More specifically, it begins by discussing the rise and decline of Chinese collectivist rural governance and its legacies (Sect. 5.2.1). It then investigates the implementation of China's de-centralised governance reform and its perhaps unintended effects on tensions and sometimes conflicts between rural residents and local governing powers (Sect. 5.2.2). Lastly, it analyses the Chinese government's efforts to bring law to the countryside, including the procedural and personnel arrangements, and their implications for how rural residents organise complaining actions and what type of settlements they receive (Sect. 5.2.3).

---

[6] In this chapter, the terms 'farmers' and 'rural residents' are used interchangeably.

[7] Articles 3, in the 1958 Regulation of the People's Republic of China on Household Registration.

[8] Articles 12, 14 and 16, in the 2004 Election Law of the People's Republic of China for the National People's Congress and Local People's Congresses. Article 14 of the 2010 amendment to the Election Law of the People's Republic of China.

[9] Mingjun and Xiaoliang (2016), pp. 3–4.

5.2.1 *The Rise and Fall of Collectivist Governance in Rural China*

This part provides an overview of the administrative history that underlies the form and content of interactions between rural residents and governing powers in China. While a comprehensive analysis of Chinese rural governance tradition and its developments throughout the twentieth century is beyond the scope of this chapter, a summary of key characteristics of China's rural governance is necessary. Specifically, it begins by describing the Chinese rural governance tradition and its approach towards managing the rural population. Subsequently, it explores the collectivisation of rural governance during the 1950s that systematically marginalised the individual and collective autonomy of Chinese farmers. Finally, it examines the dissolution of rural collective communes in the 1980s, which marked a national effort to reintroduce economic and political autonomy to rural residents.

The rural-urban divide has been a critical aspect of Chinese State governance, with urban residents enjoying greater access to social welfare and public services than their rural counterparts. Historically, the central ruling power in China did not exert its influence over the vast geographic expanse of rural regions. It usually accepted the substantial power held by rural chiefs, such as lineage seniors and wealthy landlords, to govern the rural population and administer rural affairs.[10] Rural chiefs were not part of the government system, the latter consisting of a central government and three-tier local governments at the province (*sheng*/省, or *lu*/路), prefecture (*jun*/郡, or *zhou fu*/州) and town (*xian*/县) levels. The governor and deputy governor who headed local governments were appointed by the central ruler. Although the chief governor was not necessarily from the region he governed, the deputy governor was usually locally raised and trained.[11]

The rural-urban governance divide does not imply that rural residents were exempt from taxes and duties imposed by the government. In fact, taxes paid by rural residents remained a primary source of government income. In the year 1685, for instance, the Chinese government collected 31.23 million *liang* (one *liang* being approximately 37.3 grams) of silver, of which eighty-eight per cent came from agricultural taxes.[12] In 1841, agricultural taxes contributed seventy-one per cent of the government's revenue, making it a significantly more important source of income than others.[13] Furthermore, rural residents were required to provide labour services, such as for the government's military defence or the construction of the imperial resort.[14] Although the exact ratio of rural residents in ancient China is unclear, it is estimated to have been greater than eighty-seven per cent (the

[10]Huang (2008), pp. 28–30.

[11]Mu (2011), pp. 16–19.

[12]Xue-feng (2022).

[13]Ibid.

[14]In some cases, rural residents were permitted to pay a fee to the government in order to be exempted from labour or military services. In: Golas (1980), p. 300.

percentage of rural population in 1953).[15] In perspective, the Chinese entire population reached fifty-one million in the year 1500 and exceeded 431 million in 1851.[16]

The rural-urban divide affected the differing access to public services provided by the government. In rural areas, social welfare and public affairs were not administered by government officials but by resourceful landlords who regularly made financial contributions to the maintenance of public projects, and by well-respected lineage seniors who heard and settled rural disputes.[17] These rural chiefs also determined the terms of land tenancy, supported local education, and enforced the code of conduct that rural residents were required to abide by.[18] In other words, the authority of the central power was relatively weak in rural areas throughout ancient Chinese history, as evidenced by the well-known proverb that states "Chinese emperor's power never travels further than towns."

In the early twentieth century, Chinese rural governance underwent a significant change. The last imperial government aimed to unite the Chinese nation, including both urban and rural populations, against Western colonising powers. As a result, in 1909, the government started subjecting decisions of rural chiefs to government approval, such as transportation construction plans and trades of agricultural products.[19] From 1912 to the 1930s, the Chinese Republican government further incorporated rural governing powers into the government system by paying them salaries and supervising their performances.[20] By 1953, the Chinese Socialist government had greatly strengthened its control over rural society, including monopolising the trade of agricultural output that was sold to the State-owned enterprises at prices fixed by the government.[21] The Constitution of the People's Republic of China, adopted in 1954, confirmed that rural residents must join rural cooperatives and that agricultural production and supply must be managed by these cooperatives.[22] Since 1958, the mobility of Chinese farmers from rural to urban areas had been strictly restricted under the collectivised rural governance.[23]

---

[15] The Communiqué on the Results of the First National Census (关于第一次全国人口调查登记结果的公报).

[16] Population of Xiaozong Reign in Ming Dynasty (明孝宗朝户数) and Population of Xianfeng and Tongzhi Reigns in Qing Dynasty (清咸丰、同治两朝的人口数). In: Fangzhong (ed) (2008), pp. 266 and 348.

[17] Niou (2015), pp. 230–231.

[18] Xinzhong (1997), pp. 63–65.

[19] Zulan (2014), pp. 602–603.

[20] Huang (2008), pp. 13–14.

[21] The Decision on Planned Purchase and Planned Distribution of Grains (中共中央关于实行粮食的计划收购和计划供应的决议).

[22] Article 8, in the 1954 Constitution of the People's Republic of China.

[23] There were two exceptions to mobility restrictions on rural inhabitants. The first exception allowed individuals with an admission letter from a higher educational institute to leave their place of origin and reside in the city where the accepting institute is located until the end of their studies. The second exception allowed individuals with an employment notice from a government labour department in urban areas to leave their place of origin and stay in the urban area where the

In 1958, the Chinese government implemented a nationwide rural collective commune mechanism, with the rural cooperative serving as the basic unit for managing rural production and population. This mechanism aimed to increase agricultural productivity and promote social equality. However, it ultimately resulted in widespread famine and economic hardship. Each rural collective commune governed 2000 to 7000 households and was subdivided into production teams where rural households handed in their farming tools, animals and other production resources for collective redistribution on the collective farm.[24] In the early 1950s, a production team consisted of about thirty households, and by the late 1950s, its size had grown to 150 to 200 households.[25] The production team managed the production work of its members and distributed their collective income equally.[26] By November 1958, there were 24,000 collective communes across China, where more than ninety-nine per cent of the entire rural population—that was, 120 million rural households—worked and lived.[27]

At first, the collectivised governance of China's rural economy and rural population seemed to function effectively. Rural residents readily joined the collective commune, and government subsidies for upgrading agricultural infrastructure were directed towards the most frequently used facilities on the collective farm. In 1958, the net value of grain output increased by 21.9 per cent compared to that of 1952.[28] However, the collective commune was not solely an economic mechanism for utilising material and labour resources to increase agricultural output. It also served as an administrative agency, responsible for residential surveillance of criminal suspects,[29] and mediating local disputes.[30] By the late 1950s, the collective commune had grown rapidly, but it became increasingly incapable of completing the complex economic coordination and administrative management tasks. As a result, rural welfare declined while the burden on farmers increased. In 1959, the Chinese government raised its grain procurement quota per commune by 14.7 per cent, while the actual amount of communal grain output on average dropped by fifteen per cent that year.[31]

The collectivist rural governance failed to improve the general livelihood of rural residents. In the mid-1970s, the average purchasing power of rural families remained

employing unit is located until the end of their employment. In: Article 10 of the Regulation of the People's Republic of China on Household Registration (中华人民共和国户口登记条例).

[24] Section 2 in the Resolution on Setting up the People's Commune in Rural Areas (中共中央关于在农村建立人民公社问题的决议).

[25] Lin (1990), p. 1231.

[26] Lin (1990), p. 1231.

[27] Lin (1990), p. 1234.

[28] Lin (1990), pp. 1235–1236.

[29] Article 38, in the 1979 Criminal Procedure Law of the People's Republic of China.

[30] Article 22, in the Organisational Law of the People's Courts of the People's Republic of China.

[31] Lin (1990), pp. 1237–1238.

at a level comparable to that of the 1950s.[32] The Great Famine that struck China from 1959 to 1961 had a catastrophic impact on rural society, resulting in the prevalence of poor living conditions for millions of rural households. This was further compounded by the fact that Chinese farmers were required to carry out the production plan made by the collective commune, without the power to challenge it if it appeared uneconomic or unrealistic. In 1978, the annual income per capita of rural residents was only seventy-four *yuan* (approximately eleven US dollars), which was well below the world poverty line.[33] In the late 1970s, rural residents were widely dissatisfied due to the common poverty and policy restrictions on farmers' production activities.

In 1978, a regional drought had a severe impact on cotton and grain production in the Province of Anhui. Consequently, eighteen farmers from the Xiao-gang Village, who were struggling to meet their production quotas, entered into a secret agreement with their production team. The agreement granted the signing families the autonomy to manage an assigned lot of farming land, and in return, they agreed to hand in the mandatory quota to the collective commune on time the following year.[34] In the following autumn, these families not only met the production quota but also generated a surplus, an extraordinary achievement in the region.[35] The experience of the Xiao-gang Village demonstrates the potential of household-based production to increase agricultural productivity and reduce rural poverty. In 1980, the Chinese government recognised the underground land leasing practice in the Xiao-gang Village as consistent with the socialist rural economy and therefore, could be implemented in other regions.[36]

This official recognition was a crucial turning point in the history of Chinese rural governance reforms. It paved the way for other production teams to grant leases of collectively owned land to their members for household-based agricultural production. In 1982, 78.8 per cent of rural production teams granted land leases to their members, resulting in a remarkable 11.2 per cent surge in the national agricultural production compared to the preceding year.[37] The 1982 amendment to the Chinese Constitution granted rural families the right to manage their agricultural production, use privately owned rural farmland or hilly land, manage side-line production and raise livestock for household consumption, and protect the collective economic rights and interests of rural residents.[38]

---

[32] The index of rural household consumption was measured and recorded as 102.8 RMB in 1952, 101.2 RMB in 1954, 101.5 RMB in 1975, and 110.7 RMB in 1976. In: in the Compilation of Statistics of China from 1949 to 1998 (新中国五十年统计资料汇编 1949–1998), p. 185.

[33] Jingyong (2009), p. 7.

[34] Lin (1988), p. 201.

[35] Ibid.

[36] Paragraphs 5, 8 and 11. In: Guangxiang (2013).

[37] Ibid.

[38] Article 8, in the 1982 Constitution of the People's Republic of China.

In 1983, the Chinese government dissolved over 56,000 rural collective communes across the country and replaced their governing functions with two bodies. The administrative functions of the rural collective commune, such as managing public budgeting, public security, social welfare, justice administration, culture and education, were taken over by grassroots governments at the township and county levels.[39] The villagers' committee took over the economic and social functions of the collective commune, including organising agricultural production, mediating local disputes, maintaining public order, and conveying the opinions and demands of villagers to the government.[40] By 1985, more than 92,000 township-level and county-level governments were operational, and over 820,000 villagers' committees had been established as self-governing bodies supposedly accountable to rural residents.[41]

The restructuring of rural governance in China had significant impacts on the economic, social and political lives of rural residents. It marked a departure from collectivist planning to household autonomy in agricultural production, which enhanced the productivity of Chinese agriculture and improved the livelihoods of Chinese farmers. The enforcement of the right to elect the villagers' committee in rural areas in 1988 enabled rural residents to hold local governing powers accountable for their decisions.[42] The villagers' committee, which consists of a chair, a deputy chair, and one to six members (the number of committee members depends on the size of the village), is directly elected by villagers.[43] Chinese law prohibits external interference in the appointment and replacement of locally elected members of the villagers' committee to ensure local representation and autonomy in the decision-making at the village level.[44]

The law also prohibits external interference with the decisions of the villagers' committee, highlighting a fundamental difference from the previous collectivised rural governance, where rural entities and residents were merely implementers of external commands of the government.[45] The formation and functioning of the villagers' committee is meant to be free from government interference, although this is not always the case in practice. Candidates running for village elections who receive endorsement from the grassroots government are more likely to become members of the villager's committee, which has resulted in them being perceived as

---

[39] Paragraphs 4 and 6, in the Decision to Set up the Country-level Government to Take Over Rural Administration by the Collective Commune (中共中央、国务院关于实行政社分开建立乡政府的通知).

[40] Articles 2, 6 and 7, in the 1982 Constitution of China.

[41] Qi et al. (2004), p. 61.

[42] Article 9, in the Provisional Organisational Law of the Villagers' Committees of the People's Republic of China (中华人民共和国村民委员会组织法(试行)).

[43] Articles 2 and 6, in the 1982 Constitution of China.

[44] Articles 2 and 11, in the Organisational Law of the Villagers' Committees of the People's Republic of China.

[45] Articles 3, 5 and 8, in the Organisational Law of the Villagers' Committees of China.

more accountable to the supporting government than to the villagers who elected them.[46] The opaque and closely intertwined relationship between the villagers' committee and government authorities has caused widespread dissatisfaction among rural residents (the point being explained in detail in Sect. 5.2.2).

In conclusion, the contemporary Chinese rural self-governance mechanism is a reformed continuation of the Chinese governance tradition that supports rural affairs to be organised locally while acknowledging the economic, social and political rights of rural residents. The official acceptance of household land leasing practices in 1980 marked the beginning of this effort by the Chinese government to promote household autonomy in agricultural production. The dissolution of the rural collective commune in 1983 was followed by a new self-governance model based on grassroots representation and village direct elections. These reforms have transformed Chinese farmers from duty bearers dependent on rural governing powers to autonomous rights holders. However, this shift faces several challenges, which will be analysed in the next section.

5.2.2 *Attributors to Collective Discontents of Chinese Farmers*

The evolution of the status of Chinese farmers from duty bearers to autonomous rights holders has led to a shift in their expectations of rural governing powers. To contextualise these changes, it is necessary to examine the structural factors that have contributed to collective concerns and discontent among Chinese farmers. Until recently, Chinese rural residents needed approval from the government or a higher educational institute to deregister from rural households and move to urban areas for better jobs or living opportunities.[47] Prior to 2005, over forty national and regional regulations and policies imposed restrictive clauses on rural residents that limited the enjoyment of their economic and social rights.[48] Moreover, there is a significant income gap between rural and urban residents. In 2000, rural residents earned only 37.8 per cent of the annual income of their urban counterparts.[49] This disparity has remained largely unchanged over the past two decades, with rural residents earning just over thirty-nine per cent of the average annual income of urban residents in 2021.[50]

Chinese rural governance policies have hindered the equitable development of rural society. The command economy aggravated these disparities by prioritising industrial and urban developments over agricultural and rural developments, known

[46] Yinghong (2009), p. 77.

[47] Articles 10, in the Chinese Regulation on Household Registration.

[48] Zhaozi and Chunmei (2005), pp. 71 and 160.

[49] Wenfang and Qing (2008), p. 761.

[50] Xinhua News (11 October 2022).

as *zhonggong qingnong zhongcheng qingxiang* (重工轻农、重城轻乡) in Chinese. From 1953 to 1978, the Chinese government allocated approximately one-third of the growth of the rural economy towards supporting industrial development in urban regions.[51] Even during the reforming era, government subsidies to the agricultural sector remained low, which constituted less than ten per cent of the national public expenditure until 1998.[52] Additionally, rural residents who, or whose families, used to own the so-called 'feudal property' faced exclusion from equal employment and social welfare. To gain equal access to these benefits, they had to meet socialist re-educational requirements[53] and undergo collective surveillance on both their political and work lives.[54]

It was in 1979 that the Chinese government abolished the discriminatory management of rural residents who were born into a 'feudal family'. In January 1979, the Central Committee of the Communist Party of China (hereafter, referred to as the "CPC") passed a resolution that granted full communal access to rural residents whose families used to be landlords or wealthy farmers: they were entitled to the same benefits as other commune members, provided that they had been compliant with Chinese laws and government policies, worked hard on the collective farm, and behaved well towards other members.[55] This resolution represented a significant advancement towards the political and social integration of rural residents who were previously marginalised due to their family background.

While the dissolution of collectivist rural self-governance in China was welcomed by many, it had several consequences, one of which was the transfer of fiscal power from the Central Government to local governments. This resulted in the loss of the Central Government's monopoly over Chinese fiscal revenues. Between 1990 and 1993, the Central Government retained, on average, 27.8 per cent of the national fiscal revenue but bore more than thirty per cent of the national public expenditure.[56] Consequently, the Central Government faced a challenging fiscal deficit. To address this, in 1993, the Chinese government decided to increase its share of national revenues and strengthen its power to redistribute revenues to local governments.[57]

The fiscal reform of 1993 successfully directed 55.7 per cent of the national fiscal revenue to the Central Government by the end of 1994.[58] However, it also had a lasting impact on the fiscal power of local governments, which experienced a

[51] Jingyong (2009), p. 7.

[52] Zhaozi and Chunmei (2005), pp. 71 and 160.

[53] Article 19, in the 1954 Constitution of China.

[54] Point 5 in Article 4 in the Some Problems with the Socialist Education in Rural Areas (农村社会主义教育运动中目前提出的一些问题).

[55] Paragraphs 1 and 2, in the Resolution on the Class Status of Children of Landlords and Rich Farmers (关于地主、富农分子摘帽问题和地、富子女成份问题的决定).

[56] Table 7-1 "Public Revenues and Expenditures from 1978 to 2013 (公共财政收支总额及增长速度)", In the China Statistics Yearbook of 2014.

[57] Paragraph 18, in the Resolutions on Several Issues Concerning the Construction of Socialist Market Economy (中共中央关于建立社会主义市场经济体制若干问题的决定).

[58] Kun (2020).

reduction in their share of government revenue.[59] As a result, local governments began imposing additional taxes of up to fifteen per cent on the income of rural residents under the guise of 'fees for handling local public welfare'.[60] This compounded the already heavy burden of the national agricultural tax on farmers.[61] Before 2006, the national agricultural tax was 15.5 per cent of farmers' income from food crops (such as grains), profit crops (such as cotton, hemp, tobacco, oil, and sugar), and horticultural crops.[62]

The imposition of additional taxes by local governments resulted in farmers paying up to over thirty per cent of their income to the government, which was widely complained about by rural residents.[63] In 2000, the Chinese government prohibited 'illegitimate local charges', which accounted for nineteen to thirty per cent of the grassroots governments' incomes.[64] In 2006, it abolished the national agricultural tax, with the exception of the tobacco tax, and local taxes that targeted rural residents, such as taxes on urban-rural coordination, remunerating the work of the villagers' committee, rural education, and compulsory labour quotas.[65] The abolition of these taxes reduced the financial resources available to local governments for funding public services and infrastructural development. Requisitioning rural land and leasing it to business entities has become a significant source of income for local governments. In 2014, land-leasing charges accounted for over thirty-eight per cent of local revenues, which is twice the amount recorded in 1999.[66]

In this process, rural residents have expressed dissatisfaction with how local governing powers dealt with rural land. According to the law, rural residents are entitled to a fair share of the benefits from rural land transactions.[67] However, rural residents have complained that the compensation they received for the loss of their land was considerably lower than the actual trading value of the land.[68] A survey conducted in 2011 interviewed nearly 1800 villagers from different regions who had lost their rural land, and the results showed that the compensation provided by local governments, which was 18,739 *yuan* per 667 m^2 (approximately 2677 US dollars), was less than three per cent of what the governments received from land developers, which was 778,000 *yuan* per 667 m^2.[69] Between 2000 and 2010, over sixty per cent

[59] Hongwen (2006), p. 13.

[60] Articles 3, 6, 10 and 14, in the Regulation on the Agricultural Taxation of the People's Republic of China.

[61] Zhang et al. (2015), p. 300.

[62] Article 10, in the Regulation of the People's Republic of China on Agriculture Tax (中华人民共和国农业税条例).

[63] Tao et al. (2011), p. 659.

[64] Chen (2014), p. 64.

[65] Xinhua News (6 March 2006).

[66] Jinhua et al. (2018), pp. 58–59.

[67] Article 71, in the Agriculture Law of the People's Republic of China.

[68] Chengri (2014), p. 344.

[69] Cui et al. (2015), p. 93.

of farmers' protests were triggered by shared anger at losing their land on terms perceived to be substantially lower than the actual transaction value.[70]

There are two types of land ownership in China: State-owned land in urban areas and collectively owned land in rural and suburban areas, both of which can be leased to natural and legal persons for responsible agricultural or non-agricultural uses.[71] Given the limited availability of arable land in China, cultivated land is carefully protected by the law, and the conversion of cultivated land to non-agricultural use is strictly restricted.[72] While a rigorous review procedure is required for using State-owned land for construction purposes, the review and approval procedure on the use of collectively owned rural land is relatively lenient, which is subject to an exemption clause that permits the villagers' committee to review land-use applications aimed at developing rural enterprises, rural public infrastructure, and rural welfare facilities.[73]

The exploitation of this loophole in Chinese land use and leasing regulations has had adverse effects on the rights and interests of rural residents. Business developers facing challenges in obtaining land-use quotas through the government review procedure have been known to bypass the government review by negotiating directly with villagers' committees to access rural land. These committees are sometimes considered to lack the ability or motivation to represent the interests of local farmers during these negotiations.[74] Additionally, farmers have limited access to decision-making processes related to the sale and lease of their land. This results in land lease contracts that are perceived to benefit business developers at the expense of the collective interests of farmers. For example, land use contracts fulfil the public interest clause by containing a relocation plan for the affected villagers, but also allocate a significant portion of the leased land for developing profit-driven sites, such as entertainment centers or shopping malls.[75]

In 2019, an amendment was made to the Chinese land administration law which now requires any land development plans to comply with general land use restrictions and be subject to government review and approval.[76] This amendment is a welcomed development for the protection of land rights of Chinese farmers. However, it remains to be seen how effectively local governments and villagers 'committees will enforce it. While the Chinese government generally tolerates farmers' protests as a means of external oversight over the abuse of power by local governing authorities,[77] this political culture can lead to tension or even confrontation between

---

[70] Jianrong (2011), p. 20.

[71] Articles 2, 9, and 10, in the 2019 Land Administration Law of the People's Republic of China.

[72] Articles 3, 4 and 31, in the 2019 Land Administration Law.

[73] Article 43, in the 2004 Land Administration Law of the People's Republic of China.

[74] Shukai (2017), p. 57.

[75] Yansui et al. (2014), p. 116.

[76] Articles 59, 60 and 61 in the 2019 Land Administration Law.

[77] Jianrong (2005), p. 62.

rural complainants and local governments.[78] Farmers often turn to officials from higher levels of government to resolve their land requisition and reallocation complaints, in which local authorities are allegedly the wrongdoers.[79]

In summary, the changing status of Chinese farmers to rights holders has resulted in alterations in their interactions with rural governing powers. The abolition of the agricultural tax in 2006 left local governments with fewer financial resources, leading them to requisition rural land and lease rural land to business entities without adequately considering the collective interests of rural residents. The absence of transparency and accountability in rural decision-making has caused additional anger and frustration among rural residents, resulting in numerous complaints in rural China.

5.2.3 *Sending Law to the Chinese Countryside*

As discussed in the first part of this section, the rural-urban divide has been a long-standing characteristic of Chinese State governance. Under this tradition, formal rules adopted by the government played a rather limited role, if any, in settling rural disputes. Local mediation was the primary tool in rural areas for handling disputes over marriage, family relations, farming and land properties, known in Chinese as *hunhu tiantu* (婚户田土) categories of typical disputes. The mediator in rural areas prioritised local customs and precedents over formal rules when settling local disputes.[80] Common issues resolved through rural mediation included household division and family inheritance, private loans and debts, joint care of the elderly by family members, marriage formation, and land boundary demarcation.[81]

Rural customs valued interpersonal harmony and local residents were expected to adhere to these customs to prevent the four typical types of disputes from arising. For instance, if landowners intended to sell their land, they had a duty to inform their neighbours of their plan; and the neighbours had the right to halt the sale if they had evidence to demonstrate that it would cause harm to their land and property.[82] If the parties involved did not voluntarily adhere to local customs, then they were expected to reach a settlement amongst themselves; if this attempt failed, the disputing parties would invite a locally trusted mediator to hear and settle the case. The general principle for rural dispute mediation is to minimise confrontation between the parties so that their economic and social relationships can be reasonably restored after the dispute is settled.[83]

[78] Michelson (2008), p. 48.

[79] Whiting and Shao (2014), pp. 233–234.

[80] Ibid.

[81] Huang (2010), pp. 21–24.

[82] Huang (2010), p. 31.

[83] Ibid.

The widespread use of mediation to resolve rural disputes persisted under the CPC-led border-region regime in the 1930s and 1940s. Chapter 2 presents a detailed analysis of the practical and political factors that motivated the Chinese government to promote mediation in rural areas during this period. In the late 1950s, collectivised governance was implemented in rural areas, which virtually eliminated economic and social bases underlying rural disputes related to privately owned land, family property, property inheritance, and private loans and debts.[84] The remaining rural disputes were classified into two general types. The first type pertained to free marriage and divorce, which was legally protected after 1950;[85] and the second type related to collectivised agricultural production, including the fixed price at which farmers had to sell their farming tools and animals, the assignment of production work, and the calculation of working points by the rural commune for each household.[86] The Chinese government recruited mediators to hear and resolve disputes in rural areas in order to uphold and promote government policies.[87]

These rural dispute mediators were compensated with working points, which were calculated based on the amount of time they spent on resolving disputes and redeemable as the labour output in the collective commune. However, this compensation measure became obsolete when the rural commune was dissolved in 1983. As a result, the rural dispute resolution mechanism was short of experienced mediators. To address this issue, the Chinese government assigned civil servants to take charge of dispute mediation in rural areas.[88] These civil servants followed Chinese laws and government policies when settling disputes; and in cases where there was no law or policy applicable, they relied on common sense and moral values as generally upheld in the village.[89] Contemporary rural dispute mediation serves two purposes: maintaining interpersonal relationships between the disputing parties, as traditional rural dispute resolution did, and ensuring settlements to comply with Chinese laws and policies.[90]

Since the late 1990s, Chinese farmers have been granted additional rights to participate in rural self-governance. In addition to the right to elect the villagers' committee regardless of one's ethnicity, sex, occupation, family background, religious belief, education, wealth, and length of residence in the village (as long as they are over eighteen),[91] rural residents also have the right to access administrative

[84] Huang (2010), pp. 34–35.

[85] Marriage decided by a third party, mercenary marriage and any other types of interference in the free marriage were legally prohibited with the passage of the Marriage Law of the People's Republic of China in 1950. The law confirmed and protected marriages based on the free choice of partners, monogamy, and equality between men and women. In: Articles 1, 3 and 17, in the 1950 Marriage Law of the People's Republic of China.

[86] Huang (2010), pp. 35–37.

[87] Huang (2010), p. 31.

[88] Yongjun (2013), pp. 80–81.

[89] Huang (2010), pp. 49–50.

[90] Huang (2010), pp. 56–57.

[91] Article 13 in the Organisational Law of the Villagers' Committee of China.

records of the villagers' committee such as the village election votes, minutes of the villagers' committee meetings, contracts for renting collectively-owned land, registrations of collectively-owned property, accounts of the village's collective income and expenses, receipts and distributions of government subsidies, and receipts and distributions of land appropriation compensation.[92]

Furthermore, since the early 2000s, the Chinese government has been promoting legal knowledge across rural areas, specifically regarding information on the Chinese Constitution, the Organisational Law of the Villagers' Committee, and regulations on agricultural taxation, trying to improve legal literacy and awareness among rural residents.[93] In 2008, the government introduced an open transaction mechanism to protect the property rights of rural residents by ensuring fair and transparent trade of rural land and its associated rights, such as the household right to manage contracted rural land, the collective right to manage the forestry and own the forest and wood in the forestry, the household right to develop deserted hills or valleys, the collective ownership of village business assets and productive assets (excluding land resources), and the collective and household ownership of agricultural production equipment.[94]

Despite these legislative developments, rural residents have long had limited access to impartial venues for reviewing the infringement of their rights, particularly concerning the conduct of the villagers' committee and the government. Currently, the grassroots government subsidises both the operational and personnel costs for rural dispute mediation.[95] Rural residents often distrust local dispute mediation, believing it favours the grassroots government and the villagers' committee. As a result, they tend to bypass local mediation and appeal to higher authorities at the municipal, provincial, and even central levels. The Chinese government has responded to the issue by enhancing the credibility and efficiency of basic-level courts in handling rural disputes related to the decisions and conduct of villagers' committees and grassroots governments. From the 1950s to the early 2000s, Chinese local courts were financially dependent on their administrative counterparts, making it challenging for judges to remain impartial when reviewing complaints against the government at the same or higher levels. Consequently, rural residents did not trust the court to be a viable option for settling government-related disputes until recently.[96]

---

[92] Articles 30 and 34, in the Organisational Law of the Villagers' Committees of China.

[93] Paragraph 7 in Section 3, in the Advisory Opinions on the Strengthening of Grassroots Democracy and Law-based Governance in Rural Areas (关于进一步加强农村基层民主法制建设的意见).

[94] Section 21 "Endowing farmers with more property rights", in the Decision on Several Big Issues on Promoting the Reform and Development (中共中央关于全面深化改革若干重大问题的决定); and Article 8, in the Implementation Opinions of the Chinese State Council on Guiding the Healthy Development of the Rural Property Circulation Market (国务院办公厅关于引导农村产权流转交易市场健康发展的意见).

[95] Articles 6 and 8, in the People's Mediation Law of the People's Republic of China.

[96] Weimin (2015), pp. 268–269.

In 2007, the People's Supreme Court in Beijing, in collaboration with the Ministry of Finance, expanded the pilot court budgetary reform to a national enterprise that financially frees local courts from their administrative counterparts. As of 2015, the national and provincial budgets have been the main source of funding for basic-level and municipal-level courts, accounting for approximately 70% of court expenditure.[97] If rural residents feel that a decision made by the villagers' committee violates their rights and interests, they can file a complaint with the court that has the power to issue an injunction on the disputed decision.[98]

Moreover, Chinese farmers have shown their ability to utilise their understanding of Chinese laws and government policies to protect their entitlements. For example, in 2001, a group petition submitted by farmers framed their grievances against the decisions of grassroots government in terms of rights violations. They sought redress for the violated right to review their villages' budgetary plans and expenditure accounts, and to freely elect members for their villagers' committees.[99] A study group of farmers in Hunan Province has compiled a record of centrally adopted policies aimed at reducing agricultural taxation and combating local corruption since 1998. Using this archive, they composed petition letters to the provincial authority in 2003, expressing their collective concern over the illegal and unjust financial burdens imposed on local farmers.[100]

Chinese rural residents are becoming more active in seeking legal redress collectively to protect their economic and political rights. However, some forms of collective complaints are viewed unfavourably by the court. Local judges have expressed hesitation in hearing cases involving multiple complainants about rural land transactions, fearing that court proceedings could turn into a theatrical spectacle, thereby exposing the court review to external scrutiny or influence.[101] In certain cases, rural complainants have gathered relatives and friends in the courtroom, wearing matching clothing and holding signs, and made disapproving noises when the judge interrupted the proceedings to request that the complainants present relevant points.[102]

Nonetheless, this does not mean that Chinese judges are unwilling to consider complaints from rural residents as a whole. The court has become the primary forum for reviewing disputes over decisions made by the grassroots government and the villagers' committee. A study of 204 legal actions initiated by rural residents between 2004 and 2010 found that seventeen per cent of these cases included complaints against government conduct related to the land expropriation procedure, the calculation of government compensation for rural land requisition, and the

[97] Xi (2015).

[98] Article 36 in the Organisational Law of the Villagers' Committee of China.

[99] Chen (2011), p. 36.

[100] Jianrong (2005), p. 62.

[101] Whiting and Shao (2014), pp. 239–240.

[102] He (2014b), pp. 202–206.

disclosure of relevant government records.[103] From 2014 to 2019, basic-level courts made decisions on 32,094 administrative cases against township governments.[104]

To conclude, this part discusses the legislative and institutional changes in Chinese rural dispute resolution measures. Historically, rural dispute resolution in China relied heavily on local customs and precedents, rather than formal rules established by the government. Since the 1950s, the Chinese government has integrated the work of rural dispute mediators with government intervention. This approach to resolving rural disputes is semi-formal and aims to ensure that settlements align with Chinese laws and regulations. Since the 1980s, the Chinese government has implemented farmers' political rights, including the right to access administrative records of the villagers' committee, as well as the right to free village elections. Despite these advancements, rural residents continue to face significant barriers when accessing impartial venues to review infringements of their rights, particularly those committed by the villagers' committee and grassroots government. To address this issue, the Chinese government has promoted legal literacy in rural areas and strengthened the financial independence of local courts from local governments. Over the past three decades, rural residents have increasingly utilised their legal knowledge and become more skilled in seeking legal remedies.

5.2.4 Chinese Rural Residents Demanding and Defending Their Rights

This section has analysed institutional and legislative developments underlying Chinese measures for dealing with farmers' disputes with a particular focus on farmers' complaints about rural governing powers. It begins with a detailed account of the transition from a collectivist rural governance model to a decentralised self-governance model. This has resulted in the progressive devolution of central command on the management of rural economic and administrative affairs. The government's efforts to send laws to the countryside have greatly affected the relationship and interaction between rural residents and local governing powers. It then investigates the typical causes for farmers' protests, including inequitable rural governance policies at the national level and weak decisional transparency and accountability at the local level, which have led to widespread suspicion about rural governance decisions, especially concerning the requisition and leasing of rural land to business entities. Furthermore, it examines the introduction of the self-governance principle to rural areas and the recognition of some basic rights of Chinese farmers, including the economic right to rent and manage farming land and the political right to elect and oversee the villagers' committee.

---

[103] Jie (2014), pp. 93–94 and 99.

[104] Statistics from the national judgement database 'China Judgements Online' (2014–2019).

In recent years, Chinese farmers have increasingly sought legal recourse and public support to protect their economic and political rights. Rural residents have utilised the law to demand legal entitlements from village-level and grassroots governing powers. However, Chinese farmers often have limited local resources to challenge the misconduct of local governing powers. As a result, they resort to engaging higher government authorities to seek fair and enforceable settlements for their complaints. This clash of interests and choices has resulted in varying degrees of tension between rural complainants and rural dispute resolution agencies. The case of the Wukan protests, which will be analysed in the next section, exemplifies this recurring issue.

5.3 Chinese News on Wukan: Leading Narratives and Their Implications

This section examines the role of Chinese legal rules that protect rural self-governance and farmers' economic and political rights in Chinese news coverage of farmers' protests and their settlements. A case study of the Wukan protests, also known as the Wukan incident, is conducted. The Wukan protests, triggered by the issue of local embezzlement, are emblematic of a broader concern among rural residents about the lack of procedural transparency and decisional accountability of rural governing powers. An analysis of the Wukan case sheds light on which complaints of rural residents are commonly portrayed as reasonable and which actions by authorities are narrated as normal in the news.

The first part provides an overview of the background, development and outcomes of the Wukan protests, emphasising the escalating tensions between Wukan villagers and local governing powers. The second part summarises the methods used to collect and process Chinese news reports on the Wukan protests. The third part looks into the prominent narratives about the government's responses to the protesting actions of Wukan villagers and their implications. The fourth part examines the recurring news narratives concerning the key actors involved in the settlement of the Wukan protests.

5.3.1 Tensions Between Wukan Villagers and Local Governing Powers

Wukan is a coastal village situated in Guangdong Province with a rich history of farming and port trading. Its fertile farmland and strategic location near the South China Sea made it one of the wealthiest villages in Guangdong by the early 2000s. The provincial government recognised its villagers' committee as an exemplary model for rural self-governance five times between 1993 and 2001.[105] As of April 2012, Wukan village consists of 2146 rural households with a population of 11,689.[106]

The villagers' committee in Wukan was established in 1999, but its members were not accountable to the electing villagers as these members had close ties to the township government.[107] In December 1992, the Wukan Port Development Company (*wukangang shiye kaifa gongsi*/乌坎港实业开发公司) was established as a collectively-owned enterprise to represent the interests of villagers in developing port infrastructure, rural housing, and tourism projects in Wukan. The head of the local villagers' committee served as the chief manager of the company, and from early 1993 to mid-2011, over sixty-three per cent of the collective income of the Wukan village came from this enterprise.[108]

The decision-making process of the villagers' committee in Wukan lacked transparency and failed to engage with the Wukan villagers regarding the rental and sale of local land as well as the distribution of collective income. Prior to 2009, each villager received a land dividend of 550 yuan (approximately seventy-six US dollars), in total.[109] In April 2009, a group of Wukan villagers founded an online complaint group called "Patriot Number One". The group aimed to raise awareness among their fellow villagers about the Universal Declaration of Human Rights adopted by the United Nations General Assembly in 1948 (to which China is a contracting member) and the United Nations Convention Against Corruption adopted by the United Nations General Assembly in 2003 (to which China acceded in 2005). By early 2011, "Patriot Number One" had attracted nearly a thousand villagers to study and discuss the Universal Declaration of Human Rights, the UN Convention Against Corruption, as well as the land-selling and land-leasing contracts concluded by their villagers' committee.[110]

On 21 June 2009, a group of over twenty young villagers collectively petitioned the provincial government, expressing concerns about the questionable decisions made by their villagers' committee and requesting an investigation. Despite multiple follow-up petitions, led by the most active members of the online group in the wake of the initial petition, the villagers' grievances remained unaddressed. Subsequently, in June 2011, the group appealed for wider attention and support, planning a large-scale protest. On 21 September 2011, over two thousand villagers participated in the demonstration and voiced their collective complaints before the municipal government. The following day, some of the petitioners were detained after a confrontation with the local police.[111]

---

[105] Yanbing and Zhimin (2015), pp. 80–84 and 86–87.

[106] Yanbing and Zhimin (2015), p. 80.

[107] Yanbing and Zhimin (2015), pp. 84–85.

[108] Yanbing and Zhimin (2015), pp. 80–84 and 86–87.

[109] Lu (2012), pp. 53–67.

[110] Yanbing and Zhimin (2015), p. 89.

[111] Lu (2012), pp. 53–67.

On 24 September 2011, a group of villagers from Wukan held a meeting with senior officials from the municipal and grassroots governments to address three issues: the sale and leasing of collectively-owned land, collective income and public expenditure, and the election and formation of the villagers' committee. In early October, an investigation team published a report on the misuse of public funds by the Wukan villagers' committee, which led to the suspension of two senior committee members.[112] However, the investigation did not address the other two issues: the selling of local land and the legality of the last village election, which disappointed the villagers.

On 21 November 2011, villagers from Wukan protested against corrupt land management and manipulated village elections. Slogans such as 'anti-dictatorship', 'return us human rights' and 'return us democracy' were used.[113] The government responded with oppressive measures, and between 3 December and 9 December, the leading protesters were charged with the crime of destroying public and private property and arrested by the local police. The situation further escalated with the death of Mr Xue Jin-bo, one of the arrested villagers, while in police custody on 11 December. Forensic examiners concluded that Mr Xue had died from sudden cardiac death, with no evidence of external force contributing to his death. However, Mr Xue's family contested the conclusion as he had not reported any medical complaints regarding his heart health.[114]

On 11 December, the death of Mr. Xue led to approximately three thousand villagers confronting the local police and government. In response, several hundred armed police officers laid siege to Wukan Village, leading to the climax of the villagers' collective resistance over the following days.[115] On 20 December, the provincial government intervened by sending a working team to mediate the tense confrontation between the villagers and the armed police. Following the intervention by the provincial government, the police withdrew from the village. Subsequently, on 21 December, the villagers reached a provisional settlement; the terms of the agreement included the government's commitment to publishing records of Wuhan's collective incomes and expenditures, reviewing the legality of the previous villagers' committee, and investigating corruption associated with local land lease contracts.[116]

In February 2012, a new election was held for the villagers' committee in Wukan, which was attended by local and national media. This election played a major role in restoring trust between the villagers and the government, and most villagers ceased their resistance. On 23 April 2012, the provincial investigation team released its report, which revealed that the previous villagers' committee had violated land transfer and public funds regulations. According to the report, twelve officials

---

[112] Lu (2012), pp. 53–67.

[113] Ibid.

[114] Ibid.

[115] Hualing (2014), pp. 190–191.

[116] Ewing (2012).

from grassroots and municipal governments were further investigated for their failure to detect the unlawful land sale and lease contracts submitted by the Wukan villagers' committee.[117] The report and its investigation into government officials marked the final settlement of the Wukan protests.

Essentially, the Wukan protests exposed the tension between Chinese farmers and rural governing powers. Local residents were dissatisfied with the exploitation of public resources by the villagers' committee and the lack of government oversight and intervention. The protests highlighted the issue of non-compliance with legal and regulatory standards by rural governing powers and the extent to which rural residents are excluded from the local decision-making process. Furthermore, the protests and collective action taken by Wukan villagers demonstrate that Chinese farmers are not willing to accept a passive role in rural governance. Instead, they are asserting their voice and agency to bring greater accountability and transparency to local self-governance.

5.3.2 Methods for Data Collection, Relevance Test and Data Processing

Chinese news reports on the Wukan protests and their settlements are collected from WiseNews, the world's largest Chinese news database, which captures and stores the full text of a wide range of Chinese news outlets. To ensure sufficient relevance, search terms consist of three sets of words: first, official and non-official references to the Wukan protests; second, the recurrent claims made by the villagers; and third, the names of the two leading protesters. A total of twenty-three search terms are used to collect news reports.[118] A news report is included in the search results if it meets three criteria: it is published in Mainland China, it is published between 1 January 2010 and 31 December 2013, and it contains at least one of the twenty-three search terms in the headline or content.

A relevance test is carried out by closely reading randomly selected news reports. Every first news report on every 295th p of the search result is read in detail. Approximately eighty per cent of the news reports relate to the claim, development, or outcome of the Wukan protests. Keywords in the headlines of the news reports

[117] Jian-feng (2012).

[118] Twenty-three search terms are: wukan , wukan village, wukan incident, wukan mass/group case, wukan mass group incident, wukan and petition, wukan and letter and visit, wukan and complaint, wukan and protest, wukan and assembly, wukan and demonstration, wukan and appeal, wukan and making trouble, wukan and dispute, wukan and violence, wukan and land, wukan and self-governance, wukan and village election, wukan and villagers' committee, wukan and Xu Jinbo, wukan and Lin Zuluan (In Chinese, these search terms are:乌坎 or 乌坎村 or 乌坎事件 or 乌坎群体 or 乌坎群体事件 or 乌坎群体性事件 or 乌坎上访 or 乌坎信访 or 乌坎申诉 or 乌坎维权 or 乌坎示威 or 乌坎集会 or 乌坎游行 or 乌坎情愿 or 乌坎闹事 or 乌坎冲突 or 乌坎暴力 or 乌坎土地 or 乌坎村民自治 or 乌坎村民选举 or 乌坎委员会 or 乌坎薛锦波 or 乌坎林祖銮).

Table 5.1 Composition of the cleaned corpus groups

Producer of the news	Newspaper	News journal	News agency	Web news	Size of news data (in characters)
Amount of news reports	643	27	108	0	1,352,823

that have little or no relevance to the Wukan case are used to search for similar texts, which are then removed from the data. The data that has been cleaned consists of 778 news reports, which amounts to 1.35 million Chinese characters (see Table 5.1).

The cleaned data are then processed using the AntConc software.[119] The top twenty results generated by the Word-list and Collocation methods are reported, with two exceptions. First, the results of meaningless structural particles will not be reported, including the following: and (和), de (的), in/on/at (在), be (是), with (有/与), le (了), for (为), will/would/must/should (要), yi (以), ge (个), for (对), amidst (中), above (上), et cetera(等), passive voice (被), also (也), modal verb indication (能), and negativity (不) and day/date/daylight (日). Second, the results of incomplete terms that can be understood with different connotations will not be reported either, such as ren/people/mass (人) and our country (我国). The unreported words are marked with "/" in the result list.

5.3.3 *Wukan Protesters: Legitimate Resistance or Unruly Mob?*

Wukan protests have garnered intense media coverage by both official and non-official news media and public attention. One crucial issue is how the protesters are portrayed in the news: are they legitimate rights defenders or an unruly mob? And how do news narratives interplay with the government's responses to farmers' complaining actions? To answer these questions, this part examines recurring narratives in the news about Wukan protesters, focusing on their foci and implications.

The Guangdong provincial government's decision to intervene in the local handling of the so-called "Wukan incident" on 20 December 2011 marked a fundamental adjustment to how the Chinese government addressed the protesters (as analysed in Sect. 5.3.1 above). In light of this development, the collected news reports are divided into two groups. Group A consists of news reports published between 2 September and 19 December that focus on the Wukan protests including collective petitions, protests and the villagers' resistance to the police, which will be referred to as "protest reports" below. Group B contains news reports published between 20 December and 31 January 2012, covering the period between the

[119]For further information on the corpus analysis methods used in this study, please refer to "1.4.2. On Analytical Foci and Methods" in Chap. 1.

provincial government's intervention and the first free village election in Wukan, which will be referred to as "intervention reports".

To start with, the size of intervention reports is over five times larger than that of protest reports,[120] suggesting that the government has altered its position by easing restrictions on reporting the 'Wukan incident' after the provincial government decided to negotiate peacefully with the villagers.[121] Despite the significant increase in news coverage following the provincial government's intervention, the popular phrases used in the protest and intervention reports remain neutral and do not indicate a critical or sympathetic attitude towards rural protesters.[122] The only exception is the frequent use of the term 'problem' in the intervention reports. However, it is unclear whether this term refers to government responses to the protesters or the actions of rural protesters. Hence, intervention reports and protest reports were processed using the concordance method to examine how Wukan villagers are typically portrayed in the news.

The concordance results show that Chinese news on Wukan protesters underwent a distinct change after the provincial intervention. Before the intervention, news reports tended to depict the protesters as violent and aggressive, emphasising their destructive behaviour and disregard for law and order. In specific terms, the protest reports often emphasise the aggressive behaviour of the protesters, including instances of vandalising public property (samples 1, 2, 5 and 6), crowding public offices and factory sites (samples 1, 5, 6 and 9), and obstructing government officials and police vehicles (samples 1, 2, 4 and 9). Additionally, the reports accuse the protesters of spreading rumours of police brutality towards children (samples 6 and 8) and attacking security guards and the police (samples 1, 4 and 6), which adds to a negative portrayal of the protesters in the news. In contrast, the local government's response to the protests is depicted as efficient and appropriate, with the news highlighting government efforts to quell the unrest (sample 7) and pursue those responsible for violence (sample 10).[123]

The intervention reports take a different approach. They focus on the underlying governance issues that led to the intensification of the protests, rather than portraying the protesters as a problem to be 'solved'. Specifically, the intervention reports narrate the frustrations and anger of Wukan protesters as understandable, given the long-standing malpractice by rural governing powers (samples 5 and 9). Moreover,

---

[120] Please refer to Table 5.4 "The Composition of Groups A and B" in the Appendix.

[121] It should be noted that Chinese news media do not simply receive and disseminate government opinions verbatim. As discussed in Chap. 1, the dynamic nature of both official and non-official Chinese media allows for a range of perspectives and analyses in news reports. Additionally, interviews with four reporters who covered the Wukan protesting farmers show that Chinese journalists, along with senior news editors, strive to publish stories that may not be welcomed by the government.

[122] Please refer to Table 5.5 "Top Twenty Most Popular Terms in the Data and Groups A and B" in the Appendix.

[123] Please refer to "List 1: Original Sources of Ten Randomly Selected Samples Where 'Villager' Occurs in Group A" in the Appendix.

Table 5.2 A summary of Chinese news reports on protesting farmers in Wukan

	Group A (protest reports)	Group B (intervention reports)
Recurrent phrases	Smashing government facilities; Crowding public offices and factory sites; Attacking security guards and the police; Vandalising public property; Obstructing government sites and roads.	Consultative, responsive and transparent work of the provincial working team; Ensuring the freedom and safety of protesters' representatives; Restoring the trust of Wukan villagers in the government.
Recurring narratives	The violent and disruptive conduct of Wukan protesters led to conflicts between the villagers and the government; Government measures for dispersing crowds and controlling riots are necessary.	The misconduct of rural governing powers led to the conflicts between the villagers and the government; The government's consultative and transparent measures for settling the Wukan incident are commendable.

the reports depict the efforts of the provincial working team to establish mutual trust and achieve a settlement as helpful, including disclosing their preliminary investigation conclusion to the villagers (sample 3), ensuring the freedom and safety of the protesters who met with the working team (samples 4 and 5), and offering leniency to those who were charged with administrative or criminal offences if they cooperated with the investigation (samples 4, 5 and 9).[124]

Overall, the protest reports portray the Wukan protesters as aggressive and excessive, while describing the government's measures to quell the riot and penalise violent protesters as justifiable and appropriate. In contrast, the intervention reports focus on addressing the underlying problems with village governance rather than the conduct of the protesters. For example, they highlight the absence of villagers' participation in the village's decision to sell and rent local land (sample 1), the inappropriateness of the initial government reaction to villagers' complaints (sample 2), and the problematic non-disclosure of land transaction and collective income records by the villagers' committee (sample 8). In addition, the intervention reports highlight the effectiveness of the provincial working team in restoring peace and order to the village (sample 6) and rebuilding the villagers' trust in the government (sample 7).[125]

To summarise, this part reveals a significant change in the portrayal of Wukan protesters in Chinese news reports following the intervention of the provincial government. Table 5.2 highlights a clear contrast in the depiction of rural protesters and government responses between the protest reports and intervention reports. The former tends to portray rural protesters as the aggressors and the government as the victims, while the latter takes a more sympathetic stance towards protesting farmers, who are depicted as victims of corrupt and ineffective rural governance.

[124]Please refer to "List 2: Original Sources of Ten Randomly Selected Samples Where 'Villager' Occurs in Group B" in the Appendix.

[125]Please refer to "List 2: Original Sources of Ten Randomly Selected Samples Where 'Villager' Occurs in Group B" in the Appendix.

Furthermore, the intervention reports appraise the government's consultative measures that adhere to the principles of transparency and local participation, such as inviting villagers to cross-examine the collected evidence and participate in investigation proceedings. Meanwhile, the reports problematise suppressive measures, such as the use of force and punitive actions against protesters, which are narrated as inadequate and ineffective in addressing the underlying causes of farmer unrest.

5.3.4 The Blame Game in the News and Its Implications

The Wukan protests were a complex phenomenon involving a diverse range of parties. The key actors included the locally elected villagers' committee, government authorities at the grassroots and provincial levels, and rural complainants. This section examines Chinese news narratives about four specific actors: the village cadre, villagers' committee, grassroots government, and provincial government. The Wukan protests centre on the issue of rural self-governance. The protesters were dissatisfied with the lack of public participation and accountability in the decision-making process of rural governing powers. This dissatisfaction was compounded by the government's initial inaction and perceived favourable stance towards the villagers' committee. Therefore, it is useful to analyse news reports about these key actors to discover the recurring news framings and their implications.

To start with, the term village cadre colloquially refers to members of the village branch of the CPC and the villagers' committee. A village cadre may serve the CPC village branch and the villagers' committee at the same time. Chinese news coverage consistently portrays village cadres as law avoiders and lawbreakers. The primary news narratives often centre on the wrongdoings, and in some cases, criminal activities of village cadres, such as their non-compliance with disciplinary rules and violations of Chinese rural land management rules (sample 2), private enrichment from land requisition and construction projects (sample 3), lack of participatory decision making and non-disclosure of land-selling contracts and the village's collective incomes (sample 5) and bribery to the township government seeking support for secretly decided transfers of rural land (samples 6 and 10).[126] In summary, the news typically portrays village cadres as the main cause of the grievances expressed by the complaining farmers.

Although village cadres are often portrayed negatively, the news occasionally acknowledges their contribution to the economic and social development of Wukan (sample 1). The news reports positively on the legal and professional training of village cadres as a means of preventing similar incidents from occurring in Wukan and other villages (sample 4). Chinese news on village cadres also refers to broader problems with rural self-governance. In particular, it is critical of the government's

[126]Please refer to "List 3: Original Sources of Ten Randomly Selected Samples Where 'Village Cadre' Occurs in the News" in the Appendix.

use of police force to disperse rural protesters, explaining that it fails to address the root causes of collective discontent of rural protesters (sample 7). It also highlights the lack of accountability in decision-making (sample 8) and the absence of external review on the village election (sample 9). The overall news coverage of village cadres tends to be negative, highlighting the malpractices of village cadres that lead to farmers' repeated protests and calling for more transparent and accountable governance at the village level.

Secondly, Chinese news coverage of the Wukan protests reveals two main narratives about the villagers' committee. The first narrative focuses on the misconduct and illegitimacy of the former villagers' committee, while the second narrative centres on the transparent and fair election process of the new committee.[127] The news portrays the previous villagers' committee as illegitimate and accuses its members of election manipulation and falsifying election results, which angered the farmers (samples 4 and 8). The narrative becomes more critical of the wrongdoers after the provincial working team releases its investigation report (samples 2 and 6). The news also describes the illegitimate committee as blameworthy for causing economic losses to the Wukan farmers (sample 9). In brief, Chinese news coverage of the previous villagers' committee typically presents a negative narrative.

The second narrative concerns the process of electing the new villagers' committee, highlighting the contrasts between the newly formed election committee and the former one. The new committee is portrayed as transparent, with its operation overseen by government officials and representatives of local residents (samples 1 and 7). The news also emphasises the fairness of the new election procedure (sample 3), and its positive impact on the future of village elections in Wukan and other rural areas (sample 5). Meanwhile, the news points out the challenge faced by the new villagers' committee—the long-standing governance practices that lack transparency and accountability to local farmers (sample 10). In general, Chinese news on the villagers' committee often focuses on the significance of free and fair village elections and narrates the legality and transparency of the villagers' committee as a crucial factor in evaluating its work.

Thirdly, Chinese news reports about government authorities at the grassroots and provincial levels exhibit a dichotomous framing that is both remarkable and problematic. Township and town governments are portrayed as unresponsive and unreasonable, while the provincial government's responses are generally described as consultative and commendable. This narrative emphasises the failure of lower governments to address the major complaints of Wukan villagers (sample 4), the inaction in disclosing government records about their communication with the villagers' committee (sample 7), and the approach that prioritises maintaining stability over alleviating the villagers' grievances (samples 1 and 9).[128] The portrayal

[127] Please refer to "List 4: Original Sources of Ten Randomly Selected Samples Where 'Villagers' Committee' Occurs in the News" in the Appendix.

[128] Please refer to "List 5: Original Sources of Ten Randomly Selected Samples Where 'Government' Occurs in the News" in the Appendix.

of the provincial government in a positive light accentuates its adherence to the law and the wishes of the villagers, which contrasts with the approach of lower governments. The news reports quote the provincial government's critical statement about the confrontational approach taken by the municipal and town governments (sample 1) and their inefficient responses to the complaints and requests of the villagers (sample 7).[129]

Furthermore, the news highlights the rule-based and law-abiding nature of the provincial government, which stands in contrast to the reactions of the lower governments towards protesting farmers. The provincial government is depicted as making decisions based on the Organisation Law of the Villagers' Committees and the Implementing Measures of Guangdong Province for Electing the Villagers' Committees (samples 3, 4, 6, and 9), seriously investigating financial and election misconducts at the village level (sample 2) and taking visible steps to address non-compliance issues within rural governing powers (samples 1, 5, 8, and 10).[130] The news reports mention the necessity of a long-term communication mechanism between farmers and the government (sample 8).[131] While the provincial government's adherence to the law is commendable, this portrayal fails to address the broader political context that shapes interactions between different levels of government. The narrative that distinguishes grassroots from provincial authorities oversimplifies the interactions between protesting farmers and the government, obscuring the underlying conflict between the legal and political accountabilities of rural governing powers.

Lastly, Chinese news reports often mention the concept of self-governance when describing what constitutes a successful village election. The lack of meaningful participation by villagers in their own elections is described as a significant problem that contributes to the dissatisfaction of Wukan protesters, who feel that their voices are not being heard and their interests are not being represented (samples 3, 4 and 5). The reports also portray the effective involvement of local farmers in the village election as a positive measure towards enhancing the accountability of rural governing powers (samples 1, 2, 8 and 10).[132] However, the implementation of the self-governance rule is not solely contingent on free village elections, and the news identifies two factors as jeopardising it: grassroots governments are incentivised by fiscal motives to prioritise economic development over democracy-building at the village level, and the lineage power creates competition with the elected villagers' committee or constrains its decision-making competence (samples 6 and 7).[133] While free and meaningful village election is a critical

[129] Please refer to "List 6: Original Sources of Ten Randomly Selected Samples Where 'Provincial government' Occurs in the News" in the Appendix.

[130] Please refer to "List 5: Original Sources of Ten Randomly Selected Samples Where 'Government' Occurs in the News" in the Appendix.

[131] Ibid.

[132] Please refer to "List 7: Original Sources of Ten Randomly Selected Samples Where 'Self-Governance' Occurs in the News" in the Appendix.

[133] Ibid.

Table 5.3 A summary of Chinese news narratives about the major actors in the Wukan protests

	Recurrent narratives	Implications
Village Cadres	Village cadres are portrayed as law avoiders and breakers, highlighting their malpractices as the root cause of villagers' collective dissatisfaction.	A dominant negative portrayal of village cadres contributes to the belief that the locally elected governing powers are prone to misconduct and corruption and therefore untrustworthy.
Villagers' Committee	The previous villagers' committee is accused of being unlawful whereas the new election is praised as free and fair and as helpful for restoring voters' trust in the villagers' committee.	A blaming narrative that focuses on the malfeasance of the villagers' committee overlooks the underlying problems with rural governance, such as the lack of public oversight and accountability.
Grassroots Government	The grassroots government authorities are described to be imprudent, unresponsive and ineffective in handling the Wukan complaints and protests.	A dichotomous narrative depicts a reductivist portrayal of the government's responses to farmers' protests and obscures the institutional causes of the tension between rural residents and their governing powers.
Provincial Government	The provincial government and its working team are narrated positively as adhering to the law and effectively settling the Wukan case.	
Self-governance	The self-governance principle is narrated in the context of enhancing the accountability of the local governing powers and ensuring a transparent and fair village election.	A simplistic narrative that attributes the malfunctioning of rural self-governance to the absence of meaningful village elections obscures the larger issues, such as the fiscal pressure imposed on the village.

component of rural self-governance, they are not the sole determining factor. It is also essential that the elected governing members are capable of working effectively with the grassroots government and local lineage.

In summary, Chinese news reports on the Wukan protests focus on blaming village cadres for their malpractices and misconduct, and the grassroots governments for their confrontational approach to dealing with the complaining farmers (see Table 5.3). However, it is worth noting that Chinese news does not explain the relationship between the grassroots and provincial governments, nor does it explore the accountability mechanism that shapes their interactions. By oversimplifying the complex relationship between the different levels of government, Chinese news reports reinforce a dichotomous narrative of 'bad local guys versus good high-ranking officials'. This dichotomy may obscure the underlying factors for improving the existing rules and practices for concluding farmers' protests. Moreover, the negative framing of village cadres and the villagers' committee may lead to a belief that local governing powers are untrustworthy and thus seeking intervention by a higher-level authority is necessary when there is an objection to a local governance decision.

5.3.5 Dynamic Yet Simplistic News Narratives About Farmers' Protests

This section provides a detailed analysis of Chinese news coverage of farmers' protests in Wukan, which is a significant case of rural residents demanding accountability and transparency from rural governing powers in contemporary China. The analysis assumes that Chinese legal rules protecting rural self-governance, farmers' land and political rights play an important role in the news narratives and framings. It processes a large dataset of 1.35 million characters that contains news reports published between 1 January 2010 and 31 December 2013. Upon analysing the recurring narratives in the news regarding the protesting farmers, assessment of the government's responses, and qualification of the causes for tensions between farmers and governing powers, it finds that the main news narratives simplify the complex relationship between the different levels of the Chinese government while focusing on blaming village cadres and the grassroots government for malpractices and confrontational approaches.

More specifically, after the intervention of the highest authority in the region (namely, the provisional authority), there is a significant shift in how Chinese news narrates the protesting farmers and their confrontations with the government. Prior to the intervention, the news tends to depict the protesters as aggressors and the local government as their victims, whereas, after the intervention, the news generally sympathises with the protesters and portrays them as victims of corrupt and ineffective rural governing agencies. The more recent news also describes the government's measures aimed at enhancing transparency and public participation in handling the Wukan protests as desirable. In contrast, the news often adopts a negative framing when reporting on village cadres and the villagers' committee, which can reinforce the belief that it is necessary to trigger intervention by higher authorities in seeking redress for the collective loss of farmers. Additionally, the news presents a dichotomous framing that depicts grassroots governing powers as malevolent lawbreakers and higher authorities as rule-abiding and well-intentioned, which can obscure the underlying reasons for the recurring violations of the farmers' political and economic rights.

5.4 Conclusion: A Tale of Two Tiers—Law Sent to the Countryside, Not Instituted

This chapter presents an in-depth analysis of Chinese measures for resolving farmers' protests, with a focus on the changing relationship and dynamic interactions between rural residents and governing authorities in contemporary times. The chapter identifies two tiers that underlie the form and substance of farmers' protests: one is the remarkable socialisation of legal rules that recognise and protect Chinese farmers' political and economic rights, and the other is local resistance to institutionalising these legal rules, particularly by rural governing powers. Drawing on extensive data from rural governance reform policies and results, rural dispute resolution rules and practices as well as the relevant Chinese news reports, the chapter analyses the legislative, institutional and social factors that have shaped the government's responses to rural disputes in general and collective farmers' complaints in particular.

Specifically speaking, the first section discusses China's decentralisation of central command in managing economic and political affairs in rural areas. The government's efforts to extend laws to the countryside have significantly altered the expectations of rural residents from local governing powers. Although rural residents are becoming more active in demanding their legal entitlements, they lack trust in the local dispute resolution mediator and court. This is because they view these local venues as unlikely to deliver an impartial settlement in cases where the infringement is committed by the governing power. Rural governing powers are more concerned about political accountability to the higher authority than legal accountability to local complainants. Thus, complaining farmers seek attention and support from the highest authority possible, while local governing powers fear collective complaints that bypass local remedies. This clash of motives and choices has resulted in various tensions between rural complainants and governing authorities.

The second section examines whether Chinese legal rules that safeguard the economic and political rights of farmers are commonly seen as a significant basis for categorising farmers' protests and assessing their resolutions. The analysis demonstrates that political interference has a more prominent influence than legal regulations on the narrative about farmers' protests and the assessment of the authorities' responses in the news. There is a noticeable change in the way news media depict protesting farmers following political guidance from higher-level authorities. Before the guidance, Chinese news typically depicted rural protesters as aggressors and the government as victims. However, following the guidance, news reports adopt a more sympathetic stance towards the protesters, portraying them as victims of corrupt and ineffective rural governance.

Aligned with the shifted narrative framing, Chinese news also changes its assessment of the government's responses to protesting farmers. When protesters are portrayed as violent aggressors, suppressive reactions such as the deployment of police force and punitive actions against rural protesters are depicted as normal and desirable. In contrast, when protesting farmers are narrated as desperate victims whose complaints and requests have long been neglected, the government's consultative measures that uphold transparency and local participation, such as inviting villagers to cross-examine evidence and participate in investigation proceedings, are portrayed as reasonable and desirable. However, Chinese news reports do not provide any insight into the power dynamics and political interests that influence the varying approaches taken by grassroots and higher-level authorities. The contrast between local governance being recklessly bad and high-ranking officials being responsible and good obscures the underlying factors that hinder institutional adherence to rural self-governance rules, particularly decisional transparency and accountability of rural governing powers to rural residents.

Overall, the chapter's analytical approach and findings offer valuable insights into Chinese rules and practices for managing and settling farmers' protests holistically and contextually. Those interested in advising the Chinese government on improving rural governance must recognise the growing identity of rural residents as rights holders and defenders. Despite the fact that China's rural governance reform has strengthened the governance competence of rural self-governing bodies, political authorities continue to interfere in the handling of farmers' protests. Given the evolving legal identity of Chinese farmers and the potential undermining effect of political intervention on the credibility of rural governing powers, it is important to prioritise procedural regularity and legal accountability in the management of rural disputes so as to facilitate the institutionalisation of the self-governance and rights-protecting rules in rural areas.

For those seeking to expand their understanding of the topic, the chapter covers the legislative and institutional aspects of Chinese measures for addressing farmers' complaints. However, it does not delve into the factors that initiate and shape these legislative and institutional developments. Therefore, further research is necessary to investigate the factors that motivate the central power to protect farmers' rights and local powers to comply with legal rules. Furthermore, it is unclear how news reports with a sympathetic tone relate to the decisions made by protesting farmers and the responding authorities. This could be an interesting area for future research. In conclusion, the chapter discusses the tale of two tiers within Chinese approaches to managing farmers' protests: while Chinese law has been extended to rural areas, it has not been adequately institutionalised. I hope that the chapter will serve as a valuable resource for readers interested in farmers' protests and their settlements in China, their institutional and social contexts and their impacts.

Appendix

Table 5.4 The composition of Groups A (2 Sept. 2011 to 19 Dec. 2011) and B (20 Dec. 2011 to 31 Jan. 2012)

	Producer of the news				
Corpus group	Newspaper	News journal	News agency	Web news	Size (in characters)
A (Protest reports)	54	0	8	0	57,165
B (Intervention reports)	180	5	21	0	308,648

Table 5.5 Top twenty most popular vocabularies in the data and Groups A and B

Overall		A		B	
Freq	Word	Freq	Word	Freq	Word
5150	*Society*	594	Villager	1500	Problem
4142	Problem	285	/	1486	Villager
3838	Villager	206	Incident	1437	/
3421	*Reform*	194	*Xue Jinbo*	1420	Mass
3352	/	192	Work	977	Wukan
2756	*Government*	185	/	975	/
2736	/	177	/	960	Work
2638	Incident	174	*Government*	908	Society
2458	Guangdong	173	/	896	Incident
2308	/	173	/	876	*Wukan* Village
2214	Work	172	*Wukan*	819	*Land*
2191	*Develop*	159	/	729	*Interests*
2137	/	157	/	712	Revolve
2072	/	151	/	709	/
2051	*Land*	147	/	689	*Appeal*
2034	*Election*	146	*Donghai*	650	/
1936	/	140	*Shanwei*	575	*Government*
1902	/	136	Wukan Village	525	/
1877	/	135	/	522	/
1843	/	134	/	503	/

List 1: Original Sources of Ten Randomly Selected Samples Where 'Villager' Occurs in Group A

594 KWIC results are produced from Group A with the search term defined as 'villager' and search window size set as '100' and the KWIC level set as level 1 (1R), level 2 (2R) and level 3 (3R). Ten samples are selected by the 'random selection' procedure in Microsoft Excel. The source of each selected news sample is listed below.

1. 《"心源性猝死" 嫌犯 未见 "断骨掉指甲"》, 北京青年报 | 2011-12-15报章 | A32 | 国内新闻 |
2. 《村民合理诉求全部得到落实》, 羊城晚报(全国版) | 2011-12-10报章 | A07 | 要闻 | By 王漫琪汕尾宣
3. 《广东官方回应陆丰群体性事件 村民诉求基本解决》, 中国新闻社 | 2011-12-09通讯社 | 国内新闻 |
4. 《广东陆丰在押男子猝死检方称未发现外力致死迹象》, 东方早报 | 2011-12-15报章 | A20 | 中国 |
5. 《陆丰村民为土地上访 引发打砸事件》, 南方都市报(全国版) | 2011-09-23报章| A22 | 城事 | By 陆新发
6. 《陆丰通报乌坎村民打砸事件 通报称事件造成当地多名干警受伤》, 广州日报 | 2011-09-23报章 | AII11 | 珠三角| By 秦仲阳

7. 《汕尾妥善处置陆丰乌坎事件》, 新快报 | 2011-12-10报章 | A06 | 时政新闻 | By 林良田汕尾宣
8. 《内容多风险 转发需谨慎》, 南方日报(全国版) | 2011-09-24报章 | A08 | By 闫昆仑
9. 《陆丰东海镇乌坎村发生少数村民聚众滋事故意毁坏财物案件》, 羊城晚报(全国版) | 2011-09-23报章 | A08 | 要闻 | By 王漫琪陆新发
10. 《境外势力参与陆丰群体事件广东汕尾通报事件处置情况》, 江南都市报| 2011-12-11报章| 07|国内新闻|

List 2: Original Sources of Ten Randomly Selected Samples Where 'Villager' Occurs in Group B

1486 KWIC results are produced from Group B with the search term defined as 'villager' and search window size set as '100' and the KWIC level set as level 1 (1R), level 2 (2R) and level 3 (3R). Ten samples are selected by the 'random selection' procedure in Microsoft Excel. The source of each selected news sample is listed below.

1. 《广东乌坎村村委会将重新选举》, 晶报 | 2012-01-16报章 | A10 | 时事综合 |
2. 《"乌坎转机" 提示我们什么》, 浙江日报 | 2011-12-24报章 | 03 | 要闻 |
3. 《省工作组通报第一阶段工作情况: 乌坎村问题调查取得重要进展》, 信息时报 | 2011-12-31报章 | A34 | 广东 |
4. 《广东省工作组介入乌坎事件 倾听民声解决村民诉求》, 中国新闻社 | 2011-12-21通讯社 | 国内新闻|
5. 《省工作组进驻陆丰解决乌坎事件》, 新快报 | 2011-12-21报章 | A15 | 时政新闻 | By 罗仕
6. 《拆路障拉横幅, 村民欢迎工作组》, 新民晚报 | 2011-12-23报章 | A-16 | 中国新闻 |
7. 《朱明国走访乌坎村》, 深圳商报 | 2011-12-23报章 | A10 | 要闻·国内 |
8. 《乌坎村经济50年:从围海打鱼到实业开发, 这个沿海渔村走过了一条怎样的发展之路?》, 第一财经日报 | 2011-12-27报章 | A01, A02 | 头版 | By 沈安贝
9. 《广东省工作组继续走访村民 乌坎村趋于平和》, 东方早报 | 2011-12-23报章 | A2-A3 | 大新闻, 广东陆丰乌坎事件 | 动态
10. 《汕尾市委书记郑雁雄通报乌坎事件有关决定政府收回并赔偿404亩涉事用地》, 南方日报(全国版) | 2011-12-20报章 | A16 | 广东·地方 | By 辛均庆 洪继宇

List 3: Original Sources of Ten Randomly Selected Samples Where 'Village Cadre' Occurs in the News

318 KWIC results are produced from the cleaned news data with the search term defined as 'village cadre' and search window size set as '100' and the KWIC level set as level 1 (1R), level 2 (2R) and level 3 (3R). Ten samples are selected by the 'random selection' procedure in Microsoft Excel. The source of each selected news sample is listed below.

1. 《李玉妹在汕尾调研时强调基层创先争优要务求实效》, 南方日报(全国版) | 2010-09-15报章 | A09 | 要闻 | By 周志坤 岳组

2. 《广东乌坎风波调查土地转让中村干部多人受贿一村民被抓后死亡致事件升级 维权村民曾在看守所遭虐待》, 江南都市报 | 2012-01-04报章 | C33 |
3. 《广东职务犯罪人员 村官占18.1% 省检透露, 近三年全省共查处农村基层组织人员贪污贿赂犯罪1053人》, 南方都市报(全国版) | 2013-03-22报章 | A08 | 政情By 任先博 万蜜
4. 《惠州培训千余 "村官" 市委书记授课》, 南方日报(全国版) |2012-08-25报章| A0 |要闻By 钟伟连
5. 《汕尾乌坎原8村官集体被 "双规" 》, 晶报 | 2012-04-22报章 | A14 | 中国社会|
6. 《省工作组通报第一阶段工作情况: 乌坎村问题调查取得重要进展》, 南方都市报(全国版) | 2011-12-31报章 | A07 | 重点 |
7. 《过了一道 "坎" 还有几道梁?》, 中华工商时报 | 2011-12-29报章 | 03 | 杜平| By 赵民望
8. 《破解 "乌坎困局" , 先推动产权改革》, 新京报|2013-02-15报章|A02|社论·来论|观察家By党国英
9. 《村官腐败是谁的尴尬》, 南方都市报(全国版) | 2012-04-15报章 | AII02 | 第一专栏 | 第一专栏 | By 郭巍青
10. 《广东乌坎土地转让存受贿等问题 村出纳被 "双规" 》, 中国新闻社 | 2011-12-30通讯社 国内新闻

List 4: Original Sources of Ten Randomly Selected Samples Where 'Villagers' Committee' Occurs in the News

1163 KWIC results are produced from the cleaned news data with the search term defined as 'villagers' committee' and search window size set as '100' and the KWIC level set as level 1 (1R), level 2 (2R) and level 3 (3R). Ten samples are selected by the 'random selection' procedure in Microsoft Excel. The source of each selected news sample is listed below.

1. 《广东省工作组通报调查结果乌坎村委会换届选举整体无效将尽快重选》, 京华时报 | 2011-12-30 报章 | A27 | 各地·社会 |
2. 《广东省委副书记:保证乌坎村代表人身安全》, 中国新闻社 | 2011-12-24通讯社 | 国内新闻 |
3. 《22名村民作竞职演讲 广东乌坎重新选举出村委会主任》, 长沙晚报 | 2012-03-05报章 | A13 | 中国/世界 |
4. 《汕尾乌坎村昨成立党总支部 村委会重新选举筹备小组同时成立林祖恋任书记及筹备组组长》, 南方都市报(全国版) | 2012-01-17报章 | A07 | 重点 |By 秦鸿雁
5. 《乌坎村民主选举不是独有的》, 北京青年报 | 2013-03-14报章 | A09 | 每日新闻 |
6. 《乌坎村问题调查取得重要进展》, 南方都市报(全国版) | 2011-12-31报章 | A07 | 重点 |
7. 《乌坎村重新选举出村委会主任》, 信息时报 | 2012-03-04报章 | A9 | 综合 |
8. 《省工作组通报村委换届选举问题调查情况和认定结果》, 南方日报(全国版)|2011-12-29|报章|A15|广东| By 辛均庆
9. 《乌坎村党总支部成立》, 深圳特区报|2012-01-16|报章|A11|中国新闻|By李强

10. 《乌坎, 这艘船如何驶出迷茫走向光明》, 新京报 | 2013-03-23报章 | B06 | 记者手记 |By 潘则福

List 5: Original Sources of Ten Randomly Selected Samples Where 'Government' Occurs in the News

2756 KWIC results are produced from the cleaned news data with the search term defined as 'government' and search window size set as '100' and the KWIC level set as level 1 (1R), level 2 (2R) and level 3 (3R). Ten samples are selected by the 'random selection' procedure in Microsoft Excel. The source of each selected news sample is listed below.

1. 《汕尾回应乌坎事件:村民合理诉求已落实》, 南方都市报(全国版)|2011-12-10报章|A1城事|By谭林
2. 《广东省派工作组解决乌坎事件 将进村了解村民诉求 汪洋称事件系长期忽视社会矛盾结果》, 京华时报 | 2011-12-22报章 | A21 | 各地·热点 |
3. 《汪洋治粤》, 经济观察报 | 2012-05-21报章|09|中国| 财经头条 | By 杨兴云 陈安庆 沈念祖 李骞
4. 《村民合理诉求全部得到落实》, 羊城晚报(全国版) | 2011-12-10报章 | A07 | 要闻|By 王漫琪汕尾宣
5. 《率先建立新型社会"自治"体系》, 广州日报 | 2012-03-10报章 | A01, A02 | 头版 | 头条
6. 《汪洋改革试验:GDP不再代表幸福》, 中国经营报 | 2012-04-02报章 | A10 | 经济大势 |
7. 《以信息开放推动一场改革》, 今晚报 | 2012-12-23报章 | 13 | 社会时事
8. 《这些年, 我们一起追过多少烂尾新闻?》, 南方日报(广州版) |2013-01-25报章|GC02|广州观察|By 彭晓芸
9. 《警惕先发地区陷阱》, 经济观察报|2011-12-26|报章|15|评论|社评|By 启越
10. 《朱明国称县委书记换太频 谈乌坎加强村镇组织建设》, 中国新闻社 | 2012-01-05|通讯社|国内新闻

List 6: Original Sources of Ten Randomly Selected Samples Where 'Provincial Government' Occurs in the News

508 KWIC results are produced from the cleaned news data with the search term defined as 'provincial government' and search window size set as '100' and the KWIC level set as level 1 (1R), level 2 (2R) and level 3 (3R). Ten samples are selected by the 'random selection' procedure in Microsoft Excel. The source of each selected news sample is listed below.

1. 《深化改革要敢于打破利益格局》, 新快报 | 2012-01-05报章 | A03 | 聚焦省委全会 |
2. 《广东乌坎村 原8名村官集体被"双规"》, 西部商报 | 2012-04-23 报章 | A11 | 国内社会 |
3. 《广东态度》, 南方都市报(全国版) | 2012-03-15报章 | A12 | 重点 | By 秦鸿雁
4. 《汪洋客串记者》, 第一财经日报 | 2012-03-06报章 | A01 | 头版 | By 许可新
5. 《省委领导和乌坎村民同饮功夫茶》, 新民晚报 | 2011-12-23报章 | A-16 | 中国新闻 |

6. 《26草根网帖冲出“海选”获评“南粤智多星”金点子》, 南方都市报(全国版) | 2012-02-28报章 | A06 | 政情 | By 陈良军 冯宙锋
7. 《跨过社会转型的“坎”》, 北京青年报 | 2012-01-15报章 | 每日新闻 |
8. 《林祖恋谈乌坎破局》, 财新周刊 | 2012-03-12杂志 | 66-69 | 民生 | By 屈运栩
9. 《广东团开放日汪洋妙答国内外媒体敏感问题和群众站在一起解决“乌坎事件”》, 汕头特区晚报 | 2012-03-06报章 | 01 | 头版 |
10. 《省工作组进驻陆丰解决乌坎事件 肯定村民的主要诉求合理, 具体调处土地、财务、干部和换届问题》, 汕头特区晚报 | 2011-12-21报章 | 10 | 今日看点/粤东新闻

List 7: Original Sources of Ten Randomly Selected Samples Where 'Self-Governance' Occurs in the News

521 KWIC results are produced from the cleaned news data with the search term defined as 'self-governance' and search window size set as '100' and the KWIC level set as level 1 (1R), level 2 (2R) and level 3 (3R). Ten samples are selected by the 'random selection' procedure in Microsoft Excel. The source of each selected news sample is listed below.

1. 《公开透明的选举开启乌坎未来》, 新京报 | 2012-02-03报章 | A02 | 社论·来信 | 社评
2. 《中国乡村的新乡绅时代》, 企业家日报 | 2013-09-07报章 | 12 | 名家论坛 |
3. 《过了一道“坎”还有几道梁?》, 中华工商时报 | 2011-12-29报章 | 03 | 杜平 | By 赵民望
4. 《基层民主走向进步》, 第一财经日报 | 2012-03-20报章 | A05 | 公共 | By 安卓 蓝之馨
5. 《长治久安:扩大公权还是还权于民》, 经济观察报 | 2012-06-11报章 | 33 | By 刘建锋
6. 《破解“乌坎困局”, 先推动产权改革》, 中国新闻社 | 2013-02-15通讯社 |
7. 《村民如何真正实现自治》, 南方都市报(全国版) | 2011-12-28报章 | A31 | 个论 | By 秋风
8. 《民政部副部长: “四方面”推动中国基层民主自治》, 中国新闻社 | 2013-03-08通讯社 |
9. 《乌坎事件非创新 村民自治路漫漫》, 中国经营报 | 2012-04-02报章 | A10 | 经济大势 |
10. 《基层民主选举法律不能靠边》, 京华时报 | 2011-12-30报章 | A02 | 声音 | 社评 | By 李光东

References

Article 10, in the Regulation of the People's Republic of China on Agriculture Tax (中华人民共和国农业税条例), adopted at the 96th session of the Standing Committee of the First National People's Congress on 3 June 1958 and effective on 3 June 1958. Available at: http://www.gov.cn/banshi/2005-08/19/content_24853.htm

Article 14 of the amendment to the Election Law of the People's Republic of China, adopted on 14 March 2010, replaced the disproportionate number of rural representatives before the People's congress. Available at: http://www.pkulaw.cn/fulltext_form.aspx?Gid=127960

Article 22, in the Organisational Law of the People's Courts of the People's Republic of China, adopted at the Fifth National People's Congress on 1 July 1979 and effective as of 1 January 1980. Available at: http://www.npc.gov.cn/zgrdw/englishnpc/Law/2007-12/13/content_1384078.htm

Article 38, in the 1979 Criminal Procedure Law of the People's Republic of China, adopted at the Fifth National People's Congress on 1 July 1979 and effective as of 1 January 1980. Available at: https://zh.wikisource.org/wiki/%E4%B8%AD%E5%8D%8E%E4%BA%BA%E6%B0%91%E5%85%B1%E5%92%8C%E5%9B%BD%E5%88%91%E4%BA%8B%E8%AF%89%E8%AE%BC%E6%B3%95_(1979%E5%B9%B4)

Article 43, in the 2004 Land Administration Law of the People's Republic of China. Available at: http://www.lawinfochina.com/display.aspx?lib=law&id=3673&CGid=

Article 71, in the Agriculture Law of the People's Republic of China, adopted at the Eighth National People's Congress on 2 July 1993 and effective on 1 March 2003. Available at: https://www.gov.cn/banshi/2005-09/12/content_69776.htm

Article 8, in the Implementation Opinions of the Chinese State Council on Guiding the Healthy Development of the Rural Property Circulation Market (国务院办公厅关于引导农村产权流转交易市场健康发展的意见), released by the General Office of the State Council on 30 December 2014. Available at: http://www.gov.cn/zhengce/content/2015-01/22/content_9424.htm

Article 9, in the Provisional Organisational Law of the Villagers' Committees of the People's Republic of China (中华人民共和国村民委员会组织法(试行)), adopted at the Sixth National People's Congress on 24 November 1987 and effective on 1 June 1988. Available at: https://zh.wikisource.org/wiki/%E4%B8%AD%E5%8D%8E%E4%BA%BA%E6%B0%91%E5%85%B1%E5%92%8C%E5%9B%BD%E6%9D%91%E6%B0%91%E5%A7%94%E5%91%98%E4%BC%9A%E7%BB%84%E7%BB%87%E6%B3%95%EF%BC%88%E8%AF%95%E8%A1%8C%EF%BC%89

Articles 1, 3 and 17, in the Marriage Law of the People's Republic of China, adopted by the Committee of the Central People's Government (exercising legislative powers before the adoption of the Chinese Constitution of 1954) on 13 April 1950 and effective on 13 April 1950. Available at: http://www.npc.gov.cn/zgrdw/npc/lfzt/rlys/2014-10/24/content_1882723.htm

Articles 12, 14 and 16, in the 2004 Election Law of the People's Republic of China for the National People's Congress and Local People's Congresses (中华人民共和国全国人民代表大会和地方各级人民代表大会选举法), adopted at the Fifth National People's Congress on 1 July 1979, amended in 1982, 1986, 1995 and 2004. Available at: http://en.pkulaw.cn/display.aspx?cgid=309b792df64efd67bdfb&lib=law

Articles 2, 3, 5, 8, 11, 13, 30, 36 and 40, in the Organisational Law of the Villagers' Committees of the People's Republic of China, adopted at the Ninth National People's Congress on 4 November 1998 and amended in 2010 and 2018. Available at: https://faolex.fao.org/docs/pdf/chn153710.pdf

Articles, 2, 6-8, in the 1982 Constitution of the People's Republic of China, adopted by the Fifth National People's Congress on 4 December 1982 and effective on 4 December 1982. Available at: https://www.elegislation.gov.hk/hk/A1%21en-sc.assist.pdf

Articles 2-4, 9, 10, 31 and 59-61, in the 2019 Land Administration Law of the People's Republic of China, adopted at the Sixth National People's Congress on 25 June 1986 and amended in 1988, 1998, 2004 and 2019. Available at: https://jijian.caas.cn/docs/2021-06/20210630110219559944.pdf

Articles 3, 6, 10 and 14, in the Regulation on the Agricultural Taxation of the People's Republic of China, adopted by the Standing Committee of the National People's Congress on 3 June 1958 and effective on 3 June 1958. Available at: http://www.pkulaw.cn/fulltext_form.aspx?Gid=209

Articles 3 and 10, in the Regulation of the People's Republic of China on Household Registration (中华人民共和国户口登记条例), adopted by the National People's Congress on 9 January

1958 and effective on 9 January 1958. Available at: http://www.law-lib.com/law//law_view.asp?id=1338

Articles 6 and 8, in the People's Mediation Law of the People's Republic of China, adopted by the Eleventh National People's Congress on 28 August 2010 and effective on 1 January 2011. Available at: http://www.gov.cn/flfg/2010-08/29/content_1691209.htm

Articles 8 and 19, in the 1954 Constitution of the People's Republic of China, adopted by the First National People's Congress on 20 September 1954 and invalidated by the adoption of the Constitution of the People's Republic of China in 1975. Available at: http://www.lawinfochina.com/Display.aspx?lib=law&Cgid=52993

Caixin News (2013) Press Conference at the Ministry of Civil Affairs (民政部长就保障基本民生答记者问). Published on 13 March 2013. https://china.caixin.com/2013-03-13/100500880.html

Chen X (2011) Social protest and contentious authoritarianism in China. Cambridge University Press, p 36

Chen A (2014) The transformation of governance in rural China: market, finance, and political authority. Cambridge University Press, pp 64 and 189–196

Chengri D (2014) Land and development in China. In: The Oxford companion to the economics of China. Oxford University Press, p 344

Cui E, Tao R et al (2015) How do land takings affect political trust in rural China? Polit Stud 63:93

Ewing K (2012) Guangdong Boss Bets on Velvet Glove. The Asian Times, published on 7 January 2012. https://web.archive.org/web/20120512133142/http://www.atimes.com/atimes/China/NA07Ad02.html. Accessed 24 May 2017

Golas PJ (1980) Rural China in Song. J Asian Stud 39:300

He X (2014a) Maintaining stability by law: protest-supported housing demolition litigation and social change in China. Law Soc Inq 39(4):852–853

He X (2014b) Protest-supported housing demolition litigation and social change in China. In: Hualing F, John G (eds) Resolving land disputes in East Asia: exploring the limits of law. Cambridge University Press, pp 202–206

Hongwen L (2006) A study of rural tax reform and rural governance in China. China Reform Institute on 29 March 2006, p 13. Available at: http://www.crfoundation.org/filesCser/200501.pdf

Hualing F (2014) What does Wukan offer? Land-taking, law, and dispute resolution. In: Hualing F, John G (eds) Resolving land disputes in East Asia: exploring the limits of law. Cambridge University Press, pp 190–191

Huang PCC (2008) Centralised minimalism: semi-formal governance by quasi officials and dispute resolution in China. Mod China 34(1):13–14, 28–30

Huang PCC (2010) Chinese civil justice: past and present. Rowman & Littlefield, pp 21–57

Jian-feng L (2012) Decoding Wukan: concerns about the game over rights (乌坎密码:权利的博弈引发机制深忧). The Economist Observer (8 June 2012). Available at: http://finance.sina.com.cn/roll/20120608/231812265673.shtml

Jianrong Y (2005) The origin and development of farmers' rights-defending associations: a case on Hengyang Farmers' Group (当代中国农民维权组织的发育与成长:基于衡阳农民协会的实证研究). China Rural Survey 2:62

Jianrong Y (2011) Demolition conflicts during China's social transformation: a perspective of maintaining social stability (从维稳的角度看社会转型期的拆迁矛盾). Chin Cadres Tribune 1:20

Jie C (2014) The judicial role in land-taking cases. In: Hualing F, John G (eds) Resolving land disputes in East Asia: exploring the limits of law. Cambridge University Press, pp 93–94 and 99

Jingyong X (2009) Planned purchase and distribution of agricultural products: the foundation for Chinese planned economy (中国计划经济体制的引擎: 粮食等主要农产品统购统销). J Party School CPC Xiamen Municipal Committee 107(3):7

Jinhua D, Zhiguo C et al (2018) A study of the scale and impacts of land-related fiscal revenues in China (我国土地财政规模估算及影响因素研究). West Forum 28(1):58–59. Available at: https://core.ac.uk/download/pdf/323958283.pdf

Kun L (2020) The central-local fiscal relations in China (我国的中央和地方财政关系), the report by the Finance Minister of China, published 12 August 2020. Available at: http://www.npc.gov.cn/npc/c2/c30834/202008/t20200812_307214.html

Lin JY (1988) The household responsibility system in China's agricultural reform: a theoretical and empirical study. Econ Dev Cult Change 36(3):201

Lin JY (1990) Collectivisation and China's agricultural crisis in 1959-1961. J Polit Econ 98(6): 1231–1238

Lu Z (2012) A story about Wukan (乌坎事鉴). Lens 47(01):53–67

Michelson E (2008) Justice from above or below? Popular strategies for resolving grievances in rural China. China Q 193:48

Mingjun Z, Xiaoliang L (2016) Report on mass group incidents in Chinese society in 2015 (2015年中国社会群体性事件分析报告). Study Chin Public Secur 8:3–4

Mu QE (2011) Merits and demerits of political system in ancient China (中国历代政治得失). Beijing Jiuzhou Press, pp 16–19

Niou EMS (2015) On local governance in China: from feudalism, centralised bureaucracy to self-governance. In: Fuh-sheng Hsieh J (ed) Confucian culture and democracy. World Scientific Publishing, pp 230–231

O'Brien KJ, Lianjiang L (2012) Rightful resistance in rural China. Cambridge University Press, pp 51–59

Paragraph 18, in the Resolutions on Several Issues Concerning the Construction of Socialist Market Economy (中共中央关于建立社会主义市场经济体制若干问题的决定), adopted by the Central Committee of CPC on 11 November 1993. Available at: https://www.waizi.org.cn/law/3442.html

Paragraph 4, in the "Communiqué on the Results of the First National Census (关于第一次全国人口调查登记结果的公报), published by the National Bureau of Statistics of People's Republic of China on 1 November 1954.: https://www.stats.gov.cn/sj/tjgb/rkpcgb/qgrkpcgb/202302/t20230206_1901986.html

Paragraph 7 in Section 3, in the Advisory Opinions on the Strengthening of Grassroots Democracy and Law-based Governance in Rural Areas (关于进一步加强农村基层民主法制建设的意见), published by the Ministry of Civil Affairs and the Ministry of Justice on 8 January 2003. Available at: https://www.moj.gov.cn/pub/sfbgw/zwxxgk/fdzdgknr/fdzdgknrtzwj/202103/t20210316_207482.html

Paragraphs 1 and 2, in the Resolution on the Class Status of Children of Landlords and Rich Farmers (关于地主、富农分子摘帽问题和地、富子女成份问题的决定), issued by the Central Committee of the CPC on 11 January 1979. Available at: https://ccradb.appspot.com/post/869

Paragraphs 4 and 6, in the Decision to Set up the Country-level Government to Take Over Rural Administration by the Collective Commune (中共中央、国务院关于实行政社分开建立乡政府的通知), adopted by the Central Committee of the CPC and the State Council on 12 October 1983. Available at: http://www.reformdata.org/1983/1012/6027.shtml

Paragraphs 5, 8 and 11. In: Guangxiang W (2013) HU Yaobang and the Birth of the No. 1 Document of the Central Committee of the CPC in 1982 (胡耀邦与1982年中央1号文件的诞生). Historical Archives of Hu Yaobang. Available at: http://www.reformdata.org/2013/0110/9031.shtml

Point 5 in Article 4 in the Problems with the Socialist Education in Rural Areas (农村社会主义教育运动中目前提出的一些问题), adopted by the Central Committee of the CPC on 28 December 1964. Available at: http://www.ce.cn/xwzx/gnsz/szyw/200706/13/t20070613_11731665.shtml

Public Opinion Monitoring Centre (2012) Annual Report on Mass Group Incidents of 2012 (法制网舆情监测中心2012年群体性事件研究报告). Published 28 December 2012 at: https://www.chinacourt.org/article/detail/2013/01/id/810350.shtml. Accessed 25 Feb 2017

Qi Z, Mingxing L et al (2004) Government regulation, legal control and grassroots democracy in rural areas (政府管制、法律软约束与农村基层民主). Econ Res J 6:61

Section 2 in the "Resolution on Setting up the People's Commune in Rural Areas (中共中央关于在农村建立人民公社问题的决议)", adopted by the Central Committee of the CPC on 29 August 1958. Available at: http://www.reformdata.org/1958/0829/8798.shtml

Section 21 "Endowing farmers with more property rights", in the Decision on Several Big Issues on Promoting the Reform and Development (中共中央关于全面深化改革若干重大问题的决定), adopted at the 17th National Congress of the CPC on 12 October 2008. Available at: http://www.china.org.cn/china/third_plenary_session/2014-01/16/content_31212602_6.htm

Shukai Z (2017) Regeneration of farmers. Springer Nature Singapore, p 57

Statistics from the national judgement database 'China Judgements Online', with the search conditions defined as: administrative case + township government + between 1 January 2014 and 31 December 2019. Accessed 7 Apr 2020. https://wenshu.court.gov.cn/

Table 12, in the "Household Consumption and Its Indices (全国居民消费水平指数)" in the Compilation of Statistics of China from 1949 to 1998 (新中国五十年统计资料汇编 1949-1998). China Statistics Press, 2011, p 185

Table 59 "Population of Xiaozong Reign in Ming Dynasty (明孝宗朝户数)" and Table 77 "Population of Xianfeng and Tongzhi Reigns in Qing Dynasty (清咸丰、同治两朝的人口数)". In: Fangzhong L (ed) (2008) Statistics on households, farm lands and taxes in Ancient China (中国历代户口、田地、田赋统计), Zhonghua Book Company, pp 266 and 348

Table 7-1 "Public Revenues and Expenditures from 1978 to 2013 (公共财政收支总额及增长速度)", In the China Statistics Yearbook of 2014, published by the National Bureau of Statistics of China. Available at: http://www.stats.gov.cn/tjsj/ndsj/2014/indexch.htm

Tao R, Liu M et al (2011) Grain procurement, tax instrument and farmer burdens during China's rural transition. J Contemp China 20(71):659

The Decision on Planned Purchase and Planned Distribution of Grains (中共中央关于实行粮食的计划收购和计划供应的决议), adopted by the Central Committee of CPC on 16 October 1953. Available at: http://www.reformdata.org/1953/1016/9445.shtml

Weimin Z (2015) An empirical study on the financial system of China's Grassroots Court (中国基层法院财政制度实证研究). China Leg Stud 1:268–269

Wenfang T, Qing Y (2008) The Chinese urban caste system in transition. China Q 196:761

Whiting WH, Shao H (2014) Courts and political stability: mediating rural land disputes. In: Hualing F, John G (eds) Resolving land disputes in East Asia: exploring the limits of law. Cambridge University Press, pp 233–240

Xi W (2015) A reflection on financial management of basic-level courts. Chinese Court website (7 December 2015) http://bjgy.chinacourt.gov.cn/article/detail/2015/12/id/1763546.shtml. Accessed 7 Apr 2019

Xinhua News (2006) The Abolition of Agricultural Taxes, published on 6 March 2006. Available at: http://www.gov.cn/test/2006-03/06/content_219801.htm

Xinhua News (2022) The decreasing income gap between rural and urban residents (国家统计局:10年来我国城乡居民收入相对差距持续缩小), published 11 October 2022. Available at: http://www.news.cn/fortune/2022-10/11/c_1129060653.htm

Xinzhong Y (1997) Social remedies provided by local aristocrats in the Qing Dynasty: a case on Feng-yu-yi village in Suzhou (清中后期乡绅的社会救济——苏州丰豫义庄研究). Nankai J (Philos Lit Soc Sci Ed) 3:63–65

Xue-feng S (2022) The revenue scale and structure and their changes in the Qing Dynasty (清代财政收入规模与结构变化述论). Soc Sci 01. Table 3. Available at: https://content.csbs.utah.edu/~mli/Economies%205430-6430/Jia-Qing%20Dynasty%20Fiscal%20Revenue.pdf

Yanbing Z, Zhimin Z (2015) Autonomy of local governments and social mandate in the case of Wukan rural resistance (政商关系的缔结、固化与瓦解: 乌坎土地抗争中的地方政府自主性与社会力量). Public Adm Rev 20(3):80–89
Yansui L, Ren Y et al (2014) Implications of land-use change in rural China: a case study of Yucheng, Shandong province. Land Use Policy 40:116
Yinghong Z (2009) Farmer, citizenship and state: a case research for the Shanjiaoxia Village in the Hunan Province (农民、公民权与国家:以湖南省山脚下村为例). China Rural Survey 3:77
Yongjun H (2013) Transition in rural society and people's mediation (乡村社会嬗变与人民调解制度变迁). Law Soc Dev 109(1):80–81
Zhang QF, Oya C et al (2015) Bringing agriculture back in the central place of Agrarian change in rural China in rural China studies. J Agrarian Change 15(3):300
Zhaozi R, Chunmei W (2005) The past, present and future of farmer-related challenges in China (中国三农问题). Social Sciences Academic Press, pp 71 and 160
Zulan X (2014) Historical evolution of the relationship between the state and local elites at the end of Qing Dynasty and the beginning of Republic China (清末民初国家权力与绅权关系的历史嬗变). Peking Univ Law J 26(3):602–603

Chapter 6
Conclusion: The Challenged Juridification of Chinese Approaches to Addressing Mass Actions

6.1 A Holistic and Nuanced Account of Juridification in Chinese Cases

A State governance model is not created but rather becomes a rule-based system. To explain the characteristics of the Chinese governance model, it is essential to provide a holistic and nuanced account of its governance norms, mechanisms and procedures, as well as the key institutional and social changes that interact with them. This book analyses Chinese rules and practices for addressing collective grievances from citizens for which the government is allegedly responsible. The book focuses on the dynamics of government-citizen relations and interactions in contemporary times. It details the interplay between indigenous dispute resolution traditions and external influences of accountability rules that hold government decisions accountable to the law and the public and the interplay between mass actions and accountable authorities in China.

The research on mass actions and their resolutions in China is guided by two lines of analysis. One views mass actions as a confrontation between the authorities and the complainants. This analysis concludes that the Chinese government resorts to suppressive tactics in handling mass actions and presents a systematic hostility to mass action participants. The other characterises mass actions as disputes between specific decision-making authorities and affected citizens and evaluates the effectiveness of different settlements to identify good resolution measures. However, the confrontationist and settlementist approaches do not fully capture the dynamics of Chinese measures for managing mass actions.

Therefore, focusing on formalising and institutionalising government accountability rules within Chinese governance, this book aims to address the theoretical and analytical limitations of existing scholarship. Previous studies either adopt a simplistic perspective that overestimates the monolithicity of China's governing powers in dealing with mass grievances or underestimate the impact of Occidental governance notions on Chinese measures for dealing with mass actions. In contrast, this

C.-r. Qiao, *Chinese Rules and Procedures for Addressing Mass Actions*,
https://doi.org/10.1007/978-3-031-62201-4_6

book presents two interrelated analyses. First, it outlines the historical and governance contexts that shape government-citizen interactions in China, including their contentious interactions. It also examines Chinese norms and practices for addressing citizen grievances allegedly caused by the government.

The prevailing assumption that the absence of political plurality in State governance automatically implies the absence of rule-based governance evolution is overly simplistic and fails to capture the multifaceted characteristics of China's legal and institutional developments. This multifacetedness is evidenced by the coexistence and conflict between different rules and procedures in concluding mass actions. Neglecting or dismissing the evolutionary aspects of Chinese approaches to addressing mass actions results in the omission of significant changes in their legislative, institutional and social contexts, such as the enactment of legal accountability for government decision-making, procedural separation of administrative and judicial jurisdictions in settling complaints about government decisions, and increasing legal assertiveness of Chinese citizens in seeking redress for their losses caused by government decision or conduct.

In light of these issues, the book develops a comprehensive and nuanced approach to explaining and evaluating the Chinese dispute resolution system, with a particular focus on the juridification of its rules and policies for dealing with mass actions, in which groups of complainants seek redress for injustices or losses from the governing authorities they believe to be responsible. Specifically, Chap. 1 introduces the geopolitical and research context of this book, explains its analytical assumptions, focus and methods, summarises its findings and acknowledges its limitations. The chapter provides a rationale for developing a juridification account of the management and settlement of mass action in China, highlighting the contributions of this study to the field of research as well as to policy areas related to Chinese measures to address selected areas of mass actions. Chapter 2 presents a detailed account of indigenous Chinese traditions of regulating government-citizen relations and managing grievances against ruling powers, exploring their interplay with Occidental governance accountability notions and norms throughout the twentieth century. It provides readers with the knowledge necessary to understand the evolution of contemporary Chinese rules of government accountability, and the measures used to implement these rules.

Next, the book provides empirical and new analytical insights into the socialisation of government accountability rules in the context of mass actions and their settlements from the 1990s to the present. It looks not only at the adoption of formal rules that make Chinese governing bodies legally accountable to the public and protect citizens' rights to challenge and appeal government decisions and their institutional implementation but also at how they influence the development of social norms regarding the proper ways to present complaints about the government and the appropriate responses from those responsible in China. It combines an analysis of Chinese dispute resolution traditions and their legal and institutional developments in modern and contemporary times with an examination of their impact on socially accepted relations and interactions between Chinese citizens and governmental authorities.

Specifically, Chaps. 3, 4, and 5 scrutinise Chinese approaches to dealing with three types of mass actions: collective petitions, labour actions and farmers' protests. These case studies exemplify the shifting dynamics between China's administrative and judicial powers, between government orders and legal rules, and between political intervention and legal regulation in the review and resolution of mass actions. Each case study provides a detailed examination of the legislative, institutional and social contexts for the emergence and expansion of mass actions and their eventual outcomes. These case analyses address the question of whether the institutionalisation and socialisation of accountability rules are progressing in China or lagging when it comes to collective grievances against government decision or its implementation.

The analyses and findings presented in this book are not intended to advocate a relativist argument. It does not claim that there is anything inherently peculiar about the Chinese dispute resolution system or its process of juridification, nor does it argue that the growing importance of law in Chinese rules and procedures for dealing with mass action is an inevitable development. Rather, throughout the book, I have thoroughly examined both law-based and less-law-bound aspects of Chinese measures for dealing with mass action, and also identified key challenges that hinder China's transition towards a rule-based governance system and require timely and deliberate changes by decision-makers and institutional implementers in China.

In short, the juridification account informs the formalisation, institutionalisation and socialisation of government accountability rules in Chinese approaches to dealing with mass actions. It corrects existing dichotomous and static assumptions and explanations, both conceptually and empirically. It shifts the focus to the critical question of whether the importance of law is on the rise or on the decline in the Chinese governance model in general and its arrangements for dealing with mass actions in particular. As detailed in the next two sections, there are promising signs that the institutionalisation and socialisation of law are emerging and growing in the context of Chinese approaches to managing and resolving collective petitions, labour actions and farmers' protests. However, these developments are accompanied by significant challenges. Each case study concludes with suggestions for addressing the challenges identified. Researchers, policymakers and other readers interested in the characteristics of Chinese State governance or its arrangements for dealing with mass actions will find this book a valuable resource for understanding the multifacetedness of the theme and topics covered in the book, as well as the major changes and challenges they face.

6.2 Institutionalising Government Accountability Rules in Settling Mass Actions

The modern reformation of Chinese State governance encompasses two distinct trends that have shaped contemporary Chinese rules and procedures for handling citizen complaints against the government. First, there has been a shift from a central-local division of governance to a top-down unification of governance norms and mechanisms. This transition has its origins in China's Republican era from the 1910s to the 1940s, when the then government sought to unify fragmented governing agencies and practices across the vast country in order to restore the strength of the Chinese nation. Later, the Chinese socialist government, established in 1949, furthered the conformity of Chinese State governance, with central decision-makers extending their command over local economic, administrative and social governance from the 1950s to the 1970s.

On the other hand, a counter-trend has emerged, with the withdrawal of central command from directly determining local economic, administrative and social affairs. China's central power is shifting its governance role towards maintaining an effective regulatory environment in which the decisions and conduct of the governing authorities are accountable to the law and the public. In this process, the introduction of government accountability rules has been crucial in defining the powers and duties of China's governing bodies, recognising the rights of citizens to challenge the functioning of these bodies and seek a fair review of government decisions that negatively affect their rights and interests. These two trends characterise the development of contemporary Chinese approaches to governance in general and to the management of citizen grievances in particular. They resulted in three major changes to Chinese legislative, institutional and social landscapes.

First, there is a changing relationship between complainants and governing powers in China. One significant difference between ancient and modern State governance is the political, economic, and social status of ordinary citizens. Ancient Chinese governance traditions did consider the well-being of the general population, but more in a moral sense than a legal sense. The indigenous governance principle of reciprocity requires the ruling power to be competent in governing the society. However, it did not actively specify any sanctions on the ruling power for failing to safeguard the well-being of the general public. In the 1910s, the republican government introduced the principle of people-oriented governance, which redefined the relationship between citizens and their governing powers. The 1912 Provisional Constitution of the Republic of China enshrined the principle that Chinese governing bodies have a duty to protect the economic, political, and social interests of citizens and redress government-induced harm to those interests. It led to a different conceptualisation of citizen complaints about the government in modern China.

The book presents three case studies that provide comprehensive insights into this profound shift. Chinese measures for handling collective petitions were initially guided by the mass-line doctrine, which required government officials to align with the working masses and intervene in the management of their grievances. Government petition handlers were used to settling petitions in line with government policies and officials' guiding opinions. Chinese workers used to be systematically dependent on their work units under the command economy from the 1950s and the 1980s. Work units, which are accountable to the Chinese government, exerted significant control over the professional and private lives of workers, making it uncommon for workers to voice complaints against their employer or the government. Similarly, Chinese farmers have historically assumed the role of duty fulfillers for rural and central governing powers, and this role continued under the rural collective commune mechanism that was implemented nationwide in the 1950s and dissolved in the 1980s.

Since the mid-1990s, the Chinese petition-handling procedure has shifted from protecting the interests of the working masses to safeguarding the legitimate rights and interests of individuals and legal parties. In the area of labour relation management, a transition occurred as China moved from a command to a market economy during the 1980s and 1990s, which led to a decrease in workers' dependence on their work units. Meanwhile, Chinese workers gained legal recognition and protection of their labour rights. These developments enabled workers to address grievances with their employers at labour dispute resolution venues. In the area of rural governance, China transitioned from a collectivised governance model to a self-governance model, the latter being based on direct elections for the grassroots governing body of the villagers' committee and general participation in village decision-making processes. The changes have allowed farmers to become autonomous rights holders, entitled to make their own political and economic decisions. Legal rules that protect the rights of Chinese citizens while regulating the powers of governing bodies have brought significant changes in the governance landscape in present-day China.

Secondly, there has been a significant increase in legislation-led development of Chinese approaches to addressing mass actions. This has had a great impact on the legal rights and protections available to complainants against the government. From the 1910s to the 1940s, the Republican government adopted administrative justice concepts and procedures and enacted a series of rules to recognise and safeguard the right of Chinese citizens to challenge the government before judicial and administrative review venues. The 1954 Chinese Constitution, adopted by the socialist State, further confirmed that citizens have the right to file complaints against State organs or their personnel for violating the law or failing to fulfil their duties. However, this right was not effectively enforced until the 1990s. In 1995, the National Regulation on Complaint Letters and Visits formally annulled the quasi-judicial power previously held by the government's petition-handling departments. Since then, China has implemented jurisdictional and procedural reforms to align the petition-handling process with laws-based administrative reconsideration and court review procedures. This has subjected the operation and accountability of petition settlements to legal regulations.

In 1994, the Chinese Labour Law was enacted, which separated workers' labour rights and entitlements from their political and social status. This provided robust legal protections for workers and established a tripartite labour dispute resolution mechanism consisting of labour dispute mediation, arbitration and litigation. Furthermore, the implementation of the Chinese Organisational Law of the Villagers' Committees in 1998, along with national regulations on agricultural taxes and rural land use, marked the legislative correction of past discriminatory practices against rural residents. Additionally, the government's initiatives to disseminate the law and provide judicial remedies to rural areas have significantly impacted the relationship between Chinese farmers and rural governing bodies. In summary, the legislation-led reform of Chinese measures for settling mass actions marks a significant shift in their settlement bases and processes. Statutory appeal procedures are now the primary means for addressing grievances about government decisions or conduct.

Thirdly, Chinese approaches to managing mass actions have seen the emergence of legal accountability alongside political accountability as a prominent trend. Prior to the 1990s, Chinese measures for addressing complaints about governing bodies lacked a legal framework. China's previous governance model was primarily influenced by revolutionary principles and based on political decisions, with legislation playing a subordinate role in various areas of State governance. Legal rules were systematically marginalised in resolving disputes of various kinds, and dispute resolution agencies did not take the law seriously in their decision-making. In recent decades, the role of law in the Chinese dispute resolution system has been revived. Previously, Chinese administrative power held greater influence than its legislative and judicial counterparts in settling complaints about the government. Since the 1990s, there has been a growing recognition of the need to establish legal accountability of government decisions and conduct. This has led to a more balanced approach to addressing objections to government decisions that combines political norms and legal rules in the settlement.

The case studies of collective petitions, labour actions, and farmers' protests provide insight into this developing trend. China has been reorienting its government petition procedure to become a subsidiary of statutory appeal procedures of administrative reconsideration and administrative litigation. This shift moves away from politically motivated settlements of petition cases and towards legally based ones. However, the involvement of senior officials in handling collective petitions poses a challenge to these shifts. While political engagement may ensure procedural efficiency and, in some cases, enforceability of settlement decisions, it can also undermine the credibility and effectiveness of law-based review procedures, which is evident in the issue of forum shopping by petitioners. The cultivation of a culture of public trust in statutory review procedures among petitioners is still a work in progress.

Similarly, it is widely acknowledged that the Chinese government has a duty to provide a fair and efficient settlement of labour disputes. However, the venues responsible for deciding on these settlements are bound not only by Chinese labour protection rules but also by political norms that emphasise economic and social stabilities. Labour complainants have often expressed frustration with settlement results that they had agreed to under pressure from the dispute resolution authority, the trade union, or the labour management department of the government. Chinese measures for handling collective complaints by farmers rely on national laws and regulations as an important reference during village-level dispute mediation. Court review has also been introduced and promoted in rural areas. However, rural dispute mediation and court review are often ineffective due to limited capacity or suspected partiality. This results in frequent political intervention by higher-level authorities in resolving farmers' protests.

In summary, the integration of government accountability regulations into the Chinese dispute resolution system has resulted in significant changes in how China handles grievances against the government in general and mass actions in particular. These changes reveal themselves in several dimensions. There is a growing recognition that Chinese governing bodies hold the legal duty to safeguard the legitimate rights and interests of Chinese citizens and provide venues for redressing those who have suffered losses from government decisions. Furthermore, the expansion of legislation-led reconfiguration of Chinese dispute resolution procedures has played a central role in shaping the dynamics of mass actions and the responses of Chinese authorities. The shift towards a more rule-based approach to resolving disputes is reflected in the settlements of mass actions. Additionally, the inclusion of legal accountability alongside political accountability of Chinese authorities shapes the contents and outcomes of mass actions.

However, achieving coherence between legal accountability rules and mass action settlements, as well as reconciling legal regulations and political norms, continue to pose challenges to the institutionalisation of government accountability rules in China. Decisions made by administrative and judicial review bodies are not yet consistent with applicable legal rules. Additionally, the adherence to political norms of containing socially disruptive collective actions creates conflicts with the protection of the right to appeal government decisions and seek legitimate redress. Overall, although there is a growing trend towards a more rule-based and legally accountable approach to addressing complaints about the government, reconciling conflicts between legal and political considerations in the settlement of mass actions and ensuring consistency between legal rules and mass action settlements remains an ongoing challenge to consolidating the power of law in the Chinese dispute resolution system.

6.3 Socialising Government Accountability Rules in Mass Actions

In recent decades, China has undergone a significant transformation in its social norms, placing greater importance on legal sensitivity and aligning social codes of conduct with statutory duties and entitlements. Historically, the Chinese governance principle did not explicitly emphasise the division between duties and rights of public and private parties. The dominant Chinese governance tradition relied on reciprocity, with the governed supporting their governing bodies as long as the latter demonstrated the competencies to govern the society well. However, in contemporary times, external influences and domestic changes are rapidly changing the construct of social norms regarding reasonable government-citizen interactions and proper responses of the government to citizen grievances.

It is evident that China has made a constitutional commitment to establish a rule-based governance framework. This has been accompanied by the introduction of numerous laws that regulate the Chinese economy, public administration and dispute resolution. However, it is unclear whether the legislation-led governance development has successfully reshaped Chinese social culture and effectively transmitted the spirit and contents of the law to individual and collective decision-making processes. This complex issue of integrating legal rules into social norms lacks simple or quick answers. In recent years, computational methods have advanced for collecting and processing big data, enabling the software assisted content anlaysis of vast collections of uninterrupted news reports and commentaries. This presents an opportunity to identify prevailing narratives and uncover what is commonly understood as normal and reasonable in Chinese official and non-official news.

The book presents three case studies that offer valuable empirical insights into the socialisation of Chinese government accountability rules in the context of mass actions. These studies reveal the extent to which accountability rules are present and popular in recurring news narratives and framings between the late 1990s and the mid-2010s. While news references to legal rules are becoming more common in coverage of mass actions and their settlements, the news coverage does not consistently portray the rules that protect the substantive and procedural rights of complainants and regulate the power and decision-making of governing authorities as the most relevant grounds for qualifying mass actions and assessing their settlements.

Specifically, more recent news coverage of collective petitions adopts a narrative focused on the petitioners, emphasising their shared grievances and assessing whether they receive timely responses and fair redress. In contrast, early news reports maintain a government-centric narrative, criticising collective petitions as disruptive to the functioning of petition-handling procedures in China. They justify government measures aimed at dispersing petitioners and monitoring public discontent. Similar changes are observed in Chinese news coverage of labour actions. Recurring news narratives often prioritise the efficiency of labour action settlements and their contribution to restoring the interrupted production of the concerned enterprises, rather than focusing on the compliance of settlements with labour protection rules or the satisfaction of labour complainants with the outcomes. Nevertheless, recurring news narratives are increasingly sympathetic toward labour complainants, highlighting the growing legal awareness among workers and attributing labour unrest to the misconduct of employing parties. The news also focuses more on labour protection and equal treatment rules, describing the nature and developments of labour actions in terms of the violation of workers' labour rights.

Regarding news reports on farmers' protests, there is a noticeable shift in popular narratives from describing farmers' protesters as troublemakers to justifying their complaining actions as understandable. This shift is closely linked to high-level political intervention. Prior to political support, the prevailing narrative portrays farmers' protesters as aggressors and government measures to disperse and penalise them as reasonable. However, following political intervention, the recurring narratives become sympathetic towards protesting farmers. They are depicted as victims of corrupt and ineffective rural governing powers, with an emphasis on procedural transparency and public participation in the settlement of farmers' complaints and claims.

Despite this significant change, Chinese legal rules that protect rural self-governance and farmers' economic and political rights are not framed as the primary basis for evaluating the settlements of farmers' protests in the news. Instead, the dominant news narratives use a blaming frame, portraying village cadres and grassroots officials as responsible for decision-making malpractices and confrontational approaches that antagonised protesting farmers. In addition, news narratives often use a dichotomous framing that portrays high-level political authorities as responsive, transparent and efficient in resolving farmers' complaints, while rural governing bodies are depicted as law avoiders and rule breakers. These narratives oversimplify the complex interplay of legal accountability, political accountability and economic motives of rural governing bodies, and can lead to the issue of lacking trust of rural residents in their local governing bodies.

In conclusion, the three case studies offer empirical insights into the evolving socialisation of government accountability rules in contemporary China. Although there is an increasing presence of legal references in Chinese news coverage, the news does not consistently depict legal rules as the primary basis for qualifying mass actions or evaluating their outcomes. Chinese news media have not yet established a legally relevant framing when reporting on mass actions and assessing different responses from responsible authorities. As China continues its commitment to transition towards a rule-based governance framework, it is crucial to bridge the gap between legal rules and social norms, ensuring that relevant laws are widely recognised, respected and applied in the content and settlement of complaints about the government. The incorporation of legal rules in recurring news narratives can play an important role in shaping social norms and promoting the juridification of Chinese measures to address mass actions.

6.4 Challenged Juridification of Chinese Approaches to Addressing Mass Actions

This book offers a comprehensive and detailed account of the formalisation, institutionalisation and socialisation of government accountability rules in Chinese approaches to managing and resolving mass actions. The book makes a valuable contribution to understanding the Chinese State governance model and its likely future. It employs a cross-disciplinary analytical approach and leverages a deep understanding of indigenous Chinese dispute resolution traditions and their modern transitions, as well as key legislative, institutional and social developments of government-citizen relationships and interactions in contemporary China.

The book analyses the formal integration of rules that hold Chinese governing powers accountable to the law and public since the 1980s, the institutionalisation of legal regulations on the conduct and decision of governing powers and dispute resolution authorities since the 1990s, and the socialisation of legal accountability rules in the content and form of mass actions over the last two decades. This demonstrates the juridification of Chinese approaches to dealing with mass actions. In explaining and assessing Chinese measures for addressing complaints about the government in general and mass actions in particular, it is important to consider these dynamics. The introduction of legal rules that recognise and protect the substantive and procedural rights of citizens has transformed complainants' expectations and decisions. This has, in turn, compelled Chinese authorities to provide consistent and rule-based remedies for government-induced harms or losses. Furthermore, legal rules in China that regulate the power of governing authorities are increasingly being incorporated into popular news narratives about mass actions and their settlements. This integration of legal rules into news discourse fosters sympathy and support for complainants seeking to defend their legal entitlements, suggesting changing social norms on accepted government-citizen interactions and government responses to citizen grievances.

Meanwhile, the challenges facing the progressive justification of Chinese approaches to tackling mass actions persist. These challenges include the lack of coherence between legal compliance and political considerations by dispute resolution authorities, unresolved conflicts between legal duties and political priorities in handling mass actions, and the coexistence of legal and political accountabilities in mass action settlements. Furthermore, news reports and narratives of Chinese measures for resolving mass disputes have not facilitated the effective integration of legal rules into social norms where both dispute resolution authorities and citizens who file complaints take the law seriously and work together to resist political burden and interference in the resolution of citizens' grievances against the government.

This book provides a holistic and empirically informed analysis of the changing legislative, institutional and social factors that shape Chinese measures for handling mass actions. It aims to rectify prevailing simplistic assumptions by exploring the interplay between these factors and the content, form and outcomes of mass actions from the 1970s to the present. It sheds light on the evolving notions and public expectations that decisions and conduct of Chinese governing powers are accountable to the law and the public. It also examines their impacts on decisions rendered by dispute resolution authorities and the persistent challenges to the further juridification of legal accountability rules. Particularly noteworthy are the book's extensive empirical insights into the de-politicisation of the Chinese dispute resolution system and the legislation-led reform of dispute resolution procedures for addressing mass actions and their implications for understanding what kind of citizen complaining action and resolution are commonly considered normal and reasonable in today's Chinese society.

The book presents analytical and empirical insights into the Chinese governance model and its global implications. The book is an indispensable resource for scholars and policymakers who are interested in grasping the dynamics of government-citizen relations and interactions in China. It is widely recognised that Chinese governance culture embodies pragmatism, prioritising substantive rationality and tangible results over formal rationality.[1] As former Chinese leader Deng Xiaoping aptly stated, the evaluation of Chinese governance results should be based on factual performances whether they lead to revitalising the Chinese economy and advancing social development, rather than being trapped in normative or ideological debates.[2]

For readers seeking fresh conceptual and analytical approaches to understanding Chinese rules and procedures for dealing with citizen complaints against the government, this book transcends conventional assumptions. It explores the incorporation of State legislation into institutional culture and social norms, going beyond mere considerations of the State's political form or the primacy of law. The book comprehensively explores the legislative, institutional and social factors that facilitate or hinder the juridification of Chinese measures for managing mass actions. It offers concrete techniques and detailed analyses for processing extensive data, employing automated content analysis tools and extracting meaningful insights and implications from the automated-generated results. These cross-disciplinary methods allow legal and sociological researchers to gain a deeper understanding of the popular narratives and framings that present common sense within specific textual and contextual settings.

From a policy perspective, it is important to resolve conflicts between legal compliance and political accountability in handling mass actions to establish a consistent and rule-based institutional culture. Policy efforts should aim to promote dialogue and collaboration between legal and political authorities while ensuring accessible and transparent platforms for discussion and consultation with external parties. The maturation of digital tools has made it possible to bridge the transparency gap between citizens with complaints and relevant dispute resolution authorities, which helps address the issue of forum shopping by complainants and improves the credibility of statutory dispute resolution venues amongst the public. Introducing digital databases and platforms can reduce ambiguity and secrecy in settling citizen complaints, including mass actions, allowing complainants to participate in and track settlement decisions.

In conclusion, this book illuminates the juridification of Chinese approaches to addressing mass actions, which has been maturing at legislative, institutional and social levels since the 1970s, notwithstanding significant challenges. The findings challenge and amend dominant stereotypical interpretations that often portray Chinese measures for addressing mass actions as lawless, monolithic and static. This book aims to provide a holistic and nuanced understanding of the contemporary Chinese rules and procedures for dealing with citizen complaints in general and mass actions in particular. It is hoped that readers facing language barriers, time

[1] GU Zhun: From Idealism to Empiricism(从理想主义到经验主义), the Guangming Daily Press, 2013 January, page 6.

[2] Deng Xiaoping: Key Notes Made during the Trips to Wuchang, Shenzhen, Zhuhai and Shanghai, released between 18 January and 21 February 1992, full text accessible at: https://marxism.muc.edu.cn/__local/F/8F/13/F301F7D446B74E4F17FFB6231B0_9D49D10A_BF9C1.pdf?e=.pdf.

constraints, or limited access to Chinese sources will find this book valuable. Furthermore, the book details cross-disciplinary analytical methods that combine the analysis of legal and policy data with that of massive news data, making it applicable to a wide range of contexts and topics beyond the scope and theme presented in this study.

The manufacturer's authorised representative in the EU is Springer Nature Customer Service Centre GmbH, Europaplatz 3, 69115 Heidelberg, Germany. If you have any concerns regarding our products, please contact ProductSafety@springernature.com

Printed and bound by CPI Group (UK) Ltd, Croydon, CR0 4YY
01/10/2026
02225909-0003